SWEEPING
THE PLATE

PRAISE FOR

"As a former MLB all-star pitcher for the San Francisco Giants and now as a coach of 30 years, I've had quite a few discussions with umpires—most in the heat of battle. In his book, Jim Smith does a great job in bringing out the human as well as the humorous side of discussions between coaches, players and umpires. I have known Jim more than 25 years and have tremendous respect for him and the job he did as an umpire and assigner. I know we didn't always agree on calls, but that's what makes for good stories. I highly recommend this book as a fun read with good insights on the great game of baseball. This is one call Jim got right."

—GARY LAVELLE, San Francisco Giants All Star and "All Time Appearance Leader" Toronto Blue Jays, former head coach at Greenbrier Christian Academy, and presently Head Coach at Bryant Stratton College

"As the head baseball coach at First Colonial High School in Virginia Beach for over 26 years, I didn't always see eye to eye with Umpire Jim Smith's calls. One thing we both agree on, however, is that baseball stories are often more memorable than the games themselves. If you love the game, you're going to thoroughly enjoy Jim's take on the quirky people, places and events he's encountered over the years on the other side of the plate. Good read, folks. Good call, Jim."

—COACH NORBIE WILSON, Bryant & Stratton College Bobcats Virginia Beach, Virginia

"Jim Smith and I had numerous interactions over my 44 years as player and coach at Newport News Apprentice School. This is a book that even the casual baseball fan will enjoy. Readers will see how a sense of humor can keep this game fun. As the umpires say and Jim's book proves, the best place to hide a 100-dollar bill from a coach is to put it in a rule book."

—**BRYAN CAVE**, Apprentice School Builders
Newport News, Virginia

"I was fortunate to have worked with Jim Smith when he assigned umpires for our games. The quality of his umpires and their willingness to resolve disagreements was something I didn't have to worry about. Knowing that Jim was in charge, that was never a question. That integrity and flexibility emerges in his collection of humorous officiating stories, told with great skill."

—**JOHN HARVELL**, CNU Baseball

"As president of the International League for the past 28 years, I had the pleasure of meeting Jim Smith in the spring of 2006. The late Dave Rosenfield, 48-year general manager of the Norfolk Tides, introduced us on the mezzanine at Harbor Park. I soon found out Jim was in charge of the top umpires in the Tidewater Virginia area and also of one of the largest amateur associations in the state of Virginia.

If you know Jim, he can talk baseball stories forever. So, knowing he was going to write a book, I knew it was going to be a success. In this book you will get to know Jim, not only as a player, umpire and assigner—you will get to know the person that is respected and admired by so many involved in baseball. A great read."

—**RANDY MOBLEY**, president of the International League

"In 1987 I joined EVOA, now EOA, after spending 11 years as a professional baseball umpire in the minor leagues as well as in the majors. Upon joining the organization I met Jim Smith (known to some as 'Smooch'). It was a funny nickname, but I don't think Jim kissed up to anyone; if anything, he had a reputation of sometimes turning a deaf ear to confrontations on the field. It is true that Jim did not shy away from the trouble that inevitably involves even the best umpires. This trait served him well in his later years as commissioner for EOA by enabling him to relate well to players, coaches and umpires. He guided the organization to the next level with the help of an umpire evaluation system that I designed and Jim implemented wholeheartedly. Jim's book is a GREAT, easy read, which brings back many umpiring memories."

—RICH HUMPHREY, former professional minor and
major league umpire

"As a 30-year Hampton Roads broadcaster, including being the radio voice of the Norfolk Tides, I've come to know many of the area's sporting figures. Few have as many entertaining stories and thoughtful insights into officiating, especially baseball, as Jim Smith. I should know, having also spent more than a decade working for Jim as an area baseball umpire.

With Jim, it's never been just about balls and strikes or safes and outs. As an umpire and assignor, he always knew how to connect with the people in the game, and I think you'll find that personal touch in this array of amazing stories. You'll enjoy the read!"

—PETE MICHAUD, Norfolk Tides broadcaster

"Being a baseball player and coach in the Tidewater area for 30 years, I thought that I heard every good and funny baseball story from the area. That was not true until now. After reading Jim Smith's new book I can truly say that is true. Great and enjoyable read for anyone that likes to laugh and likes a good baseball story. Grab a copy and enjoy."

—ANDY WISSINGER, assistant coach
Christopher Newport University

"I've served as athletic director at Kempsville High School in Virginia Beach since 2010 and have known Jim since 2002. I look forward to his book release because if you love baseball coaching and umpiring, you'll find Jim blends these two vocations together so you appreciate both perspectives. The coaches' interactions with the umpires make for many funny stories and some fond memories."

—TIM WOLF, athletic director, Kempsville High School

"As longtime head baseball coach at the University of Mount Olive in North Carolina, I had the good fortune to get to know Jim a few years back. Jim has such a passion for the game and is a genuine gentleman. Talk about someone that knows the game of baseball, the ins and outs of umpiring and running an organization; wait until you read his book, and you will see exactly what I mean."

—CARL LANCASTER, University of Mount Olive

"I have found in my time as a player and coach that this baseball thing is infectious. After playing and coaching competitively for almost 28 years, I think a lot of the lure to baseball comes from the people you meet and the stories created along the way. The most entertaining stories emanate from on-field encounters and off-field shenanigans. Jim Smith's book does a great job of capturing a lot of these memories that will resonate with true fans of baseball. His stories will remind readers why they love and respect the game."

—SCOTT SIZEMORE, former MLB player

"I am president of a number of minor league teams, including the Norfolk Tides. Jim and I have sat together at Harbor Park trading baseball stories for at least the last 15 years, often including our late GM, Dave Rosenfield, who was in the Tidewater area for over 50 years. Jim has a great recall of his baseball life, which provides many insights and humor into the people he has encountered along the way. His book will bring you many a smile and is an easy read. Jim's memories demonstrate that he has a knack for reaching people and bringing out their best."

—KEN YOUNG, owner of Norfolk Tides

"I was fortunate enough to play in the big leagues for 8 years, including as an all-star. After retirement I got to know Jim Smith in my work for the Baltimore Orioles. I see Jim when I am in town and at Harbor Park for the Orioles' Triple-A games. We both always get to the game at least 1 hour early, sit in the same place and talk baseball right up to the first pitch.

I highly recommend his new book as a great baseball read with good insights in the game of baseball. Jim's book is not only a book with memoirs—the way he ties in players, coaches and umpires makes this book unique. This is a 'PERFECT GAME' for the reader."

—LEE THOMAS, former major-leaguer and all-star,
now special assistant to the general manager of
the Baltimore Orioles

"As a general manager in the International League for seven years and a veteran of several professional sports leagues, I have had countless interactions with umpires and league officials. Jim Smith was a true asset to the Tides when called upon in a pinch. Whether we needed umpires for a high school, college, minor league game or major league exhibition, Jim was always there to ready to help. He is still a steady fixture at Harbor Park and baseball fields throughout the area. Jim's stories told in person are a joy to hear and have now found their way into his new book, *Sweeping Off The Plate*. Just as I have, I'm confident baseball fans will enjoy his warm and humorous storytelling from someone who has really done it all in baseball."

—JOE GREGORY, general manager for the Norfolk Tides

"As a former umpire in EOA and later as a professional umpire and now a trainer and coach to minor league umpires, I understand how umpires affect the growth of young players and the flow of the game. I experienced firsthand Jim's commitment to those purposes, and I know his readers will enjoy *Sweeping Off The Plate* as it captures the essence of what one dedicated umpire and leader can do to positively impact the game and those who both play and officiate it."

—LARRY REVEAL, Minor League Baseball
umpire evaluator/intructor
MiLB's umpire academy curriculum coordinator

Sweeping Off The Plate:
Umpiring Stories Told
After the Dust Settles
by Jim Smith

© Copyright 2018 Jim Smith

ISBN 978-1-63393-678-2

Published by

 köehlerbooks™

210 60th Street
Virginia Beach, VA 23451
800–435–4811
www.koehlerbooks.com

SWEEPING OFF THE PLATE

UMPIRING STORIES TOLD AFTER THE DUST SETTLES

Jill
I really hope you
enjoy all the stories.
especially
JIM SMITH yours
"The Mayor"

VIRGINIA BEACH
CAPE CHARLES

TABLE OF CONTENTS

IN MEMORIAM

Over the many years I have been privileged to umpire and assign baseball games in Hampton Roads, many of our umpires have left the area, some have retired from umpiring, and sadly, some have passed away. Without meaning to omit the contributions of any of our deceased umpires I do want to mention several.

Lee Sheldon was a friend to everyone. He was one of the most sincere guys you ever wanted to meet and never had an unfriendly or harsh word to say about anyone. He passed away after a courageous battle with cancer at a much too early age.

Mike Brown was one of our strongest. He was an outstanding role model for many of our umpires, young and old. Technically sound and always in the right place, Mike should have had a lot more games in his life when we lost him.

Preston Harding, Jr. was a student of baseball and also of football. Equally comfortable on either field, he was an official's official. Preston understood the role of an official in making sure the game was played fairly and with the integrity Preston himself demonstrated. He was always willing to guide younger officials and made many valuable contributions to all of our umpires in meetings and clinics.

Bob Campbell was perhaps the most respected umpire ever to serve our association, with a forty-year career in the field and a legacy of postseason honors second to none. He was known for demanding strong effort and hustle from everyone with whom he worked and those he instructed. He more than ably led our development system, almost from its inception, bringing his wisdom and on-field experience to many aspiring umpires.

The Eastern Officials Association (EOA) dates back over fifty years. Richard "Bullet" Alexander may not have been EOA's founder, but he was its inspiration. A firefighter by profession, Bullet was best known as Hampton Roads' top local umpire, an informal but nonetheless valid honor he held for many years. When the Tides needed a fill-in umpire, Bullet often was their man. He shaped our organization and helped it grow into one of the leading local umpiring associations anywhere. He had a rare combination of love of the game, desire to contribute to umpiring, and ready humor. He touched the style of hundreds of umpires. Every one of them misses him.

THE BROTHERHOOD OF UMPIRES STANDS STRONG
EVEN WHEN WE LOSE SOMEONE.
(L-R:) LEE SHELDON, BOB CAMPBELL, AND BOB BARRY

FOREWORD

Who is Jim Smith? Chances are many of you already know him, but I am sure there are many out there who do not. Hopefully, his journey will become much clearer as you go through his book. It will take you from his start in baseball as a Little Leaguer in rural Greenville, North Carolina to his years as a very successful teacher, referee, umpire, and baseball commissioner in the much larger area of Hampton Roads, Virginia, home to nearly two million people.

I first met Jim more than forty years ago. We umpired, refereed basketball, and laughed together for fifteen seasons. Then I decided to acknowledge the demands of my law practice and spend more time raising two softball players who would wisely become competitive swimmers. Jim would have an unsuccessful surgery that unhappily ended his on-field and court time. We were out of touch for a number of years, but then, one night in September 2005, we were sitting next to each other at an awards banquet. He had just been elected as the new baseball commissioner, and he asked me if I would come back to umpiring. Like many properly trained husbands do, I went home and checked with my wife. She said yes, under two conditions: you only work two days a week and keep your Sundays free. Deal. With that, Jim and I were back together.

This memoir contains many stories, and each chapter will provide numerous excerpts from each stage of Jim's remarkable career. The hardest part of editing this book was to choose which stories to include and which to cut out. Many are hilarious, others are serious, but importantly, all are true—with one exception. Not knowing who would be reading the book, Jim chose to remove all the profanity, which, like it or not, is as much a part of baseball as learning how to spit. For any baseball person, the blanks will be easy to fill in.

One precaution all of Jim's successful umpires knew was that there are two Jims. One side of Jim appears only on a rainy day during which there are hundreds of cancellations. His phone conversation will last at the most ten to fifteen seconds, sometimes more like five. If you are not near a computer and need to call him, he only needs one piece of information: your game site. We learned not to tell him it is raining where you are for fear he will immediately say goodbye and hang up. Now the other Jim, on a beautiful, sunny day, will talk your ears off until another call comes in or you say *Please, I have to go.*

Jim had many names in the officiating business: Jimbo, Smooch, Chief, Commish, The Boss, the Mayor (how he got that one is another story in itself). However, whatever name people chose to call him, they always intoned it with the respect that he had earned. When he first took over as commissioner, he said he wanted to emphasize two things: making Eastern Officials Association one of the largest, strongest, and best trained umpiring groups in the state, and making it always put an umpire's family first. He accomplished both.

Jim Smith did so much for the development of baseball umpiring in Hampton Roads. Hopefully, you will either remember some of these people and stories yourself or laugh or be touched when you read them. Most of all, as you turn these pages and see these photos, please appreciate how one high-energy and dedicated man's accomplishments could improve so many people's lives through the sport he loves.

Bob Barry
Norfolk, Virginia
April 2018

INTRODUCTION

Many people don't get the opportunity to reflect upon their career in an in-depth way, looking back into their own playing days as well as reconnecting with umpiring friends. I have enjoyed this walk around the base paths of my memory lane. My hope, as I put my favorite stories down on paper (well, actually, into Microsoft Word), is that these recollections of days on the field will resonate with anyone with a passion for the game. I also hope it will create some informative and at times poignant and humorous reading. As we know, just about all umpires love to tell their stories from the field, or "war stories," as we often call them. Sometimes we tell them accurately, sometimes with a bit of embellishment, but I assure you the stories which follow are as accurate as my ability to call 'em as I saw 'em.

Whether during my time umpiring or when I served as the commissioner for our association, my life in sports has always been about the players or other umpires, not me. Fortunately, for the past forty-plus years, I have been able to work with and learn from some of the top officials and sometimes coaches in the sports world.

For some of these stories, I was not able to come up with the exact date, and some may be out of chronological order, but it's the story, not the date, that's most important. Also, for some of the stories, I will delicately leave out the names of the coaches, players, and school. Discretion may not have always been my strongest virtue, but fortunately, I have advisors.

One thing I tried to do after every game was write down notes about the game I umpired or, during my basketball career, refereed. Doing this helped me reference things I needed to work on. If I had a bad game, I noted it. If I had a good game, I still wrote down something I could work on. I still have those notes to this day, and they helped me with many of the dates and facts about the stories in this book.

Unless indicated otherwise, most of these stories occurred in the state of Virginia. All the scholastic games took place in Virginia. Except for my early days in North Carolina, all the recreation games were also in Virginia. All my college games were either in Virginia or North Carolina.

After some of the most memorable games, I asked game management if I could keep a baseball. It took my wife and me years to find the right curio in which to put them, but that finally happened in 2004. The reason it took so long is that I wanted a cabinet with lighted shelves for mementos of my own playing as well as each category of game I officiated, my recreation umpiring memories, then scholastic and college. The last shelf holds balls signed by great players like Whitey Ford, Bob Feller, Joe Morgan, and others.

Although many of today's players and coaches use profanity during questionable plays or heated arguments, I prefer not to use profanity in this book and will substitute the word "bleep" in whatever form it must appear. You can fill in the rest from the context.

Let's get started as I dust off the plate and some great memories for your enjoyment.

CHAPTER 1

"HEY, BLUE!"

I was born in Raleigh, North Carolina on August 23, 1949, to two wonderful parents. I didn't get on the ball field that day, but it didn't take long. My parents both worked full time to help support my three sisters and me. During my early years, Dad had to do a lot of traveling, so the weekends were our special time together. But Raleigh was not where my high school days would begin.

We stayed in Raleigh until my father found a new job in Greenville, North Carolina, working for the local TV station. That transition was tough, as I was leaving all of my friends. Raleigh had just built a brand-new high school (Enloe High) that was right down the street from our house. I had been looking forward to attending a brand-new school that looked more like a university. It took a while, but I finally adjusted into playing at Rose High, a name which would turn out just as sweet. There, I lettered in football, basketball, baseball, and track.

After graduating from Rose High, I ended up going to and playing baseball at East Carolina University (ECU) in Greenville, North Carolina. I had received offers from The University of North Carolina, UNC-Wilmington, and North Carolina State to play baseball, but due to my extended battle with mononucleosis during the latter part of my senior year, I guess you could say I coughed up those other offers. That story will follow a little later in the book.

SUMMER BALL AND THE DAY I THREW IT ALL AWAY

At the end of my sophomore year in college, one of our pitchers and I were invited to play in a summer league composed of college players from various parts of the Mid-Atlantic region. The name of the team was the Stancel Chapel Dodgers. In those days we didn't have all of the summer leagues like we do now, so I was just happy to be playing. Our college coach also wanted us playing somewhere. I was the number two catcher on the team and having a blast.

We played doubleheaders every day Saturday and Sunday, and the stands were always packed. Our stud catcher would catch the first game, and I would catch the second.

1968 SOPHMORE YEAR ECU BASEBALL TEAM. 2ND ROW, 4TH FROM RIGHT

What was so frustrating for me was that the other catcher was so good the LA Dodgers offered to make him what we called a bonus baby with $350,000 to sign. Back in 1969, that was very big money. But he didn't take the offer. He just loved being a good ole country boy playing baseball. Even more, perhaps, he loved his home cooking and didn't want to leave it. At the time, he had one of the best arms I had ever seen. He threw to second, like MLB catcher Tony Pena, from his normal crouch and never stood up. No one stole on him. If they tried, he would gun them down. I wish I had his arm and had gotten the offer he got, as I would have been gone in a heartbeat. I could hit with him for power and maybe a higher average, but he was the better defensive catcher.

There were some serious perks of playing for the team that summer. Whether we were in violation of NCAA rules, I do not know and never wanted to ask. Since the drive to our games was about two hours each way, our host team fed us after every game and filled up our cars with gas while we were playing. Not to mention, and we certainly didn't, that the owner gave us $50 for a single game and $100 for a doubleheader. Now $200 for the weekend, free meals, and free gas put in our cars sure helped out on the tuition side. The Dodgers helped out with uniforms, too.

Unfortunately, before it was all over, it was I who paid the biggest price. Near the end of the season, I heard something in my arm or shoulder pop, but I did not know what had happened. All I knew was that the powerful throw to second that I used to have was gone. When I returned for my junior year, the coach tried me some at first base, but we were already strong at first. That is when I made a decisive change in my life. I decided that I better get my teaching degree because playing professional baseball was not going to happen. I became a statistic, one of the many college and minor leaguers who just do not make it to The Show. Odd, wasn't it, that my decision which followed the pop I felt may have been my first call to the aspiration of umpiring?

KICKED OUT OF STUDY HALL

I was the type of student who liked to get my homework done before I went to bed or get up early enough to get it done before I went to school. This was also a parental requirement, and trust me, I never wanted to test my parents.

FOOTBALL DRILLS

During my junior year, I had first-period study hall. Since my homework was always done, I would occasionally put my head down and rest. Not a good idea with the biology teacher that was in charge of the study hall. She wanted you working no matter what. When I told her my homework was done, she told me to find something to do. I told her I knew just what to do, put my head down and rest.

She said, "Young man, don't you get smart with me or question my authority. I don't care if you are a star athlete."

I told her she should not question me either.

Wrong response. Off to the office I was sent.

I was very fortunate that one of my coaches was in the office when I arrived. After chewing me out, he told the principal he could use an assistant during the time I was supposed to be in study hall. That was approved, but no one knew that Coach Best took me out to the field to work on pass catching during football season and to the gym to work on free-throw shooting during basketball season. He was my coach for both sports.

Guess who I had for study hall my senior year. Yep, the biology teacher. Same teacher and same period. As I walked through the door, I asked her if she thought it would be a good idea for me to just head to the office. She agreed, and I again became a pass catching, free-throw-shooting assistant. Score one for the athlete.

TOUGH LOVE

If you think you had it hard, strict, or tough growing up, consider these three strikes on a young man's freedom.

Strike One: Chores

Every person in the house had theirs, and they came with rough consequences if not completed. Other than keeping my room clean and bed made, my main job was the yard, but wow, was that a lot. Leaves and pine straw collected in the fall, and then, of course, there was the grass the rest of the year. Forgetting to cut the grass or making excuses was an ejection offense. Just an FYI, both our front and back yards were both the size of a major league outfield, and we didn't own a John Deere.

Strike Two: Date Night

Until we were eighteen, curfew was 11:00 sharp. That was by dad's watch, not ours, which, on date nights, I am convinced he deliberately caused to run fast. Fifteen seconds late, and you were confined to the dugout for a month. We soon learned to be in the house by 10:45. Being three months shy of driving age my sophomore year meant I could not drive to the junior/senior prom with my date, who was a junior. She was very understanding that my parents had to take us, but with the dance ending at midnight, you guessed it, I still had to be home by 11:00 PM. How embarrassing, but there was no collective bargaining agreement about time, and economically, I didn't want to become a free agent.

As a senior, I would not turn eighteen until August. Guess what time I had to be in. Correct, 11:00 PM. That meant to leave the dance, take your date home, and be in the house by 11:00.

In the town where I grew up, the day after prom, we would drive to a cottage at a beach (sixty miles away). This was a lot of fun, except for one thing. Anyone going to the beach had to come over to the house and listen to my dad's underage drinking and driving speech. Seemed like a real downer then, but somehow age and my own parenthood have made that speech feel a little bit shorter and a lot more relevant.

Foul Ball and Still Alive: Transportation Woes

Speaking of cars, my sister and I had to platoon (share use of) an old car to get back and forth to school. It was an Opal, which I am sure most of you have never heard of. Getting to school was easy enough, but since I was playing sports all year, I let her have the Opal to drive home. I would usually end up walking home after practice or possibly getting a ride from one of my teammates.

When the manager bought a veteran car for us, a stick shift, we soon discovered that my sister did not know how to drive a stick. I had the option of teaching her or having the car all to myself. What an ethical challenge that was. Dad gave her thirty days to learn to drive it, or it would be mine. So I became her hitting coach, and she met the deadline by one day.

To my surprise, someone rewarded my good-faith efforts. The manager had noticed my sister and me working hard to solve our transportation problems, so he ended up buying me a small motorcycle. Wheels at last: maybe only two of them, but so be it. I finally had the green light to run on my own.

Strike Three, I'm Out: The Lost Newspaper

My dad always wanted the best for me, and when I decided I wanted to concentrate on baseball and especially catching, he did everything he could to help me become the best catcher I could be. I had a fast and strong arm to second, and very few runners stole on me.

In the summer of 1964, when I was fifteen, we had several weeks of steady rain, which also meant we had a lot of games to make up. As we were short on pitching, I told my coach I would like to pitch. He reminded me of what my dad had said, either pitch or catch, but not both, as the mechanics of the throws are completely different. But I finally talked him into it. All I had was a fastball with no windup. I ended up throwing a perfect game. The next day's local newspaper read "PLANTERS BANK SMITH THROWS A PERFECT GAME."

I was scared to death that my dad was going to see that headline and be upset, not of course about the perfect game, but about my disregarding what he had been telling me for the past year. "If you want to play in college or have a shot at professional baseball, pick one or the other." I decided the smart thing to do was to get rid of the newspaper. Wrong. Dad was a traveling salesman at the time, and when he got home on Friday night, he loved to read his newspapers. When he didn't see that newspaper, he started asking questions. I played dumb, thinking I had gotten away with it, perfect game and perfect cover-up, but sure enough, my defiance and scheming came back to haunt me. He drove to the newspaper office and got another copy. When he got home, he asked me one question, "Boy, who is the new kid named Smith on the team?"

I figured out that wasn't really a question. That was the last time I ever pitched.

CHIPS OFF THE OLD BLOCK

In 1965, my dad got laid off from a job trying to implement a radio program for the local TV station, WNCT Channel 9 in Greenville. He was such a great salesman that the station wanted him to do advertisements in the FM radio format. The idea was about two years ahead of its time, but they were trying to be the first to break ground in this side of the business. He was promised his old job or another position at the station if this program didn't work. They were supposedly holding his old job open, in case it didn't work. They lied.

None of the children knew this at first. We just saw Dad leaving and figured he was on his way to work. One day I detected a worried looked on my mother's face, so I asked her what was wrong. She hesitated but finally told me what was going on and that we were down to the last of our money for rent and food. Dad was too proud of a man to ask for help, so I went to him and offered. He refused, but I told him we had no choice. Keeping the family in the house or putting off college was a no-brainer of a decision for me.

I took the $2,000 I had inherited from my grandparents for college and the money I earned working on Saturdays and gave it to Dad. I remember the day like it was yesterday. We all cried, as that meant I might not be able to pay for my college tuition. But family comes first.

Roughly nine months later, Dad started a new job with Charles Chips Potato Chips. He set up his own routes and serviced the Greenville and Winterville areas of NC. He ran routes seven days a week until he retired. Everyone knows my "gift of gab," but you should have met my father. He could sell you oceanfront property ten miles out *into* the ocean. He gave me one of the Saturday routes, and I would usually clear about $150. Now, $150 in those days was like $600 today. With my umpiring job and this money, I was able to make enough to continue with my college career.

In 1972, two years after I started my teaching career, both of my parents drove up to Virginia Beach. They did this often, but this time was different. My Dad pulled me out to the back of the house to our garden, and he handed me an envelope. In it was $4,000. The exact amount he borrowed. It was so emotional that I had to help Dad keep the tears back. Then I could see that wasn't going to happen. I just told him it was okay to cry, and I was just glad things worked out for the entire family. This was so touching and so private that I am sure this is the first time my sisters or anyone else has ever heard this story.

THE STATE TROOPER MUST HAVE BEEN A FAN

One night, several of my teammates on the ECU baseball team and I decided to go to the movies. When we got there, we discovered the theater had some electrical issues and was closed for the night. Since Greenville only had one theater, we decided to go to a neighboring town, Wilson. When we got there, ironically, they were also having problems but were only running thirty minutes behind. Thinking we had enough time to watch the movie and get back to Greenville, we decided to stay. All would have been fine, except there was a major wreck on the only road home. It closed for traffic for about forty-five minutes. When we got rolling, I was trying to make up time by doing seventy-five in a fifty-five mile-per-hour zone. No troopers—boy, was I lucky. As we approached the hill where the dorms were, the speed limit dropped from fifty-five to forty-five. I slowed to sixty and was hoping my luck would hold out.

It didn't. All of a sudden, in my rearview mirror, I saw police lights come on. The trooper came up to my car and asked me if I knew what the speed limit was on the hill and if I knew how fast I was going.

I said, "Yes, sir, it is forty-five, and I was going sixty, but can you hurry up and write my ticket?"

He asked me what my rush was. I told him we were all on the ECU baseball team and curfew on nights before game day was 11:00.

He looked at his watch and said, "That gives you guys ten minutes. You will never make it. Follow me, but remember, if you lose tomorrow, you get your ticket. If you win you only get a warning, and by the way, I have duty at your game tomorrow."

With his flashing lights on, we made it with one minute to spare. Good thing too, as we got a bed check that night.

Sure enough, the very next day he was there and made sure we saw him. Prior to the start of the game, he approached me with a broad grin and said, "Don't worry about the ticket; just do your best." The guy must have had a heart for baseball.

A CAROLINA BOY FINDS THE OLD DOMINION

In 1971 I graduated from ECU and started looking for a job. With nothing open in the surrounding area, I reached out to my former high school basketball coach, Nelson Best, now a principal in the Wilmington, North Carolina area. He was getting ready to open up a brand new high school the following year and wanted me, but that was a year away, and he had no openings that year. He then made a phone call to his brother-in-law, the job recruiter for Norfolk, Virginia public schools. I interviewed with him the next day, and as fate would have it, ended up getting a job.

ANOTHER SCHOOL NAMED ROSE

I taught in the Norfolk Public School System for thirty-six years. I was fortunate enough to do it in the same building, Rosemont Middle School, which is very rare, until I went out on disability March 24, 2004. I served as the department chair for the last twenty-eight years, which helped give me the knowledge, organizational and leadership skills I would need to later serve as commissioner of two sports.

OPPORTUNITY KNOCKS ME OVER

Even though I umpired a little while in college, I guess my real start in umpiring came unexpectedly one spring day in 1971. It was a fateful opportunity, one that I could not have recognized at the time, but it was still one of those life-changing days that you can never forget. More about that later.

INTO THE TWENTY-FIRST CENTURY

From 1971 to 2004, I juggled teaching, umpiring, basketball refereeing and assigning basketball. Most of all, I learned and acquired experience while making lifelong friends and contacts, in multiple sports on multiple age and skill levels. I assigned basketball for twenty-eight years, prior to taking over the commissionership in baseball in 2005. At that time I stopped assigning basketball and got heavily into the baseball assigning.

BUT WHO'S COUNTING

Over my thirty-six-plus years of umpiring and assigning, I had the honor and pleasure to officiate over 7,500 games—315 college games, 656 scholastic games, and the rest were recreation, but who's counting? In those days, you worked seven days a week. On Saturdays and Sundays, you were liable to get four games each day, maybe five. Recreation games were some of the most fun to work because you could interact with the fans. You couldn't do that in scholastic or collegiate games. In this book, I will share with you some of the most memorable games.

BASKETBALL TOO

As mentioned earlier, in addition to teaching, umpiring baseball and refereeing basketball, I also served as the adult, AAU and summer/fall scholastic basketball commissioner for twenty-eight years. As the assigner, I assigned over forty thousand basketball games. I have accidentally erased the data on the number of basketball games I worked as an official, but they were numerous and probably close to the same as my baseball schedule. I was lucky enough to referee basketball for thirty-six years and work eleven VHSL State Tournament Basketball games. All these choice assignments came thanks to our scholastic assigner, the late Dick Bowie, the Little General, whose life ended much too soon and will be mentioned later in one of the baseball stories.

A SUITE TRIP TO TEXAS

In the summer of 1997, I was contacted by a group out of Texas that ran the National 3 on 3 *Hoop It Up* Basketball Tournament. They were coming to Norfolk and wanted to know if I would assign the officials. Norfolk was one of the regional sites leading up to the World championships.

I took the opportunity and continued to assign the tournament for the next four years, and in November of 2000, I was asked if I wanted to fly to Dallas, Texas for four days to work the National Finals. What a great

2000 DALLAS, TEXAS HOOP-IT-UP WORLD CHAMPIONSHIPS

thrill. They put each official in an individual suite large enough for two families. They also gave us several uniforms, bags, and numerous other gifts as a token of their appreciation for coming to town. The flight, food, and nightly entertainment were all free, even including a trip to a Dallas Mavericks game.

A COACHING WHO'S WHO

During my time working basketball, while assigning and working local AAU National Tournaments, I was also fortunate enough to meet some of the great basketball coaches of our time. I'm talking about Pat Summitt (University of Tennessee), Geno Auriemma (University of Connecticut) Gail Goestenkors (Former Duke University and now Texas Coach), the late Dean Smith (University of North Carolina), Mike Krzyzewski (Duke University), Wendy Larry (Old Dominion University), and Tara Vanderveer (Stanford University).

THOSE GUYS MADE THE NBA!

I was also fortunate enough to meet and develop great friendships with four NBA referees: the late Jess Kersey, the late Nolan Fine, Tony Brothers, and Leroy Richardson. Both Tony and Leroy are still active in the NBA, and Tony has worked the NBA finals the last two seasons. I keep in touch with both of them. Both have invited me to go see them work, and now that I am retired, I plan on taking them up on it. Both also generously volunteered their time for the Hoop it Up tournament.

THE STATE FINALS

1975 WITH DAD AT THE VHSL CHAMPION-
SHIP FINALS AT SCOPE IN NORFOLK, VA

I realize this book is mainly about my life as an umpire and baseball assigner, but I did officiate basketball games for thirty-four years and assign officials for them for twenty-eight years before switching over to baseball. In mid-February of 1988, my basketball assigner had me working all the district and regional finals leading up to the selection of the officials that would be working the state semis and finals. I can't remember the date, but I can remember the game just like it was yesterday. That morning I received a letter from the state office informing me I would be working the state finals that year at the Scope in Norfolk, Virginia.

Words cannot explain how excited I was, my first state finals. That night I was scheduled to work the regional finals at Oscar Smith High School in Chesapeake Virginia with Dennis Nixon and Phil Nelson. I knew I better put on a good show. The place was packed, and my assigner was there. We were working three-man mechanics, and midway through the second quarter I slipped on a wet spot and pulled my hamstring. At first, I didn't think it was bad, but as we approached halftime, I told my partners I could not rotate and to please keep me in the "C" position the rest of the game.

At halftime, our boss, Dick Bowie, came in there and chewed us out for fifteen minutes. This was normal, but I didn't say a word to him about the hamstring.

After the game, the trainer brought ice in, and he wanted to know what it was for. Here came my second butt-chewing. He said, "Jim, you have the state finals in less than two weeks. Why didn't you come off and let them finish two-man?"

I was speechless.

He said, "How bad is it?"

I told him I didn't know, but it felt worse than any other time I had pulled a muscle.

The next morning my right leg was black all the way from my tush down to my toes. I could hardly walk and could see my dream of working the state finals going out the door.

Fortunately, I had great connections with many of the trainers in the area, and two immediately went to work on me every morning before school and every day after school. The game was two weeks away, and when I could not even jog two days before the game, I was ready to turn the state assignment back. And yet both trainers said, "You will be ready."

I said, "How? I can't even jog."

They told me we would meet four hours before game time, do some treatment, and then basically tape me from my butt to my ankles, give me some Tylenol or Advil, and I would be okay for two hours.

The night of the state final I went out in the hallway and could not believe I could actually jog. Not one hundred percent, but I would say seventy percent. When I got out on the court, I was more nervous about jogging than I was about the game. It hurt to jog, but I then knew I could make it through the game if I was careful. I was working with two Northern Virginia high school officials that also regularly worked NCAA games, so I was the rookie. Everything went fine until the last second in the game, when one of the officials blew her whistle on a play that happened right in front of me. Had she not blown her whistle, the game would have been over, and the winning team would have been state champs and 26-0. Instead, the other team went to the free throw line, hit two free throws and sent the game into overtime. As it had to be, that team won in overtime, and the team that would have won and been 26-0 was now 25-1 and state runner-up.

We were escorted off the court and quickly taken into three different rooms. All of us were asked to give our explanation of what happened. The senior tournament official and observer questioning me asked me why I didn't have a whistle on that play.

My response was, "We had let that play go for thirty-one minutes and fifty-nine seconds without calling it, and I was not calling minimal contact with one second to go in the game."

"Did you hear your partner's whistle?"

"Yes."

"Do you think it beat the horn?"

"No, that it was impossible because with the electronics we were using the whistle keeps the horn from sounding."

They said, "You are one hundred percent correct. Did you offer your input?"

"Yes, but when I approached my partners, they said they had it."

After we all had been questioned, they brought us back together in one room. What followed was a painful but important lesson in officiating teamwork. The lead observer said this is the way we should have handled it:

"All three of you needed to get together to make the final decision, not two of you. There was no way the whistle beat the horn. Since the horn sounded, the horn had to come first, and Jim is the only one that got that correct."

I did not find out until then that my partners' conversation with the losing coach had erroneously stated that the whistle beat the horn. Had they changed the wording and said the foul occurred before the horn, instead of the whistle, we would have all been okay.

"If you call a foul out of your area, you need to be one hundred percent sure on the call, and since all three of you had been letting them play all game with some contact, our supervisor said he would have let that play go." He thanked us for coming and said, "Some games are easy to call, and some are tough; you guys had a tough one. However, that one call did not cost them the game. They had plenty of other opportunities to score."

My assigner was sitting courtside, about twenty feet from the play, and he said I was one hundred percent right in not blowing the whistle. Considering the often harsh critic that he was, I truly appreciated his confirmation. Then he proceeded to ask me about our session with the tournament observer.

What made this bittersweet was this was the first and only time my entire family, including my mother and father, got to see me referee a state final. We were booed on the controversial call and every call during overtime. We were also booed as we were leaving the court. I was hurt that my children, even though only they were very young, saw their dad being booed. When I explained the call to my family and the input the evaluators gave me, they were elated. Officials work as a team just as much as the athletes. Sometimes players and fans don't appreciate that concept, but officials who progress in the ranks of officiating surely do.

CHAPTER 2

BECOMING A
SPORTS OFFICIAL

How I got started in umpiring is probably going to be one of the toughest questions to answer. Even I'm not sure, but there were many hidden signs of this unenviable behavior before my beginnings in 1969 at eighteen years old and my serious start in 1971.

I started playing Little League in 1958 for Austin Produce in Raleigh, North Carolina. My most memorable year was 1960, when my dad coached me. He was a yeller and always on the umpires, but his motives were good, just wanting the best for us. The umpires often asked if the coach was that way all the time. I told them yes, and that he also was the same at home. That is when they found out that he was my father. After expressing their regrets for my no doubt tender ears, they often told me I ought to become an umpire and then, they laughingly said, I could "toss my own dad." I confess that at the time, I found the thought quite appealing. Little did I know that umpiring would soon dominate my future.

RALEIGH LITTLE TAR HEEL LEAGUE
AUSTIN FRUIT & PRODUCE
COACH
SPONSOR
SUMMER - 1960

1960 LITTLE LEAGUE TEAM COACHED BY MY DAD

OUR PERSONAL SANDLOT

Our front and side yard in Raleigh was laid out perfectly for both playing football and baseball. Our only stipulation was that we had to plant grass seed at the end of each season. We were all glad to do that, as it provided us with a football and baseball field. So as not to cross the street and get hit by a car, we played the road as the home-run fence. Better to ding a passing vehicle or, worse yet, break a windshield than get run over. Anytime we had an odd number of players, either one of my friends or I offered to be the umpire. Talk about putting your foot in your mouth. I found out quickly that every time you made a call, someone was going to get upset. Most of the time, as young as we were, we walked away laughing after the game, as youngsters always did in this age of crewcuts, narrow ties and innocence, or at least mostly so. Wally and the Beaver could have played ball in our side yard, and Eddie Haskell could have come over to harass them. Afterward, we would all go down to the

BRETT GRIFFIN AND ME IN 1960

local pharmacy to get a drink or milkshake. However, some days, when someone didn't think the person umpiring made the right, game-winning call, there was dead silence, and everyone went home unhappy. No pharmacy trip that day. The importance of good umpiring had begun to emerge for me in the significant form of missing a root beer float or maybe a limeade.

MY PROMISING SENIOR YEAR, BROUGHT LOW BY MONO

A little background about my high school playing days may also illustrate how being around officials could have played a role in my eventually getting into officiating. I played four sports at Rose High from 1964 to 1967. I was fortunate enough to play for two great coaches who just happened to officiate both baseball and basketball in their spare time. Their names were Nelson Best and Bud Phillips. They were my coaches for football, basketball, and baseball. They worked us hard, but they knew each game. We felt their background in officiating gave us a great advantage, and when they called our intra-squad scrimmages, they called them just like a real game.

Coach Phillips and Coach Best often went to scout or observe other teams on our off nights and allowed me to go with them. We would sit in the stands and not only watch the players but also discuss the officials.

I give both of them credit, but especially Coach Phillips for helping me with my hitting. He worked with me on my swing and was very instrumental in my senior stats. I was having one of my best years ever. I was hitting .667, with a .774 slugging percentage. I had three home runs, a triple (yes, I could run back then), two

1966 ROSE HIGH SCHOOL
MUGGING FOR THE CAMERA

HE WAS OUT!

1966 ROSE HIGH SCHOOL ALL CONFERENCE CATCHER

FIRST ROW: Ronnie Johnson, William Moye, Malcolm Williams, Jimmy Smith, George Garrett, Leon Peaden, and Mike Aldridge SECOND ROW: Kent Leggett, Russell Cayton, Tom Basnight, Dennis Harrington, Billy Calloway, and David Hahn

1967 ROSE HIGH SCHOOL BASESBALL TEAM

doubles, and seventeen singles. That resulted in 16 RBI, twelve runs scored and eight stolen bases, but who's counting? Okay, I was. Even though I was only able to play half the year, I was fortunate enough to receive All-State honors for the state of North Carolina. I mention this because, with those stats, I could not envision anything other than playing in the major leagues.

It was not to happen. Mononucleosis did, and I swear to this day that it wasn't from too much kissing.

I could not believe this was happening my senior year, and so like anyone else, I asked the doctors how someone in such good shape could come down with mono. At first, the docs thought my falling asleep in class was just due to not getting enough sleep. They finally decided to do a blood test. One simple blood test two months earlier and my case would not have been as bad as it was. I was distraught with my doctor, but there was nothing I could do.

My mono ended up being so bad that I was homeschooled for the last two months of the year. I was so appreciative of a lady by the name of Vivian Little. Every afternoon around 3:00 PM, my mother would greet her at the door with the work I missed in school that day. If I had to take a test, she didn't leave until I was done. She is the one that made sure I could walk across the stage on graduation day.

LOST SCHOLARSHIP

Fortunately or unfortunately, by coming down with mono in the spring of my senior year, I lost potential scholarships offers off to NC State, the University of North Carolina, and UNC Wilmington. I ended up playing at East Carolina University with a teammate named Tony Guzzo (from Virginia) who then went on to big-time college coaching at several Division 1 Schools (Virginia Commonwealth University and Old Dominion University), Billy Smith (from Pennsylvania), and Lenny Dowd (from New Jersey). We all thought we were all going to end up in the major leagues, since we were the best catchers from four different states. The real world set in when we found out there was a junior All-American catcher named Russ Nixon in front of us. I got my playing time, but never my dream call to play pro ball.

That was the point in my life, even though I loved baseball and wanted to play in the big leagues, where I realized I had better study and get a degree. That is also where thinking about umpiring as a part-time job entered into my mind. So yes, one could say that my umpiring was born of failure, and many have since said I never improved!

COACHING AND TEACHING

Moving forward to the summer of 1968, I had the privilege of coaching a team that went to the thirteen-to-fourteen-year-old Teener World Series, and that gave me another indication about getting into umpiring. Coaching younger teens helped me with the job with which I would fall in love for the next thirty-six years, teaching middle school children.

The regular-season team I coached during the spring and early summer ended up being league champions. Our league rules stated that the coach of the league's regular-season champs would also be the all-star coach. Some parents had reservations about me, being an eighteen-year-old, traveling around the country and supervising thirteen-year-olds, so I asked a good friend of mine and a baseball guru to join me in coaching the team. He accepted, so along with my co-coach, Johnny Holt, taking the lead, we coached the Greenville All-Star Championship Team and took them on a four-week journey around the Southeast.

This just reinforced my instinct that teaching middle school children was what I wanted to do. Seeing and helping these young men go through their homesickness was an enriching experience. We took second place in the national championship game, losing to West Allis, Wisconsin 3-2. We had twelve hits in the game to their two. However, we hit into five double plays which just killed our offense. Russ Smith, our star pitcher, had a no-hitter through five innings. He ended up with a two-hitter. Talk about a heartbreaking loss. We outplayed them, but this shows how the game of baseball goes. It is far more unpredictable than the other major sports.

One of the highlights of this journey was our welcome-home celebration. Roughly ten miles out of Greenville we started to see state troopers and local law enforcement vehicles pull in front of our bus. We also noticed no traffic from the opposite direction. The troopers had blocked off the road from all other traffic and were escorting us to Guy Smith Stadium for an enormous celebration. This sent chills through every one of us, players and coaches alike. When we arrived, we were greeted by at least half the town, including the mayor, TV stations, and all the parents. We enjoyed a cookout second to none.

Joe West, who is now Cowboy Joe, the senior umpire in the big leagues, was our catcher, and longtime American League Umpire Steve Palermo worked the plate for the game. Watching and talking to Steve Palermo throughout the Series made me further think about umpiring. Another one of our star pitchers that needs to be mentioned and helped get us to the championship was Jimmy Bond. During the regular season he was the star pitcher for my league championship team and someone with whom I still keep in touch now 50 years later.

NEWSPAPER REPORTER

Another opportunity to see the officiating side of sports was having the honor of working for our local newspaper, *The Daily Reflector*. In 1967 as a freshman at ECU, I was given the opportunity to cover both our high school and ECU football games. I was given a camera and told to go shoot pictures of the game. As soon as the game was over, I had to rush back to the newspaper office and get the film developed. I was given my choice of which pictures would be featured in the newspaper the next day. It was neat seeing your name appearing in the paper. I did this for three years to help pay for part of my college tuition. During that time I was able to see and meet several Miss Americas and Miss North Carolinas. However, being the sports nut and on the sidelines for all the games, I most valued

1969 MY COLLEGE DAYS WORKING ECU FOOTBALL GAMES FOR *THE DAILY REFLECTOR*

talking to the officials, before, during and after the game. Seeing that they were getting paid for doing something they loved just fascinated me. I thought to myself, "I can do that."

1968. PLAYING WITH MY DAD IS A MEMORY I WILL NEVER FORGET

PLAYING WITH DAD

One of the biggest thrills for my dad was when I played with him on the church softball team from 1968 to 1970. Even though I was a catcher in baseball, I played shortstop for the church team because of my glove and arm. He pitched, and I tried to keep him out of trouble with the umpires. This was no small assignment since he tended to argue calls and get in trouble with the umpires almost every game. Can you imagine anyone would argue with an umpire?

We went undefeated, and all the churches said I should not have been allowed to play because I was also playing collegiate baseball at ECU. However, the church league rules said any church member was eligible to play. I still have that picture of Dad and me on my desk. They also thought it was unfair for me to play and be associated with the umpires doing our games. What they could not understand is umpiring is different when comparing baseball and softball. I umpired baseball, not softball.

STUDENT TEACHING

The last story that I would like to share in this section and another possible influence toward officiating has a funny twist. I was in my senior year as a health and physical education major at East Carolina University and getting ready to go out and do my student teaching. I was assigned to Jimmy Grimsley, a great gentleman and a sports official as my supervisor. In those days student teachers were assigned two different schools with each experience lasting eight weeks.

The first school to which I was assigned was Chicod. I had heard about some schools having grades one through twelve housed in the same building but never thought that is where I would start off. They were closing the doors to Chicod halfway through my assignment, and so even though it was all new to me, it was strange teaching in a school that was about to shut down and also a school that housed all twelve grades.

Mr. Grimsley decided that even though Chicod was closing in nine weeks, it would be great for me to experience the beginning of my teaching career in such a unique situation. To top it off, he picked the right day to come out for my first official observation.

In between classes, two guys, both about six foot two and 250 pounds, were getting ready to fight each other over a girl. After all, that's what high school guys do. Several experienced teachers tried to stop it, but neither boy would listen. The crowd was building when the principal arrived. Even then, actually especially then, neither of the pugilists would back down. Something hit me—no, not a punch—and I asked the principal if I could try to intervene. He said I better stay back since I was inexperienced in handling these type of situations. But just as they were starting to fight, I stepped in.

"Guys, before you get blood all over the floor, can you tell me what you are fighting about, and then you can continue with the fight."

Everyone looked at me like I was crazy. The fighters said they were arguing over who was the better athlete.

"That has nothing to do with girls . . . but let me pick a neutral sport and after school whoever wins gets to go out with her."

Just then, the girl they both wanted to date walks up with another guy. The sport I picked was hitting baseballs. Both ended up crushing the ball and ended up making the baseball team at their new school.

Afterward, both the principal and Mr. Grimsley called me into the office and reminded me that I should have stayed out of it but asked how on earth I had come up with the sports competition idea. I told them all I was trying to do was defuse the situation by changing their mindset. Ironically, both guys decided if the girl was sneaking around with someone else, she was not right for them.

During my second experience, I was assigned to D.H. Conley in Ayden, NC. Every time he came out to observe me, Mr. Grimsley would spend at least an hour telling me what I needed to work on to become the best teacher I could be. He also saw a propensity for officiating, so he ended every session with at least another hour talking about that. He related to me how breaking up that fight at my first school was kind of like defusing a coach.

As Mr. Grimsley being one of the top officials in the local area, I valued his input. I only had one semester left in school, but he advised me to take an officiating class if at all possible. He just happened to be teaching a class the next semester, and I immediately enrolled in it. He used my fight scenario in one of his lessons. *Hmmm,* I have wondered years later. I must have some innate talent for calming down irate managers and coaches that emerged that day at Chicod.

CHAPTER 3

WHAT WAS I GETTING MYSELF INTO?

In 1969, at the ripe old age of eighteen and as a sophomore in college, a gentleman by the name of Dan Gordon, who had watched me play both in high school and now in college, was in need of umpires for Little League games. He gave me a rulebook, hat, shirt, and old-fashioned balloon chest protector and told me to go to Elm Street Park and umpire the game. The next day he sent me to Guy Smith Stadium to umpire. I had no clue what I was doing, so I guess I fooled a lot of people who thought a former local high school player that was now playing at East Carolina University must know the game. Well, maybe I did—sort of.

Any time a coach came up to me with a rules question, I quoted them something like Rule 4.7, exception C, paragraph B. They always bought it and never knew I had no idea what that rule was or what I was talking about. I would go home that night and look up the proper rule, just in case someone called. A little knowledge, sometimes even very little, and sounding like you know something is a powerful thing.

1976. ELM ST. PARK WHERE I FIRST STARTED UMPING

I used this line throughout my career whenever a coach was being a butthead and didn't want to leave. Thank goodness most of them never took the time to read the rulebook. I will say this, had they asked me to repeat the rule number and exceptions after the game, I could never have given it to them. Confidence and appearing to know your stuff has always been an essential part of umpiring. I think the way I was able to pull this off was that I learned which rule applied to each situation. For example, if the rule pertained to a batter, I would always start off with Rule 7. If it referred to a runner, I would start off with Rule 8. If it applied to a pitcher, I would start off with Rule 6. Knowing the headings for the nine main rules was my salvation in my earlier years.

NOT A BLEEPING COMMENTATOR

In 1971, I graduated from East Carolina University, yes really, and moved to Virginia Beach, Virginia to start my teaching career at Rosemont Middle School in Norfolk. After lunch one day, Natalie Caddell, one of our secretaries, said I had a phone call from a gentleman named Hollis Drake. She asked if I knew who he was, and I told her no. I almost didn't take that call but got curious. I wondered who he was and how he got my name. He said he was given my name by a fellow umpire that heard I had umpired and played ball in North Carolina. He asked me if I would be interested in umpiring, and I told him maybe.

I took Hollis up on his offer, and with no formal training, he sent me and one another guy named Talmadge Dunn off to umpire at $5 a game. Three weeks later, the league president called Hollis and wanted to tear up the contract and give us $10 a game if Hollis would guarantee the two of us coming every day. Hollis called me and asked me what was going on. He wanted to know what the heck this guy was raving about, so he sent me with Nolan Fine (EVOA umpire and former NBA referee) and another prominent local official, Dick Bowie.

I was working games with nine- and ten-year-olds for two weeks and then suddenly jumping to games with seventeen- and eighteen-year-olds. After one game, both Nolan and Dick said, "Sit down, young man."

Dick said, as only he could, "You are not a bleeping commentator, you are an umpire. It is not high inside or down; it is a ball or a strike. You don't go out and explain balks in the higher level games, just call them."

After that night, I knew one of two things. Either I was not worth a damn, or I needed to make some drastic changes. I decided to do the latter.

LEARNING FROM HOLLIS: I GOT ONE HIGHER THAN THAT

Hollis continued umpiring top-flight high school ball and in 1971 had a great interchange with a young Granby High School player named Bob Barry. Stepping into the time machine for just a moment, Bob is now in his fifty-first year of umpiring, has been my friend for forty of those years, and is my collaborator for this book.

Back to the 1970s: at a game with arch-rival Maury High School, Bob was pitching and had already had a bases-clearing triple to put the game out of reach. Hollis was working the plate.

He knew Bob had already started umpiring for our association when he turned sixteen. Bob had one more at-bat that day, and Hollis had seen enough pitches. Hollis also wanted to see how young Bob would react to an umpire with whom he did not agree.

The first pitch to Bob came in about shoulder high, and Hollis called, "Strike one."

Bob bent down to tie his shoe (which didn't need tying) and said quietly to Hollis, "That was pretty high."

Hollis replied, "Get back in there. I got one higher than that."

Next pitch is neck high. Bob doesn't turn around but says, "Really, Mr. Drake?"

Hollis said, "I got one higher than that."

Now the catcher hears all of this and is laughing. He gives a really high target for the next pitch which is about the top of Bob's helmet. "Strike three," bellowed Hollis.

Bob knew he'd been burned and turned to look at Hollis, but before he can say anything, Hollis says, "Kid, you want to be an umpire? I got one higher than that!"

Bob went off to college after that year, but he and Hollis would umpire together many times over the years. Whenever they would work with each other, or when Bob went by Hollis' customary seat at Met Park and later Harbor Park in Norfolk, Hollis would smile his well-accustomed grin and say . . . well, you know what he said, "I got one higher than that."

BACK TO MY LEARNING CURVE

Shortly after that butt-chewing from Dick Bowie and somewhere in the early to mid-'70s was when my serious start in umpiring began. Our umpiring association, and in particular Richard "Bullet" Alexander and Hollis Drake, brought in clinicians and Major League Baseball umpires to train us. Joe Brinkman and John McSherry (two of the best major league umpires ever and friends of Bullet) started coming up from Florida. They set the building blocks and helped train us to be where we are today. They came up every year for about six years and put on a Friday to Sunday umpiring clinic for us. They always brought along two triple-A-level umpires to help run the clinics.

What a learning experience! They broke down film on us and gave each of us copies, along with their phone numbers in case we had any questions.

Again, Bullet made sure one of the big league came up every year to train us. Bullet and John remained the best of friends until their respective passings, and today are probably still calling games in that highest of leagues together, up where the Man Upstairs is the Commissioner. We miss them both.

Bullet was the person that was probably the most instrumental in my training. He was my mentor and the one I will always give credit for getting me to the level I attained. I would, with no hesitation, say that Bullet was the one person most responsible for training ninety-five percent of the umpires in the Tidewater area and solely responsible for getting our local umpires to the collegiate level.

Bullet was also the one who got my son into umpiring and made sure he learned the correct way to do things. Anytime I had a game near Bullet's house, we would always stop by and see Bullet and his wife, Frances. I will never forget the day Bullet asked Frances to go out back to the shed and get Ryan a book Bullet had written about umpiring. He even signed it for Ryan. Talk about loving someone; Ryan was like a son to Bullet. On the way home, I told Ryan he was lucky. I never got one of the signed books from Bullet.

Larry Reveal (now director of Minor League Umpire Development) and Rich Humphrey (who worked in the major leagues for several years and many years in the high minors) were two more big-time umpires that passed on many skills to all of us. I was also fortunate enough to have been able to work all three levels of games with them (recreation, high school, and college). You always learned something each time; they made sure of that by quizzing you after the game.

VERY REVEALING

Speaking of Larry Reveal, I want to share a story about overzealous adults not keeping their priorities in order. One of our league presidents called me one night to complain about an umpire who would not allow a thirteen-year-old boy to play with a cast on his arm. He said the boy had already played in four games without anyone even mentioning it. Our umpire called me as well and explained that although there is no rule in the applicable rulebook prohibiting playing with a cast, he sidelined the player based upon the umpire-in-chief's authority to make rulings on matters that come up and are not covered by the rules. Good decision, I thought.

Unfortunately, this was not the end of it. The league wanted the kid to play! So I called Larry to get his take. He agreed that there was no rule on casts, but like me, he asked what parent would want their thirteen-year-old to risk further injury to himself or others, and what league would allow that?

We went back and forth with the league about who would bear liability if a second injury occurred. Our lawyer was not excited about a release of liability from the league standing up if we were sued by a parent of a different child injured through contact with the cast. Eventually, the league decided to allow the boy to play, a bad call, but this time not by the umpire. We continued to umpire his games since no rule prohibited casts on ball fields. This one was a real head-scratcher, but evidently, the league's position was cast not in plaster but in stone.

BACK TO BULLET

Each year, if you wanted to continue umpiring college baseball, you were required to attend the NCAA clinic as well as some of the local collegiate clinics. If you didn't attend, you didn't work college baseball. One of the main presenters was always Bullet Alexander. He was that well respected among the collegiate and professional umpires.

In March 2002, Bullet was able to get MLB umpire Jeff Nelson to start coming up to do clinics for us. He came up for several years, but then said the association knew what it was doing and felt we could save the expense of bringing up an MLB umpire and continue to do the things we did well. He also told us his phone line was open anytime we needed to call him concerning a rules or mechanics question. To this day Jeff is still one of the top MLB umpires and works the playoffs every year. Several times, we have also taken him up on his offer regarding rules or mechanics questions.

The highest compliment anyone could pay us was hearing from the likes of John McSherry, Joe Brinkman, and Jeff Nelson that we have one of the best umpiring associations in the United States. Nearly every one of our umpires has another full-time job and only so many hours to give to learning and improving his umpiring skills. Even so, with the kind of help we were able to receive from some the greats of the game, and with the mentoring we offer from our members, some of whom measure their experience in not years but decades, we have achieved something really valuable. Our impact is not just to the association's members, but more importantly, it's for the customers we serve, the young and older ballplayers of Hampton Roads.

CHAPTER 4

THE FUN GAMES

Before starting these stories, I would like to touch on how I learned to umpire recreation games. Recreation games were always the fun games to umpire if you just kept things in perspective. You needed to manage the game first and then know how to work with the coaches and the fans. The latter two were the biggest challenges. People often comment about the fans getting on umpires. Well, that's true, but it's especially true of younger parents who are overly protective of little Johnny or his sister. Older baseball parents have seen more and are more tolerant, at least up to a point.

DEALING WITH VOLUNTEER COACHES

The first challenge new umpires face is dealing with the coaches. Recreation league coaches are volunteers, and many have—well, let me be charitable—incomplete knowledge of the rules. They see coaches yelling at umpires on TV and think that is the way things are supposed to go. Let's get this straight. The late Earl Weaver of the Baltimore Orioles was not a good role model for recreation league coaches. The first step is to defuse the behavior of overly excited coaches, getting them to talk quietly. Good umpires will let them speak first and just listen. Sometimes they end up talking themselves right out of the argument. Sometimes they only come out for the sake of looking like they are representing their team.

If the umpire thinks the coach is just not going to calm down, it's time to turn him, so he is facing the fans. That way if he starts using profanity or bumps the umpire, he will be heard by others and can't deny it if he gets ejected. Coaches don't realize or sometimes forget that just like them, many umpires are just getting into umpiring. They are also the ones who overlook the games are supposed to be about the kids, not them.

AND THEN THERE ARE THE FANS

The second challenge umpires will face is the fans. They need or want all calls to go their way. If they don't, Mom and Dad need someone to blame other than their less than proficient son or daughter. It's just not possible that Johnny looked at that called third strike right down the middle. That leaves the umpire to be their scapegoat.

Interestingly, you can always tell when the coach's son or daughter comes up to bat as the intensity rises, both from the coach and the player's mother. It is the same thing when any of the other coach's son or daughter came up to bat. If they don't swing at the pitch, it absolutely, positively must have been a ball, and even if they did swing and made an out, it was because the umpire got the previous two pitches wrong, putting the kid in a two-strike hole. Same thing when the coach's kid is on defense. If his child is pitching and it was anywhere near the plate, it has to be a strike. Same with close plays at first or any other base. The umpire just about always has fifty percent of the fans disagreeing with his eyesight, judgment, and sometimes his integrity.

LADY AND THE TRAMP ER, UMP

So how does an umpire handle all these scenarios? It takes patience and years of training. You have to learn what works for you without coming off as arrogant. You can give new umpires suggestions, but they need to know there is no one particular way to handle things. Guide them and let them develop their own technique. Even though we don't teach carrying on conversations with fans in recreation games, many umpires do. Sometimes it helps the fans to see that you are human. What one has to remember is if you talk to one side, you need to talk to the other side also.

I always shared with our new umpires one of my techniques. One day I had a lady just eating me alive. Not knowing what to do, I decided to go over to the fence one inning and tell her I was sort of in a bind. I said that with my son on the other team and their head coach being my brother, I needed to make sure they won tonight, or no one would speak to me when I got home.

The lady was shocked and didn't know what to say. I just walked away. She immediately went to the league official to lodge a complaint. He laughed and told her I was messing with her like she was doing in a different way with me. I went back over two innings later, and she asked how the family was.

I told her "Great, and yours?"

I must have had her for three or four more games that year, and she always laughed and said, "How is the family doing?"

Will that work for everyone? No, but at least it did on one good night. We always say if you can handle recreation parents and coaches, you can handle almost any game. With the volume of games I did, the teams usually got to see me three or four times a year. They also got to know me over the years as their sons and daughters moved up to the next level. The two real good things about umpiring recreation games are time limits and mercy rules. These keep the games from going on for hours and can be real lifesavers.

THE GOOD WIFE WAS NOT JUST A TV SHOW

Now I would like to continue my storytelling adventures with three of the most important memories of my early officiating career. It wasn't about the games; it was the birth of our children.

What a day August 8, 1983, turned out to be. My oldest daughter, Ashley, was born at 6:44 AM. I received a call a few hours later to work the Jim Catfish Hunter Thoroughbred World Series (nineteen-to-twenty-one-year-olds). My wife gave me the okay, so I left the hospital around 11:00 AM to go work my game at 1 PM. Bullet Alexander, my assigner, saw me walking in from the parking lot with my base gear and asked me where my plate stuff was.

I said, "In the car."

He said, "Go get it, you've got the plate and are getting the opportunity of a lifetime today. We are going to see how well you can handle pressure."

Talk about being nervous. But Bullet helped me relax and said, "I know you can do it, or I would not have put you in the game."

These teams and players were considered some of the best college players who played ball in the summer. I had a team from Palo Alto, California playing one from Chesapeake, Virginia. I made it through the game without any controversy, but boy, was I nervous the entire game. After a short post-game discussion, I dashed back to the hospital to see my beautiful newborn daughter.

Our next child, Lauren, was born on February 18, 1987. At 6:25 AM. Dick Bowie, our basketball assigner, called to congratulate both my wife and me, but that didn't last long as he soon asked if I wanted to work a playoff game that night. Again, this presented another amazing opportunity! I did the game and hurried back to the hospital.

Our third child, Ryan, was born on June 12, 1991, at 3:22 PM. Yes, this was during the baseball season, but miraculously, I had no game and just had a wonderful day at the hospital with Ryan, my girls and my tired but happy wife.

PERFECT GAMES

I was lucky enough to have been able to umpire three perfect games in my officiating career. One in recreation in 1985, one in college in 1989, and one in high school in 1997. My first was on July 17, 1985. The perfecto occurred in the State Bronco Tournament Finals game with twelve-year-olds. The pitcher,

Brian Strealau, struck out all twenty-one batters he faced. Again, these kids were only twelve years old, but they were the best in the state, and to think not a single batter walked, grounded, or flew out. It was unbelievable, and I was pleased to be a part of it.

HURRICANE CHARLIE GAMES

On August 17, 1986, we worked one of the most memorable National Senior Baseball World Series Tournament games ever. This tournament consisted of some of the best college baseball players from some of the powerhouse colleges and universities all over the United States. It was such a big event that it attracted numerous scouts for every game.

It had been raining off and on for two days as Hurricane Charlie was working its way up the east coast and supposed to hit our area in three hours. We had to move all the remaining games from Met Park (former home of the Norfolk Tides) to Old Dominion University due to the field flooding. The AAA team was also due back in town later in the week, and the grounds crew needed time to repair any damages from the hurricane. We started the second semifinal game in nasty, rainy conditions around 2 PM, thinking we could get it in. LaGrange, Illinois was down 7-6 but rallied and took the lead from Churchland/Western Branch (a Virginia team) in the top of the seventh and last inning. They went up 8-6. However, in the bottom of the seventh inning, the game had to be called, as by that time the rain was coming down sideways. Since the game was official after five innings, by rule the score of the game reverted to end of the sixth inning (the

1986 NATIONAL SR. BASEBALL WORLD SERIES DURING HURRICANE CHARLIE

last completed inning), and the Virginia team ended up being declared the winner.

The visiting team was furious and made a phone call to Tournament Headquarters to try and get the ruling overturned. Their appeal failed. I was umpire-in-chief for that game, and as you can imagine, I caught a ton of grief from the Illinois teams. You could say I would not be on their Christmas card list.

1986 NATIONAL SR. BASEBALL WORLD SERIES DURING HURRICANE CHARLIE— NO HELP FROM BLUE

Once the hurricane hit the coast that night, it weakened and picked up speed. Luckily on the next day after a short delay and after heroic work by a superb grounds crew, we were able to play ball. We started the game around 10:00 AM, keeping in mind the team from California had a 2:00 flight that could not be changed. Both agreed to play nine innings or until 12:30, whichever came first, no matter whether it was in the top or bottom half of the inning. This would allow California time to get to the airport to catch their flight. At the end of the seventh inning, right at 12:30 PM, with California ahead 7-6, the players tipped their caps toward each other, and the visitors ran to the bus to get to the airport to catch their flight back home. God was with us that day, as we were able to play through the light rain from the backside of the hurricane. I was lucky to get a call from the assigner and be able to work both the semis and finals.

CHEATERS MAY PROSPER BUT EVENTUALLY GET CAUGHT

The next story I would like to share proves that cheaters get caught more often than not. We were at Cascade Park in the South Norfolk area of Norfolk, Virginia, doing a Palomino Tournament game (ages seventeen-eighteen). A team from Tennessee was always the powerhouse up to that time. They seemed always to win and win by a large margin. One night in late August, one of the teams got word that one of the players on Tennessee was not the same player that they listed on their affidavit of eligibility. The tournament director, Flash Gordon (not the sci-fi hero), decided to do a little checking into it. For the sake of the story, we will use the fictitious names Jim (eighteen years old) and John (nineteen years old). Jim was the name listed on the affidavit. John, his older brother, was a much better player but looked a lot like his brother.

Mr. Gordon decided to call Tennessee and see who answered the phone. The person answering the phone, not knowing who was on the other line, introduced himself as Jim. When asked if he could speak to John, an innocent and unprepared Jim said, "He is in Virginia playing baseball."

Goes to show, cheaters eventually get caught. PONY baseball revoked the Tennessee players' franchise, and that is the last time they fielded a team.

TIMING IS EVERYTHING

The next story is a very short one but will illustrate one very key word in umpires' lingo, **timing.** I was working first base in a tournament game. We were in the bottom of the seventh inning with a runner on third and a ball hit down the first baseline, approximately six feet foul. All of a sudden the ball hits a rock and kicks inside first base, making it a fair ball. The ball caroms into right field and the runner on third scores the winning run. However, my partner called the ball foul as it hit the rock, which killed the ball, sending the batter back to the plate and the runner back to third.

Imagine trying to work your way out of this situation without having to throw the coach out. He came to me asking if I would help my partner, but I told him once the ball is called foul, it remains foul. We go into extra innings, and wouldn't you know, the other team scores and wins the game. Talk about needing to have a police escort to your cars; this was one of those games. Again, good timing is a skill that we teach all the time. Take your time, let the play happen, and then make the call.

FLASH GORDON

For those that ever had the honor of working a PONY tournament game for Flash Gordon, this was one of the classics. This was a Colt tournament game somewhere around 1980 that started off at Cascade Park in South Norfolk. It had rained all day, and the field was soaked and just not playable. So Flash, with his many connections, called the Coast Guard and asked if they would send over a couple of helicopters to blow the field dry. The Coast Guard rescued the terrain, and two hours later we were ready to play ball. Just as we got ready to start playing, here came another storm. Not being able to get the helicopters back, Flash pulled another trick out of his bag. He had the field spread with a quantity of gasoline and set it on fire to dry it out. That worked, and we were ready to play ball, except for one thing . . . here came another storm. Now Flash started calling around to find another field. We finally got Great Bridge Middle School as the only dry field in Tidewater. We started the game around midnight and ended around two o'clock in the morning. Now that was determination, and during the several periods of lightning, you might say it was Flash out of the pan and using the fire.

Usually, after a game, umpires sit down and discuss the game while drinking a beer and a few might do some things they would prefer not to report. However, not after this game. Given the late ending, my partner got in his car, rushed home, got his wife, kept her in her pajamas, and brought her back to the ballpark to make sure that she knew he was actually working a game at 2:00 in the morning. True story that umpires still tell today.

ADULT BASEBALL

This story took place in our local adult league called the Tidewater Summer League. Mike Mungin is still a very good friend of mine, and even though both of us have retired from active baseball, we stay in touch. Mike was a terrific pitcher in his younger days. He played on the Green Run High School State Championship Team here in Virginia Beach and then went on to pitch for the Oakland Athletics. He stayed with the A's until arm problems ended his career. He then pitched in the local adult league (Tidewater Summer League) for several more years. The league consisted of college students home for the summer looking for a place to play, college graduates who still wanted to play during the summer, and some who had played small stints in professional ball. To umpire these games, you really needed to have umpired on the collegiate level.

One night, Mike and the other pitcher, also with some pro experience, were both throwing gas in the upper eighties to low nineties. On numerous occasions that night, the opposing pitcher had no idea where his fastball was going. He ended up hitting three of Mike's teammates. Mike was cruising along in the fifth inning of a nine-inning game, throwing pitches anywhere from six inches above the knees to six inches below the knees and working on a no-hitter. Bob Campbell was working the plate, and I was working the bases.

As mentioned previously, Mike had just watched three of his teammates hit with pitches, so he decided to retaliate. Instead of hitting the victim in the tush, Mike hit him in the middle of the back with a 9oh-mph fastball. The benches cleared. Mike tried to say it had slipped out of his hand, but I told him, no one with his control that night was going to miss that high. He had to go, or the game would likely have gone nuclear. We ended up getting control of that situation with no further ejections. He went on to be one of the better HS Coaches, and we still laugh about the play. Several years ago, he finally admitted what we had all instantly known: it was intentional.

VISITING IN THE VALLEY LEAGUE

As mentioned earlier, each summer umpire, working their way up to college ball, wanted to work in the Valley League, located in the mountains of Virginia. My first Valley League game was on June 25, 1993, with Bullet Alexander. We had two good teams that night, and the locals packed the stands. The stands down toward first and third were no more than twenty feet away from you at most of the parks, and the locals would start on you from pitch one. Umpire baiting was their summer entertainment in these rural towns. Thank goodness Bullet had prepared me. He said that on any pitch or call that did not go for the home team, they were going to let you know about it. Bullet had the plate for the first game, and I was on the bases. I thought Bullet, a former minor-league umpire and one of the top umpires on the east coast, could get away with just about anything. Wrong: they were on him all night, as it seemed like every pitch they whined that he missed.

Two nights later I had my second Valley League game, also with Bullet. I figured it was now my time to be eaten alive, and they would leave Bullet alone. Wrong again: they were on him all night, as it seemed like every call he had was a banger that went against the home team. As for my fun on this lovely June night, I had to throw out the catcher and coach for arguing balls and strikes. The funny part about this story is I did not get booed; I was cheered. Here is the catch: both ejections went against the visiting team.

My night did not go entirely without controversy. In the fourth inning, I got yelled at on a swinging bunt play up the first baseline. The pitcher fielded the ball going up the first baseline and tagged the batter-runner. I was blocked out and did not see the tag, so I called the runner safe, no tag. The crowd erupted, and the coach came flying out of the dugout demanding I go for help. I did, and fortunately, Bullet saw a tag. I went from being a bum to getting a standing ovation. Again, the call went for the home team, but I am sure the applause I received was just a coincidence.

MUCHAS GRACIAS, AMIGOS

On August 8, 1993, I was fortunate enough to work the Mustang World Series Championship game in Virginia Beach. Puerto Rico beat Great Bridge (Virginia) 8-2. The unique thing about this game was that none of the Puerto Rican fans spoke English, and both of the coaches struggled with English. Having taken Spanish in HS and college, and with my wife's Hispanic family background, I was able to communicate with all. For them, just the honor of someone trying to communicate in their native language meant the world, not only for them but for me also.

WORKING WITH A BIG-LEAGUE UMPIRE

The next two stories are about games with a professional umpire named Rich Humphrey. Rich was an umpire that worked in the minors but also had some time in the big leagues before retiring and deciding to go back to working his roots, recreation baseball. He also became one of our association's instructors and evaluators, as well as the chairman of the Baseball Committee.

One night, Rich was a last-minute fill-in for a game scheduled at Plaza Little League. When I found out that I was working with Rich, I was about as nervous as I had ever been. I had never worked a game with an umpire that had been in the major leagues. I will always remember his statement to me at the car, "Relax, we both put our pants on the same way." He then told me he needed my help, as it had been a long time since he had worked a recreation game. He said he was going to rely on me to help him with the recreation rules.

The one play that I will never forget and mechanic that I carried with me throughout my entire umpiring career dealt with pop-ups around first base. After the game, Rich asked me who had ball responsibility on the pop-up at first. I looked at him and told him that I was sure that my answer was going to be wrong, so I asked him to give me his reasoning.

His comment was, "There is no right or wrong answer. It is no one's ball until you communicate with each other."

His further advice was, any time you have a pop-up around first base, with nobody on base, he liked to give the ball up to the plate umpire. That releases the base umpire to go ahead and come on the inside of the diamond. By doing this, the base umpire does not get in the way of any fielder trying to catch the pop-up, as well as being able to get out of the way of the batter-runner. If the base umpire does take the ball, then the plate umpire, with all the heavy gear on, has to take the batter all the way into second or third. Not a great way to make friends with your partner. Anyone that ever umpired with me from that day forward very seldom ever saw me take ball responsibility on pop-ups around first. That depth of analysis and reasoning differentiates professional and longtime college umpires from the guys who labor in the obscurity of recreation and even high school fields.

The second story about Rich deals with intimidation. Not only me, but most umpires seemed to be intimidated when working with Rich, I guess mainly because most of us had never umpired with a major league umpire before. Rich had a classic line after every game, "evaluate yourself and then evaluate me." Most of us were afraid to say anything about Rich, fearing intimidation.

I will never forget one night in late July. Rich and I were doing an adult game at Lake Taylor High School where the lights were not quite equivalent to a pair of candles. Generally, with no runners on base, a ball hit to left-field or left-center field was the plate umpire's responsibility for catch or no catch. Having worked this field numerous times and knowing how bad the lights were, I told Rich that any ball from the left fielder over toward the right-field line was going to be my ball responsibility. He looked at me like I was crazy, but I told him, after the third inning he would understand why. Sure enough, around the third inning, it got dark, and he realized why I was taking all flyball responsibility. Once it got dark, any ball hit to the outfield was a guessing game for the plate umpire and in most cases for the outfielders.

After the game, he asked me the usual questions to evaluate myself and evaluate him. I told him the one thing that I screwed up was communication on a pop-up around first base. He agreed. He then asked me to evaluate him. I told him I thought his timing was horsebleep and strike zone was not one of his best jobs.

He looked at me and laughed and said, "You are finally there, aren't you."

"What do you mean?"

"You are no longer intimidated by me."

"You are one hundred percent correct."

He told me that he had not umpired for the past three weeks and knew that his zone and timing was off. He also said that if I had told him that he had a good game, he would know I was not telling him the truth.

WORKING WITH A BIG-LEAGUE PITCHER

I will never forget the honor of umpiring games for Gary Lavelle, a former San Francisco Giants pitcher, when he pitched a summer game in one of our local adult leagues. Being behind the plate calling pitches for him was an honor, and let me tell you, he still could bring it. The ball had incredible movement. As he was walking to the mound, he said, "Don't pinch me; give me as much as you can for the old timer." Well, he didn't need my help or anyone else's.

For many years, Gary was the Head Baseball Coach at Greenbrier Christian Academy and led the Gators to conference and state titles almost every year. We remain very good friends, both as a former umpire and assigner.

NATIONAL AAU TOURNAMENT EJECTIONS

One of the highlights of my recreation umpiring days was working several of the National AAU Tournaments. Both were in the 16U age bracket. Nelson Adcock, one of the top officials for AAU baseball, was the one that was most responsible for bringing the tournament to the Tidewater area for five straight years.

The first tournament was in August 1998. There was only one memorable game here. I was working the tournament championship game at Old Dominion University. The two teams were East Cobb (Atlanta) and Knoxville, Tennessee. It seemed like East Cobb had a coach for every player on the team. They had a head coach, two separate base coaches, pitching coach, hitting coach, outfield and infield coaches and not sure how many more. In one game, I kept hearing complaints that umpires call "chirping" on any close pitch. I finally figured out in about the fourth inning that the catcher was signaling to the pitching coach anytime he thought I missed. I told him that if he had a problem on a pitch, he needed to ask me, not shove it up my rear telling the coach I missed it.

I should have known at the end of the inning he would tell his pitching coach., who came out fuming and told me not to accuse his catcher of relaying signals. I told him I knew what the signals were, and it left him speechless. I told him the next time a pitch was close, and his catcher went to his mask with his glove, and he opened his mouth, they both were done. Like most coaches, he wasn't speechless for long and asked if I was threatening him. I said no. He said you better not be. I told him that was enough, knowing he would take the bait. Rather than understanding that was his last warning, he told me not to tell him how to coach. I told him there was no need for me to do that because he wouldn't be coaching anymore today.

"I have never been thrown out of a game before."

"Well, you have been now."

He then had to get his money's worth saying, "Do you know who I am?"

"Yes, you are the coach that just got ejected."

"I am the pitching coach for Georgia Tech, and I am getting paid to coach these kids, so they deserve good umpiring. I know when an umpire is missing pitches. My catcher would never lie; catchers never lie."

By this time the tension had increased, and frankly, I was done with this pretentious guy but also somewhat amused. I told him that I was a college-level catcher at East Carolina, so he shouldn't bring the catcher stuff into that argument. As we are taught to do, my partner came and got between us. I started walking away, and my partner escorted him to the gate.

The second tournament ran from July 25 to August 4 of 2001. This was a much larger tournament, and we had teams from all over the United States. The games I umpired had teams from Los Angeles and Sacramento, California; Houston, Texas; Seattle, Washington; Philadelphia and Pittsburgh, Pennsylvania; Boston, Massachusetts; Columbus, Ohio; Middletown and Knoxville, Tennessee; and four or five other states.

I had several very memorable games in the tournament, all of which resulted in ejections. You never like ejections in national tournaments, but some of the teams must have been able to get away with murder with their home associations. The most memorable one was between LA and Houston Texas. We didn't find out until mid-way through the game that they had already played each other twice earlier in the year and had very bad blood toward each other. There was a lot of chirping between the two teams, and I had to issue a team warning in the third inning for pitchers throwing at batters. The Houston coach took exception to it and came out to argue with me. Two batters later, I called a balk on his pitcher. He went off on me, telling me I had no clue what a balk was. I ejected him, and he told me I would never work another one of his games, and he could guarantee me of that. As I was leaving, I called my commissioner, explained what had happened, and told him the report would be sent to him later that night. He asked me if I wanted their next game, and I said sure. Both the team and I had a thirty-minute drive to that site. You can imagine the look on the coach's face when I showed up at home plate.

The next ejection happened in the York, Pennsylvania and Franklin, Tennessee game. I ended up throwing out both the head coach and catcher for arguing balls and strikes. They didn't even try to hide it. The coach asked the catcher where the pitch was, and he said it was a strike, even though I had called it a ball. I got both together at the end of the inning and told both of them I was not sure how they did it in their home state, but if they had a problem with balls and strikes, we were going to handle things a little different today. They just didn't get it, and the coach continued to yell out to his catcher if he thought I missed it. Each time, the catcher yelled back to his coach it was a strike. Both ended up getting ejected and couldn't seem to understand why. What part of "don't argue balls and strikes" didn't they get?

The last ejection occurred in a game between Davidson, Maryland and Seattle, Washington. In this game, I was working the bases. The coach for Seattle came out to argue a call at second base. We went nose to nose, and he ended up pulling the old "flip the bill of the hat" trick. That was an easy and automatic ejection. He asked me for what, and I told him I had been down that road in a college game and knew what he was doing. After the game, he followed us to the parking lot, held up his phone and yelled over to me, "Seven-Eleven is on the phone, and they have found a job that you are qualified for."

That night he wrote a letter of apology and hand-delivered it to me. He apologized for both the hat incident and comment made in the parking lot. He said he had been way out of line, and his wife had said if he didn't apologize, he would need to find another way home three thousand miles to Seattle after the tournament was over. Amazing, isn't it, the power wives sometimes wield over their husbands.

FREE PASS TO THE BAR

Somewhere in the early '90s, Nick Sessoms, one of my very close friends, coached the Kempsville Palomino team (seventeen-eighteen-year-olds) for many years. Nick was also one of the best softball players and exceptional athletes to come out of Virginia Beach. The best games in this league were always between Kempsville and Lynnhaven. Umpires fought for that game. In those games, everything was strictly business, and there were at least five hundred fans in attendance. Only the top umpires got these games, and they better bring their "A" game that night. In most of the other games, Kempsville would be ahead by at least fifteen runs by the fourth or fifth inning. Since these games were during the hot and muggy summer days, about the fifth inning, Nick would pick a semi-close play and come out and say it was time for him to go. He would carry on with his hands waving in the air looking like he was chewing us out, all the time telling us a couple of jokes. He was one of the best joke-tellers you ever ran across.

He would make a big show and then say, "Toss me, and the first round is on me." He would then head back to the dugout and tell his players that he didn't think he did enough to get tossed, but they would be okay. What many never knew and may not know until now is this was all staged. There was a bar about two blocks away that we always went to after the game. Nick just made sure he got an early start.

DON'T GET OFF WORK EARLY ON GAME DAYS

Nick had a son named Rob, an exceptional baseball player who ended up playing at Old Dominion University. After his college playing days, Rob decided to continue playing in our local summer league. One day, Rob got off work early and made the mistake of going out drinking. When he came up to the plate the first time, he said, "Jim, I can hardly see the ball. Help me out this first at-bat, and I should be okay the next time up."

I said okay and went out to the pitcher to tell him to walk him kind of intentionally. He obliged.

The next time Rob came up, he lined a single to right. I called time and brought him back to the plate. He asked why.

I said I had called time, making the ball dead. I really hadn't, but I told him, "Now you and the pitcher are even."

He ended up grounding out. We still laugh about the story every time we see each other.

LATE TO THE PLATE

This story comes from Jeff Aldridge, then a Little Leaguer whose memory of a day long ago stuck with him. I never told him my hands were stinging.

Jim, when I heard you were doing a book, I asked to share a story where you were umpiring a Little League game that I was playing in. I didn't know you well, but I knew you were a star catcher and played at both Rose High School and ECU around the time my brother Mike did.

I remember one game in particular when I was pitching, and you were umpiring behind the plate at Guy Smith Stadium. My catcher that day was late getting on his gear, and no one from the bench came out one inning to warm me up. You put your protector and mask down, squatted behind the plate, and motioned for me to go ahead and throw to you.

You were barehanded, and so I just barely tossed the first warm-up pitch.

You threw it back and said, "Go ahead and bring it."

I said, "I don't want to hurt you."

You said I wouldn't so I threw the next one a little harder.

You said, "That was a little better, but this time, give it all you have."

I don't want to sound like I'm bragging about my ability then, but for a Little Leaguer, I threw pretty hard, and the last thing I wanted to do was hurt or show up the umpire.

I threw the next one about half speed, and you said something like, "Come on! I said show me what you've got!"

I reared back on the next one and let it go, throwing as hard as I could, and you caught it, didn't flinch, and tossed it back to me and said something like "That's more like it, good pitch!"

Then on the next pitch, you told everyone you were throwing it down. The catcher said he would throw it, but you told him you had it, and if he got dressed quicker the next inning, he could throw it down. You better believe our catcher got dressed fast from then on.

THE TRUTH MAY BE PAINFUL

Here comes a painful memory from a player who understood the game, especially the inside edge of the plate better than most.

My name is David "Red" Lindsay, and I met Mr. Jim Smith while playing for the Tidewater Drillers. I was always thrilled when I saw Mr. Smith walk up to do one of our games. You always knew you were going to get his very best effort and a great game from him.

As a player, I was hit by a lot of pitches. One summer, I was hit by twenty-five of them. This one evening, I was hit by a pitch, and dropped my bat and sprinted as hard as I could to first base. Mr. Smith brought me back to plate. Even though I had basically jumped into the path of the pitch, I had to ask Mr. Smith, "How do you expect me to hit now? You have just told the pitcher he owns the inside part of the plate."

Mr. Smith smiled at me and said, "Red, get your tail back in this box; you know what you did."

I picked up my bat and stood at the edge of the box for a moment. I barely turned and lifted my head and smiled at Mr. Smith through the corner of my eyes, just below the bill of my helmet, so no one could tell I was talking to him—and said, "Yeah, I know, great call!"

Mr. Smith is my all-time favorite umpire. He gave you his very best. If he missed a call, which was extremely rare, he would admit it and move on. I have always had so much respect for him. I always will.

CONFUSED, CONCUSSED, OR MAYBE BOTH

In the summer of 1982, I was working a seventeen-year-old Palomino recreation league game with Moses Wheatley. Supposedly, there were two real good teams, and at this age, you would think they could pitch and catch. WRONG. For those that do not know, the distance from the pitcher's plate to home plate is sixty feet six inches. If only the pitchers knew that.

In the first two innings, I would estimate getting hit with at least ten pitches that bounced five feet in front of the plate. All should have been easily caught or stopped by seventeen-year-olds, but that is another part of the story. Both starting catchers were out of town playing in other tournaments, so I was working behind two non-catchers. Neither knew how to or perhaps even cared to block pitches in the dirt. Not wanting to get hit, even with all their gear on to protect them, they bailed on me.

Somewhere in the third inning, here came a fastball that bounced five feet in front of the plate. The catcher basically fled and did an ole, and I turned to try and stay behind him and took the pitch squarely and sadly on my unprotected left ear. I was down for the count—for about ten minutes, and if it was a prize fight, it would have been a knockout. Anyway, this was long before anyone cared about concussion protocols, and when I came to, I insisted on continuing. There happened to be a nurse in the stands, and she came out insisting I go to the hospital, thinking since blood was pouring out of my ear, I might have suffered a concussion. Two innings later, having no memory of the previous innings and a massive headache, I gave up and let them take me to the hospital. Sure enough, when I got there, the concussion was confirmed. My wife was called to come and take me home.

While we were still at the hospital my assignor, the late, great Bullet Alexander, called me. I remember his comment like it was yesterday, in the way only he could say it, "Jim, what in the hell are you doing turning your head?" There was no "Are you okay" or "How do you feel?" What a great laugh we had.

So I turned around and shot back at him "Alright, Smart A_____. What would you have done?"

He told me there were four things I could have done: 1) insist on new catchers, 2) grab ahold of the catcher when he started moving away, 3) go behind the mound and start calling pitches, or, what he would have done: 4) call the game on the grounds that these so-called catchers were making a mockery of it, and I was not out there for target practice.

This was one of many lessons learned from Bullet. What fun other coaches had for the rest of the summer with their one-liners.

"Jim are you sure you're over that concussion?" said one. "'Cuz you're not seeing the ball real well today."

Another loudmouth yelled, "We will be glad to take you to the doctor again, cause you sure aren't seeing real well."

One of my favorites was a coach who came out to argue on a pitch and with deadpan face said he told his catcher to let the next high one over the inside corner to just go by so he could get a new and decent plate umpire! Tough crowd.

THE DAY I WAS A RECREATION LEAGUE PARENT

2010 NABA (National Adult Baseball Association) vs. Umpires All-Star Game—In 2008 the league president for the NABA teams and I thought about putting together a players-versus-umpires game. We thought this would be a fun day for all. As we were soon to find out, it may have been fun, but it was a highly competitive game that would carry bragging rights for a year.

They would select their best players from all fourteen teams, and we would take our best-playing umpires, many with former high school and some with college experience. In 2008, the players took us lightly, and the umpires beat up the All-Stars something like 22-1. In 2009, they came back and beat us with a walk-off hit in the bottom of the ninth.

So 2010 was the rubber match. We only got six hits that day off one of the top pitchers in the league, Will Somerindyke. My son, Ryan, got three of them and shocked all of us. One of them happened to be the game-winner as we would find out two innings, after what I will describe next. Talk about being a proud papa.

Near the end of the game, the NABA team had the winning run on second base. Their batter hit a deep shot to center field that had two-run homer written all over it. I just turned my back in frustration. All of a sudden, I heard our guys leaping for joy. Our center fielder had made an over-the-shoulder catch at the fence. What I didn't know was Ryan had moved from right field to center field and was the one who made the catch. What a great father-son moment! I will never forget it! Who said an umpire could not also be a fan?

CHAPTER 5

SPRING GAMES
WITH JACKETS

The strange thing about most of the high school games during my career was we seemed to always be in long johns (as they were called in the old days), gloves, and anything else we could put on to stay warm, with very few days in short sleeves. I think the "weather gods" liked messing with the games in our part of the state. However, before going into the stories, I will say I was lucky enough to work eighteen VHSL state playoff baseball games. The reward here came from having the right mentors and listening to what they had to say. Later in the book, you will see the ways I tried to give back as a veteran umpire and then as commissioner.

One of my favorite scholastic catchers to umpire behind was Jimmy Hunt, who played at Princess Anne High in Virginia Beach, Virginia. He always kept the balls off the umpires, and all umpires loved to do his games. He was also fun to communicate with as the game progressed. All he wanted to know was where the zone was going to be that day. If he knew you were having a bad day, he never changed the way he thought about you. If the pitcher had an attitude, he took care of it for you. After high school, he went to Virginia Tech, where he played for four years. After college, he came back to coach locally as an assistant at First Colonial High School and then moved on to become head coach at Princess Anne High School.

While Coach Hunt was still in high school, his dad kept score for the team. It seemed like he would ask for the count after every third pitch, and if he thought you missed it, which was often, trust me, he would let you know about it.

One day, I told Jimmy I was going to have some fun with his dad. Every time he asked for the count, I was going to give him the wrong count. In the meantime, I would visually give the batter the real count. In the third or fourth inning, the elder Hunt came up to me and asked if I was okay. I told him that since he was always asking for the count, I would have some fun with him that day. No problem from that day on. He just went to asking every once in a while.

Coach Van was the Princess Anne head coach, and during one particular game, he got hit in the head and knocked out by a foul ball. After he was medically cleared to coach again, he was required to wear a batting helmet. To make sure he stayed one hundred percent safe, I tasked Mr. Hunt with making sure any time Coach Van got close to the edge of the fence to pull him back. I guess he appreciated this duty, because he never asked me about the count again.

THE LINEUP CARD GAME

This game was between Salem and Kempsville, played at Salem. I was working the bases that day, and my partner was working his first varsity game. I was sent there to work with and evaluate him. During the fourth inning, Kempsville's Coach Ray Barlow approached the plate umpire with a lineup change. I could see my partner was struggling with the changes, but I wanted to give him time to work through it. Coach Barlow had already won four state championships, was a bear of a man with a voice to match, and was real well known around the area, but he was also known to play mind games. This was going to be one of those days.

While Coach Barlow and the plate umpire were standing on the first baseline talking about the changes, I noticed the assistant coach start out to the mound to talk to the pitcher. I stopped him before he crossed the line and told him only one coach could be out there. Here comes the crazy part. He was putting in a relief pitcher, but before the new pitcher got out there to get in his warm-ups, the shortstop threw three pitches to the catcher. Then the second baseman threw two pitches. So now I thought I would sit back and watch the circus. Before it was over, the first baseman threw a couple of pitches and then walked off laughing.

Neither he nor anyone from Kempsville got the final laugh. As we broke up the conference, I told my partner the shortstop was the new pitcher because once the substitute takes the pitcher's position, even in warm-ups, he is in that spot and is required to pitch to the next batter until that batter is retired, gets on base, or is injured. Coach Barlow certainly knew the rule but argued. I quickly explained what had gone on and what the rule was. He then said the kids were just having a little fun. I told him he was responsible for his team's actions, and I would be glad to end his day early if he wanted to continue arguing. He promptly signaled the shortstop to stay on the mound, and from that day on, he and I got along great.

THE NOTE GAME

One game occurred back in the early '80s. First Colonial's Coach Norbie Wilson and I commonly referred to it as the Note Game. What I need to interject here is that Coach Wilson and I played ball against each other in college. After college and to this day, he and I are the best of friends and talk often. Coach Wilson had been chirping for several innings about safes and outs, so I gave him a warning. Knowing him and loving to work Coach Wilson's games, I should have known that would never work.

Several innings later, here came Coach Wilson, flying out of the dugout to question another call.

I tossed him.

He said, "For what?"

I said, "For running and not walking."

With mock sincerity, he said, "I apologize, sir."

I thanked him and told him he was still done and his runner was still out.

Now you need to know that an ejected coach is prohibited from communicating with his team in any way. I should have known something was up as he had one of his student managers walk to the building with him. I continued to see the student manager go back and forth and finally saw him hand a piece of paper to one of the assistant coaches on the field. I pulled a piece of paper out of my own notepad and wrote Coach Wilson a little note.

"Coach Wilson, if I see your manager make one more trip to that building, I am going to forfeit the game. Then I am going to confiscate all your notes and send them to the VHSL office."

I asked the manager to go give it to Coach Wilson, wherever he was hiding. Now read on, so Coach Wilson can provide you with his version of the Note and some other good stories.

Time to throw you readers a changeup. I'm Norbie Wilson, and I have many Jim Smith stories to tell Here's what really happened in the Note Game back in the 1980s. After all, how often does a coach get an opportunity to talk about an umpire?

THE NOTE

I had already been warned once by Jim to stay in the dugout. I should have known better, but I stormed out on the field one more time; yes, I had been out before, to dispute a call. Jim tossed me from the game and told me to leave the premises immediately. Before I left the field, I called my student team manager to join me in exile. I went into the high school building and settled next to the window in the second-floor math room, so I could be inconspicuous but still see the game. I then proceeded to send notes back and forth to the dugout through my manager. After about thirty minutes of this, my manager returned, somewhat concerned and somewhat breathless, with one more note and a very sheepish look on his face. When I opened it, there in Jim's handwriting was this terse message, "Send one more note to your players, and you will forfeit the game."

I had to chuckle. Busted! Sharp guy, that Jim Smith.

THE BALK

Our team was playing Tallwood High School, then coached by the legendary Ray Barlow. I was always intimidated by Ray. He had won four state championships at Kempsville High School in the 1970s, and now, in the 1990s, he was trying to build a winning program at Tallwood. I was pumped!

We were much better on paper than they were, but they were starting a crafty left-hander against us. I believed he "balked" every time he threw a pickoff attempt to first base. In fact, he picked off three of my runners in the first two innings.

I kept going to Jim Smith, the plate umpire, and Bill McInnis, a seasoned umpire who was covering his first game in Virginia Beach. I got no satisfaction from either one. They ran me back and forth between the two of them for at least four innings, smiling and chuckling as my blood pressure kept going up and up. Finally, I just said *the hell with it!* and we started going the minute the pitcher lifted his leg. We just "outran" the pick and won the game going away. Not one more runner got picked.

After the game, I stopped by where the two "bums" were changing out of their umpire gear. They stood there laughing at me! Jim said, "Why didn't you start running on the first movement earlier?! I would have!"

They had been pulling my chain the whole game. Jim was just trying to see how Bill would handle me since I didn't know him, and it was Bill's first game in this area. Jim beamed with his approval, and Mr. McInnis went on to become one of the best umps in our region.

BOB KYLE

First Colonial High School was playing Manor High School in a non-district game at our place. Manor was coached by one of my long-time friends, Bruce Phelps. We had some good-natured battles over the years, and there had always been a mutual respect between us.

The umpires for the game were Jim Smith and Bob Kyle. Bob had thrown me out in the last game we had with him. He was behind the plate, and our greeting to one another at home plate was a little strained. I was still steamed about my previous ejection, and Bob, Jim, and Coach Phelps all knew it.

In the top of the second, we called for a fastball on the outside of the plate. Our catcher never moved his mitt.

"Ball one!" called out Mr. Kyle.

I looked at my catcher, and he dropped his mitt—a sign that Mr. Kyle had missed the pitch. I called the same pitch again, and again it hit the same spot.

"Ball two!" said Mr. Kyle, who looked right at me for a response. I just stared back at him.

After the batter walked, I immediately went to Jim Smith. His exact comment was "Don't come down here to talk about a fellow umpire, and I'd advise you not to stare or say anything to Mr. Kyle."

"Well, thanks for all your help, Jim!" I replied.

"Thank YOU, Coach Wilson," said Jim.

I didn't take his advice, and when I walked past Mr. Kyle, he motioned that was my first time out and charged me with a visit to the pitcher. I told him very quietly to use his finger in his anal region; I'm just saying as a suppository or something of that nature. He tossed me, as he should have.

Jim Smith and Bruce Phelps were waiting in the parking lot after the game to joke me. They asked me what part of Bob Kyle saying "play ball" at the beginning of the game pissed me off.

As I said many years later to Jim, I liked and respected Bob Kyle, but he threw me out of two games, and I had a total of only six tosses in twenty-six years.

BENCH-CLEARING GAME

Bayside High School was playing a game at Salem High School somewhere in the midst of the 80s to determine who was in first place. I was on the bases for this game. Throughout the game, there was a lot of trash talking that both my plate partner, Bob Campbell, and myself had to monitor. During

BOB CAMPBELL—EVOA ICON AND
ONE OF MY CLOSEST FRIENDS

the game, the catcher from Salem kept stirring things up. Salem was leading the entire game and was up by three runs going into the fifth inning. Bayside ended up scoring three runs to tie the game. One of my former middle school students, Ramon Estevez (Poppy as we called him), came up to bat. He hit a line shot down the first baseline and ended up scoring an inside-the-park home run to tie the game up.

While approaching the plate, he ran over the Salem catcher, to which the catcher naturally took exception. Both players started after each other, and Bob got in between them to try and stop anything else from happening. Both benches cleared and came on the field. Both Bob and I blocked what we could, but they all went after each other. As I was trying to get ahold of Poppy, the Salem coach grabbed him from behind. Big mistake, as Poppy was six foot two and about 250 pounds. As Poppy started to swing, not knowing who had laid hands on him, I yelled, "Poppy, this is Mr. Smith, don't do it."

He stopped, and I got him out of the way, fearing for what might happen if he hit anyone. He was also an All-State linebacker that went on to play college football, and I didn't want this to have any effect on him getting his scholarship. Then, out of nowhere, a fist from another Bayside player went by Bob's head and contacted the catcher from Salem. At this point, both Bob and I stood back and started taking numbers to see who and how many would be ejected. To say the least, the next game for both teams was played with reduced squads. The Salem coach also had to sit out for grabbing a player from an opposing team. I am thankful for both the coach and Poppy that Poppy was one of my former students and listened to me. This could have gotten very ugly.

STATE CHAMPIONSHIP GAME

My first and only Virginia AAA state championship final was June 8, 1985. The two teams were Manor High out of Portsmouth, Virginia and J.R. Tucker High out of Richmond, Virginia. I was fortunate enough to get the plate assignment. My partners were Ducky Davis and Bob Hood. The umpires in our association didn't get to work very many AAA championship games, because prior to around 2010, the state office always used neutral associations to work them. Our area was such a hotbed for talent, starting back in the days with Michael Cuddyer and going through the Uptons, that our teams were almost always in the semis or finals. This shut our umpires of the top-level, AAA playoff games. Don't get me wrong, working A and AA championship games was an honor, and we got a lot of them, but AAA was the best talent in the state, and I remember very well how special it was to have the plate for the championship game.

WHEN YOU TURN AROUND ON AN UMPIRE

I am not sure about the date on this one, but I would guess probably the late '80s. Nathan Thomas was one of the exceptional athletes in our area at that time. He was in middle school, but his parents had held him back a year, making him a year older than his classmates. With his talent, size, and age he had no business playing middle school baseball. His parents asked me to write a letter on his behalf, which I did. He got a waiver with the help of my letter and was allowed to play high school ball while still attending a middle school. The middle school coach did not like my letter and fought it, but I was doing what I thought was best for the young man.

It was definitely the right move, as Nathan was one of the top first basemen in the area for all four of his years in high school. He crushed the ball at the plate and was one of the leading hitters in the region. In his junior year, Coach Wilson was in need of a left-handed relief pitcher. Nathan was what he needed. He was left-handed and had never pitched in his life, and so he had a young and very live arm that somehow stayed around the plate. The scouts started to notice and had Nathan played his cards right may have had a future in the major leagues. He went on to sign with the Cubs, but being hard-headed as he was, he didn't make it. He wanted to hit, and they signed him as a pitcher. They cut him. Again, since he was a left-hander with movement and a ninety-plus mile-per-hour fastball with a young arm, they gave him another chance. Again he wanted to hit, but this time got into a little trouble, so they had to cut him again. They gave him a third chance, but due to some personal battles and his insistence on hitting, they finally had to give up on him.

I saw Nathan about two years ago, and he seemed to have straightened out his life. We still talk about his first encounter with me in recreation ball. He was thirteen at the time and turned around on me on a pitch that I called a strike. His dad, a good friend of mine, yelled from the first base coaching box, "You better swing at the next one."

I told the catcher to go out and tell his pitcher to throw one in the dirt. He did, and I called it strike two. Nathan turned again to question the pitch. Again, his dad yelled, "You better swing at the next one."

He didn't, and I called strike three. The next time he came up to bat I told the catcher to go tell his pitcher to throw all three at least a foot off the plate. He did, and I called all three strikes. His dad said, "I told you to swing."

The third time up, Nathan said "I understand." We had already set it up for the pitcher to throw these three high and away like he was intentionally walking the batter.

After the third strikeout I said, "Now we are done." Never turn on an umpire.

THE BALK/NO BALK GAME

I will never forget the balk game at First Colonial in April 1989. My partner, Bill McInnis, had just returned to the Tidewater area that year, but had been an umpire here previously and umpired and assigned abroad for the past ten-plus years. On this day, Tallwood High, the visiting team, had a lefty with a great pickoff move. In the first inning, we had a pickoff attempt at first. It was my call all the way, but I thought I would have fun with the coach. I told him it was Bill's call. Before he left to go talk to Bill, he asked me, "Is this guy new or any good? I have never seen him."

I told him yes, he had just been out of the area.

As soon as he got out to Bill, Bill told him it was my call and sent him back to me. When he got back to me, I told him this was a strange situation, and it was Bill's call, so back he was, off to see Bill. Of course, Bill again told him it was my call, so again, he was coming back to me. When he got back to me, I told him it had been my call all along. He just threw his hands up in the air and laughed. We had a blast running him back and forth.

He ended up getting three guys picked off at first that day. After the third one, he knew it wasn't going to do him any good to come to me, but he walked out quietly anyway. He said, "Jim, he's got to be balking."

I said, "No, he's not, but if we are missing the balks, I would highly suggest telling your base runners to shorten up their lead. That way you won't get anybody else picked off."

Again, he just laughed and walked away. Being the intelligent coach that he was, he told his runners, "We are not going to get that call today. I want you to take off on the pitcher's first movement, and don't stop until you get to second."

Great coaching move, as the pitcher's move to first was very good but slow and deliberate. It worked to perfection as the team ended up stealing three bases the rest of the game. I will tell you, to this day, it still was never a balk.

FAIR IS FOUL

The next story I would like to share with you was a high school regional playoff game at ODU in the mid-1990s. The two teams playing were First Colonial and Mills Godwin. I was working the plate with two umpires from another association, with whom I had worked many times before.

The bases were loaded, and we had a line shot hit down the third baseline. The third-base umpire did not call it foul, so everyone thought it was a fair ball. He just turned and watched the ball roll to the fence. The FC coach had all of his runners running. Finally, with the batter-runner on second and all three runners on base having crossed the plate, the third-base umpire called the ball foul. Talk about an uproar. It took all of my power to keep the coach in the game. He kept saying, "How can you let three runs score and the batter gets to second, and then say it was foul?" Not a bad point!

We got together and talked, and my partner said he had orally called the ball foul, but never sold it. I told him that when he never put his hands up to signal a foul ball, everyone in the ballpark thought it was fair. He then asked me my opinion, and I told him I had the ball fair, but if he truly vocalized the ball foul, we could not reverse it.

When I thought everything was over, the FC coach walked by and said to the third-base umpire, "Let's get one right today."

The umpire responded with "Don't you ever accuse me of cheating."

The FC coach said, "I am not accusing you of cheating. I am saying you just can't see."

Well, the FC coach may have gotten that wrong, because plainly, the umpire could see. He just couldn't **speak.**

HIGH SPEED UMPIRING

In June 1993, I had the plate for the Eastern Region AAA Semifinal at ODU. Kecoughtan was ranked seventeenth in the Nation, Kempsville upset them 6-1. What a game! One hour and twenty minutes, no errors by the players or, of course, by the umpires.

SET-THE-ALARM-CLOCK GAME

Somewhere in the mid-'90s, I was working a high school game at Cox High School. Their pitcher, Jason Dubois, who went on to play at VCU and with the Cubs, was throwing a great game. In the fourth inning, he threw one right down the middle. It could not have been any prettier, but I called it a ball.

The pitcher's coach, John Ingram, who always sat on a bucket close to the plate, unsurprisingly said, "Jim, where was that pitch?"

I said, "Right down the middle; if you have an alarm clock, set it for me, and I will wake up."

At the end of the inning, he came up to me and said he was speechless and didn't have a comeback for me. He said that was the best one-liner he had heard in years. We have talked about that play whenever we see each other.

WHAT'S WRONG WITH THAT PITCH?

Coach John Ingram, mentioned just above, had the dubious pleasure of watching me from the dugout a whole lot of times. After I retired, he had this to say including his memory of the perfect pitch I missed.

As a high school baseball coach in both public school and private school, I have had the privilege of knowing Jim Smith as an umpire, baseball commissioner, and friend for over twenty years. Jim umpired many of my games when I coached at the public-school level, and even though he is a friend and excellent umpire, he was a bad-luck charm. We seemed to play our worst and make the most mistakes when he was umpiring (even though that had nothing to do with his umpiring). I was still thrilled to see him walk onto the field.

Besides being a solid mechanical umpire, one of the best attributes of a great umpire is that of not being noticed during a game. Jim was there for the kids and did not let his ego get in the way of the game. Many umpires seem to feel that they are there for a show and to show how much in control they are. Jim was never like that. He maintained complete control of the game in a manner that let one know he was in charge, but never in a way to demean the coaches or players. Mechanically, Jim was a competent umpire; he was always in position to make a call (one of my pet peeves about other umpires was not being in the proper place to make the call). As an umpire, Jim had all the attributes that made him an umpire you wanted at your games. He was professional, personable, accurate (most of the time), and willing to listen to a coach.

As a coach, I often disagreed with umpire's calls (isn't that normal?) and would call time out to discuss them. Often, when I disagreed with Jim, I would rush out on the field as though I was angry and tell him that I was doing this to let the players know I was backing them up and then calmly ask him what he saw while making it seem I was angry. We laughed about that at a later time.

The other thing I will always remember shows a side of him that is seldom seen in umpires and says a lot about his self-confidence. We were playing in a particularly important game at home, against Green Run in 1994, and the game was close with every pitch being important. Our pitcher threw a perfect strike that hit the catcher's mitt exactly where it was placed.

I yelled (probably not too nicely), "What was wrong with that pitch?"

Unafraid to admit he missed the pitch, he replied, "Not a damn thing." Local baseball has missed Jim Smith since he retired.

HIGH SCHOOL PERFECT GAME

As mentioned previously, I was lucky enough to work the plate for three perfect games in my officiating career. One was a recreation game in 1985 mentioned previously, one in college in 1989, and this one in 1997.

This one, my last, was on April 8, 1997, in a game at Cape Henry Collegiate. Thom Ott from Greenbrier Christian Academy (GCA) struck out the first twelve batters he faced and sixteen for the game. At the end of the game, I had no idea what had just happened until Coach Lavelle from GCA shared it with me. Thomas went on to be signed by a Division 1 School and did well for them. Good thing I didn't know about the perfect game. I would not have wanted to repeat my alarm-clock call.

RAIN, RAIN, GO AWAY

On May 18 and 19 of 1999, we had torrential rains and were not able to finish the Beach District Postseason Tournament as originally scheduled. Finally, on May 20, we were able to get the second semifinal and final games in. The only catch was that because of regional championship play, we had to have a winner at the end of that night. That meant playing two games back to back.

Kempsville and Tallwood played first. The winning run was scored on a Kempsville suicide squeeze in the bottom of the tenth inning with an oh-two count and two outs. Talk about catching someone by surprise. It fooled everyone, especially me. Had the batter missed the pitch or not beaten the throw to first, we would have been heading into the eleventh inning. This situation created the rarity that the runner could have been safe at home, but the run would not have counted if the batter had not also been safe at first. I called "safe" at the plate, and the runner did beat the throw to first. Game over.

We turned around and played the district championship game thirty minutes after the completion of the semifinals. Kempsville was no doubt tired from the first game, and at the end of the long evening, First Colonial won, and everyone else yawned. Game end time, 1:00 AM the next day.

THE EYES HAVE IT

In the late '90s, I had the opportunity to work the VISAA championship game at ODU. The VISAA is made up of all the top private schools in the state of Virginia. Bob Campbell had the plate, and Bill McInnis was on first. I worked third. The game was between Greenbrier Christian Academy and Bishop O'Connell out of the DC area. This was back in the days where they took the appeal rule for missing a base out of the team's hands and put the responsibility on the umpires. One of the dumbest rule changes ever. It was changed back several years later.

In the bottom of the seventh, GCA had a runner on second, with no outs and down by one run. There was a deep fly ball to the outfield, but the runner didn't tag up and advance. We should now have had a runner on third with one out. The coach was so upset he changed the runner at second. The next batter up got a base hit that would have tied the game, had the runner been on third. We now have runners on first and third. Then we had a steal play putting runners on second and third. Thinking we might have a squeeze play, I moved from what umpires call the C position behind and to the left of the mound to D position on the third baseline.

The very next pitch was hit a ton out of the ballpark, but foul down the left field line. The third baseman asked if he left early, and I said yes.

He said, "He is out, isn't he?"

I said, "No, the ball was foul."

The very next pitch was hit to shallow right field and was caught by the right fielder for out number two. Knowing that the play at the plate, if the runner on third tagged up, was going to be close, I "cheated" and left my position to get an angle twelve feet down the line toward home. Sure enough, he tagged up and was a good three feet to the right of me when the ball was caught, meaning he gained at least fifteen feet early.

The team from Bishop O'Connell was yelling from the dugout, "Appeal, appeal, he left early." They played real baseball and did not use the new rule where the umpire made the call. As soon as all play ended, I called time and called the runner out.

Then the GCA coach went crazy and told me there was no way he left early. I explained to him where I was for the angle and that I would never have made that call unless it was one hundred percent obvious he left early. I also told him he left early on the pitch before and the whole Bishop O'Connell team was yelling on that play, but the ball was foul.

After the game, as we were heading to our cars, we had to pass the coach for Bishop O'Connell who was talking to Coach Tony Guzzo (head coach at ODU). He wanted to thank me for having the guts to make that crucial call against the home team. He said he really thought he was going to get "homered" by the local umpiring crew. Coach Guzzo said that is why he loved the three of us. Whether on the road or at home, we called the game the same.

Standing with the coach was a player and his mother. The player also complimented us. I said if that was the case, then why the profanity toward the first-base umpire on a call earlier in the game? He claimed amnesia. His mother asked me to tell her what he said.

I said, "No, your son will tell you."

He finally came out with "I was telling our shortstop the umpire at first stinks and just bleeped up that call," but he used the f-word. This was on a ball the shortstop had bobbled and threw late to first. She thanked us and made him apologize. The coach also told him, even though they were state champs, he would have laps the next day.

NEAR NO-HITTER, NEAR PERFECT GAME

On May 24, 2000, in the Beach District semis, Cox High School went in as the #2 seed against Kempsville, the #6 seed. Matt Liffick was pitching for Kempsville and gave up a leadoff single up the middle in the bottom of the first. Okay, where do we go from here? **The next twenty-one batters went down in order.** Kempsville won 12-0, and working behind the plate, I almost had my fourth perfect game.

SNATCHING DEFEAT FROM THE JAWS OF VICTORY

On June 6, 2000 in the state quarterfinals at Fairfax, Virginia we had Mills Godwin vs. Oakton. The umpiring crew was all from my association in Hampton Roads. Jeff Doy was on the plate, I had first base, Ducky Davis was on second, and Robert Turner was on third.

This was Ducky Davis's last scholastic game after forty-one years of umpiring. I asked the host school if they would recognize him for his contribution to baseball, He got a five-minute standing ovation from everyone in the stands. Tears flowed in all the crew's eyes, especially mine. In our area, Ducky was known as the "Second Dean of Umpires" (our first being Bullet Alexander). His present-day job is a scout for the LA Dodgers. I am proud to say he was then and still is one of my best friends.

Now to the game and one of the strangest endings I have ever seen in all my years of umpiring. Mills Godwin went into the bottom of the seventh inning leading 3-1. With two outs, the batter hit an easy bouncer back to the pitcher. The pitcher bobbled the ball allowing the runner to be safe at first. The baseball gods punished Mills Godwin that day, as the next batter hit a home run to tie it up. With new life, the next batter came up and also went yard. Mills Godwin goes from needing one out to reach the state semis to losing by one run. No one asked to interview the Mills Godwin pitcher. Good thing.

WOULDN'T HE LOOK GREAT IN A BRAVES UNIFORM?

Each year during spring break, when the kids are out of school, our area coaches, spearheaded by Coach Gary Spedden, put together a tournament called the Beach Blast. Teams from all over the state are invited. On April 8, 2001, I was working a game at Kempsville High. David Wright and his Hickory High teammates were their opponents. I was working the bases, and as you can imagine, there were quite a few scouts there.

Being a diehard Atlanta Braves fan, I looked over at the fence and saw a scout with a Braves hat on. So as not to be out of line or draw attention to myself, I looked straight forward and said, "What a great hat and team."

He said, "You must be a Braves fan."

I told him I was.

The scout asked if I had worked many of David's games and if I had, how did I like him?

I told him there were not enough accolades to describe him. I told him he was a great player, but his off-the-field demeanor was what I most admired.

He said it is too bad the Braves didn't have the first pick as he would look great in a Braves uniform.

I agreed.

The scout had to leave in the sixth inning to go catch his flight, but he asked me to relay a message to David. He said to tell him great game, but he forgot to sprint out of the dugout just one time all day. He also said to tell him the Braves would love to have him.

When the game was over, I asked the Hickory coach, Steve Gedro, to have David come over to the umpire's cars after the team meeting. He did, and I relayed the message about not sprinting out to his position just once to David. He was floored and said, "I didn't?" I told him I didn't notice it, but a scout did. Little things can make a big difference. In David's case, however, crushing the ball all day must have made the scouts the most interested. As we in Hampton Roads like to say about David, "The rest is history."

JUSTIN JONES AND THE HIDDEN COACH TRICK

On May 29, 2002, Keith Buttolph, working his last game for our association, an umpire from the Peninsula, and I were working the Great Bridge versus Kellam AAA Region Semifinals at Old Dominion University. I had the plate. The real highlight of this game was that I had the pleasure of having Justin Jones pitch in his last scholastic game. Justin was one of the top lefthanders to come out of Tidewater, with one of the quickest moves to first we had ever had seen. In this game he was dead on, and no one even knew the umpires were there. After the game, the Cubs drafted Justin in the seventh round and signed him shortly after the end of the season. Also playing in this game was future major leaguer Ryan Zimmerman.

After Justin finished his pro career, he came back to help one of our well-known, local Virginia Beach high school coaches, St. Clair Jones, at Kellam High School. Justin did a great job with the pitchers and never gave any of the umpires any problems, except this one particular day at Princess Anne High School. Since I was at the game, I was able to observe everything firsthand. Justin was coaching first base and started chirping in the first inning about balls and strikes. Randy Jones, one of the area's top high school and college umpires, had the plate and let him go for about three innings. Finally, he ripped his mask off and said, "That is enough."

Justin stopped for one inning and started again, chirping even louder.

Randy said that was enough and tossed him.

Instead of leaving the ballpark as required by National Federation Rules, Justin hid behind the dugout and started working with the next pitcher that was coming into the game. I stepped closer to the dugout to make sure he saw me. As soon he saw me, he knew he was wrong, got his jacket, and at a rather quick pace walked toward me. When he got up to me, he said, "Are you going to report me?" If I did, it would have meant more than a one-game suspension.

I said, "Are you going to try that trick again?"

He said, "No, sir."

So I told him, "Then this conversation was over, and I never saw you." Respect was gained for both of us that day.

MY LAST GAME

THE LAST GAME I UMPIRED

The last game I ever umpired was on March 23, 2004, Princess Anne at First Colonial. I had the plate and my partner, Pete Cartwright, had the bases.

Coach Norbie Wilson called this the upset game of his career, as you will read later. First Colonial High School was hosting Princess Anne (P.A.). P.A. was coached by Jimmy Hunt who had been Coach Wilson's assistant coach for many years. He was like part of Coach Wilson's family, but while he strongly supported his move to head coaching, he knew P.A. was rebuilding. Most of his players would have had trouble making FC's very talented team.

Because of that, Coach Wilson was very loose and maybe

overconfident before the game. When Pete and I met with the coaches at home plate, I mockingly said, "I gotta tell you Coach Wilson, P.A. is going to win today because Coach Hunt paid us off." We all got a big chuckle out of that, and Coach Wilson walked back to his dugout feeling pretty good about the game to be played. As the game unfolded, FC couldn't throw, catch, hit or get a good break. P.A. went on to win in what has been called one of the biggest upsets in Beach District history.

Coach Wilson was very gracious to his former assistant coach and his elated team as both shook hands after the game. He said he didn't get a chance to get out to the parking lot to discuss the issue with us, because immediately after the game he had his team take the field for a full-blown, three-hour practice. To this day he says he wondered if a certain umpire had put the "whammy" on him with his pre-game joke (baseball coaches are notoriously superstitious).

THE UPSET

This is the way Coach Wilson remembers this remarkable upset. Somehow I'm not surprised he recalls my home plate comment fourteen years later.

> First Colonial High School hosted Princess Anne High School on our home field back in the late 1990s. Princess Anne (P.A.) was coached by Jimmy Hunt who had been my assistant coach for many years. He was like part of my family, but while I strongly supported his move to head coaching, I knew his team was rebuilding. Most of his players would have had trouble making our very talented team. Because of that, I was very loose and overconfident before the game. When Coach Hunt and I met with the umpires, Jim Smith and Pete Cartwright, at home plate, Jim mockingly said, "I gotta tell you, Coach Wilson, P.A. is going to win today because Coach Hunt paid us off." We all got a big chuckle out of that, and I sauntered back to my dugout feeling pretty good about the game to be played.
>
> As the game unfolded, our team couldn't throw, catch, hit, or get a good coach, and P.A. went on to win in what has been

called one of the biggest upsets in Beach District history.

I was very gracious to my former assistant coach and his elated team as we shook hands after the game, but inside I wondered if a certain umpire had put the "whammy" on us with his pre-game joke (baseball coaches are notoriously superstitious). I didn't get a chance to get out in the parking lot to "discuss" the issue with Mr. Smith and Mr. Cartwright, however, because I immediately had my team take the field for a full-blown, three-hour practice!

MLB STARS

I was lucky enough to have umpired at the time Tidewater was producing a lot of the future MLB Star players and fortunate enough to have been assigned to work many of their games. Some, but not all, are David Wright, Justin and BJ (now Melvin) Upton, Mark Reynolds, Ryan Zimmerman, Michael Cuddyer, and Justin Verlander. There are many others from our area that also made it to the big league for a short period of time, but these are the best-known ones whose games I umpired.

THE LONGEST ARGUMENT IN BASEBALL HISTORY

(As told by Coach Morrison)

I was coaching at Bayside High School in the late 1990s. We were playing Princess Anne High School at their home field. Jim Smith was working the bases in this game.

He made a terrible call at second base, at least in my opinion. It had to do with a slide play at second. After the call, I came storming out onto the field to let Jim know how bad he had blown it. Jim stood smiling, almost excited that I was coming at him so animated. He let me tell him how bad his call was. Then he politely told me he saw it differently. I told him he must be blind and continued to verbally abuse him. At this point I started to wonder why he had not thrown me out.

I had no idea he was having fun with me and setting me up. It concerned a then-new sliding rule that had been put in for the safety of high school players. Since coaches did not have to go to the rules clinics in those days and I didn't ave a new rulebook, I was totally unaware of the new rule requiring players to slide directly into the base (different than the then-professional rulebook, which has now also been changed).

As I was walking away, Jim called to me, "Ian, is that all you got?"

I stormed back at him, and we ended up chest to chest. I remember telling him he better toss me or this was going to go on forever.

Jim smiled, gave me that look, and said, "Is this still the best you can do? However, this argument is over, and I would appreciate you heading back to your dugout."

Since Coach Hunt started yelling about losing sunlight, I decided to quit the argument.

That is when Jim said, "We were going to finish the game, even if we had to use flashlights." As a side note, this was after daylight savings time kicked in, and Coach Jim knew we had an extra hour of sunlight.

So I got all the way back to the dugout, and I heard Jim say, "You are done." I started racing back out to Jim, and he stopped me dead in my tracks. He told me that he had dumped my scorekeeper, not me. I asked him why. His response was he needed me in the game, not a scorekeeper.

Since this comedy/argument/ejection had gone on for almost fifteen minutes, he quickly explained the new rule to me and told me he had an extra copy of the rulebook in his car. I appreciated this as no one heard us.

Jim is the type of umpire that never gets too excited. He accepts the fact that part of a coach's job is to come out and argue or question a close play. Jim would let you argue, but he expected four things: 1) keep your hat on, 2) don't kick dirt, 3) don't point at the play or be overly demonstrative, and most importantly 4) don't bump him. Yelling was okay, but only to a certain extent. Many umpires nowadays are too quick to eject coaches. To this day Jim and I are still good friends, and I respect him for the umpire he was.

MICHAEL CUDDYER PITCHES IN THE SE DISTRICT
TRN GAME AND THEN SIGNS HIS PROFESSIONAL
CONTRACT 2 MONTHS LATER.

THE REASON I'M LAUGHING
IS BECAUSE I JUST TOLD HIM
HE WAS ARGUING WITH THE
WRONG UMPIRE.

PREP UPDATE   April 30/May 1, 1992

Staff photo by LAWRENCE JACKSON

Craig Simpson of Bayside leaps over First Colonial's David Ogle while trying to pick off his opponent.

TOUGH CALL IN AN EXTRA INNING GAME WITH BOTH TEAMS
FIGHTING FOR FIRST PLACE.

SOME OF THE BEST

Following are some more of the high-profile games in my career, most of them on the plate. By the way, many of the umpires in our association said I had the cleanest, most seldom used-looking plate equipment of anyone. I just can't quite understand why? Anyway, most of the games involved a lot of our local players, soon to be college and then professional, battling each other. Some of the others were post-season playoff games or players that went on to play college baseball.

May 31, 2000: AA Regional Finals at Poquoson
Duration of the game: a speedy ninety minutes first to last. Umpires love to finish in less than two hours: every minute less than that is a sign of moving a well-played game skillfully along. Grafton scored the only run of the game in the third inning on a mental mistake. Runners on first and third, one out, ground ball to the shortstop. He underhanded the ball to the second baseman, covering the bag for the second out, who then rolled the ball to the mound thinking it was the third out. The runner on third raced home for the only run of the game.

March 20, 2001: Opening Day of the 2001 Season,
Kempsville vs. Ocean Lakes
At the time, two high school pitchers, soon to be college and then future professional players, battled it out on a high school field— Justin Jones vs. Mike Ballard. Ocean Lakes won 2-1, scoring two runs in the bottom of the sixth inning. Only three hits allowed in the game by both pitchers.

May 1, 2001: Cox vs. Ocean Lakes
Again, two future collegiate and soon to be professional pitchers throwing against each other—Jason Dubois for Cox and Billy Bray for Ocean Lakes. Such a great game, it took ten innings. OL scored three runs in the top of the tenth inning to win it. One week later, Billy Bray would be signed by The College of William and Mary.

May 15, 2001
Western Branch beat Hickory and David Wright to force a playoff game for the Southeastern District Title. This was David Wright's last regular season high school game. He would end up signing in the June draft of that year. Scott Sizemore, another future major leaguer, also played for Hickory that year.

May 24, 2001
First Colonial beat Kellam 7-6 in the Beach District championship game. We had three future big-league players in this game: David Winfree and Mark Reynolds for First Colonial and Ryan Zimmerman for Kellam. Not too many peope get the honor of umpiring a game with three future big leaguers in it.

May 30, 2001
Ocean Lakes beat Denbigh 7-0 in the Eastern Region semifinal to advance to the school's first state tournament. Pitching that day was Billy Bray. He retired twelve of the first fourteen batters he faced and had a no-hitter for four and two-thirds innings.

May 27, 2002: AA Regional Finals, Powhatan at Poquoson
The significance of this game is we were invited to go in the backyard of another umpiring association that thought they were working the game. It put us in a funny position, but both principals and the state office wanted us in the game and not the local association. The other association had several of its umpires at the game watching us. We had several crucial calls in the game, one being a home run on which I had to overrule one of the base umpires that went against the home team. The main thing was we wanted to get the calls right, and even though they went against the home team, the coaches were glad to have us there. After our performance in that game, we were invited to go back over there the next two years.

May 15, 2003: Kempsville at First Colonial
Final game of the season, and First Colonial was undefeated. Everything that First Colonial hit was right at someone. Just

one of those days, but to be so close to a perfect season had to hurt them. Would have been nice also for the umpiring crew to witness a perfect season. Kempsville won 8-2. First colonial star David Winfree was held hitless.

May 27, 2003: Regional Quarterfinals at Old Dominion
Menchville upset First Colonial and ruined the matchup everyone wanted to see between First Colonial and Great Bridge. This was also David Winfree's last game before moving on to Clemson and then pro ball. First Colonial came in as the favorite to win not only the game, but also the tournament. One side note, David Winfree had only struck out twice all season. He struck out twice this night.

June 3, 2003—State AAA Quarterfinal
Even though I did not know it at the time, this would be my last state tournament game. A botched surgery took me out of umpiring March 24, 2004. The game was Robinson vs. Lee Davis, and I was glad I got to plate it. Robinson, out of the Alexandria area, upset Lee Davis 8-0.

JIM SMITH, COLLEGE ADMISSIONS COUNSELOR

Coach Gary Spedden remembers a role I must have had in steering one of his players to William and Mary and great success there and beyond in professional baseball. Unless you happen to be a fan of Bucknell baseball, here's what happened.

Spedden's Recollection

In 2001, while at Ocean Lakes, we were chasing a district championship. Our team that year was blessed with three Division 1 left-handed pitchers. Two were early college signees, and the third, Bill Bray, was more of a late bloomer. In May, we were playing a key game against the Cox Falcons. Jim had the plate. We won a close game, and I recall Jim coming up to me post-game and asking about Bill's plan for college. Jim was one of the top umpires in the association and did both our games and college games. He had been working at William and Mary and knew that coaches Jim Farr and Ryan Wheeler were looking for a quality left-hander. Bill Bray was an outstanding student in our math-science academy who was verbally committed to Bucknell. I told Jim that I would speak to Bill to see if there was any interest, and Jim contacted Coach Wheeler to tell him that he had seen a potential player. At Bill's next start, Coach Wheeler was in attendance. Bray pitched us to our first district title, and Coach Wheeler was interested. Bray ended up visiting William and Mary and signing with them. After three years, he was a first-round draft choice of the then-Expos and went on to pitch several years in the big leagues. Jim's part in that shows that he was not just another guy calling balls and strikes.

Smith's Recollection

I was assigned a game at William and Mary on a Sunday, April 24, 2001. The first base coach was Ryan Wheeler. He was always asking who I had seen down in our Tidewater area that had potential Division 1 skills. I told him I loved a player by the name of Billy Bray at Ocean Lakes High School. Everyone seemed to know about a player by the name of Mike Ballard and one other stud they had, but at the time Billy was supposed to be the number-three man on the pitching staff. I told Coach Wheeler I'd had Billy on the plate three times in the last two weeks, that I loved him and the way he changed speeds and locations. Coach Wheeler agreed with me, but said Billy was ready to sign a four-year ride to Bucknell University on Wednesday. I asked him how he and Coach Farr let him slide through the cracks or had not heard about him. I knew he had a great arm and knew how to work the plate. In my games, he never threw one down the middle of the plate. Again, he agreed with me and said they would love to have had him, but it was too late. I said, not if he has not signed yet.

I asked Coach Wheeler if I could talk to Billy about William and Mary's interest, yet make sure I was not violating any NCAA rules. I told them I had Ocean Lakes in two days and would call his coach on the way home that night if we were in compliance with the NCAA. I called Coach Gary Spedden, and he called me back within the hour and said Billy was interested and would see me on Tuesday. Billy and I talked that Tuesday, and toward the end of the game, I saw both Coach Farr and Coach Wheeler standing by the bleachers. A couple of weeks later, Billy ended up signing with William and Mary. After finishing his college career, he played pro ball and pitched in the major leagues, ending up his career with the Cincinnati Reds.

One last note concerning William and Mary shows an umpire's eyesight is not always that great. W&M was playing at ODU on February 19, 2002. Coach Farr came out to the mound to make a pitching change. I asked him for the name of the relief pitcher. The look on the face was of total shock. He said, "I always knew umpires couldn't see, but Smith, you take the cake. That is Billy Bray, the guy you helped to change his mind and sign with us." He had gotten bigger and stronger to the point that I didn't recognize him when he started out of the bullpen. Coach Farr never let me live that down. William and Mary won the game 15-0, hitting two grand slams in the game. Come to think of it, I didn't have to see that well that day anyway.

Spedden Again: Lightning Strikes

In 2012, while still at Ocean Lakes, we were playing a game at Kempsville High School. Our team was young and struggling, and we were fighting to get a road win. Jim was in the stands, as commissioner, evaluating officials. We had a lead and the skies began to threaten. As the clouds thickened, thunder rumbled. I approached the student activities coordinator and then the officials working the game to express my concerns. The coordinator said that we had to continue playing unless we actually saw lightning. I remember vividly disagreeing with this and throwing my hands in the air in Jim's direction. I thought that, even though the decision was not his, he would somehow be able to fix the situation.

We continued to play, and the home team took the lead. After that, we were retired in the top of the fifth inning. Two pitches later, magically, lightning was seen in the distance, and the game was stopped. I was furious. The skies opened up, and the game was not resumed. It was an official game, and we lost. It is, I believe, the most upset that I have been on a baseball field.

Later, either that night, or the next day, Jim and I spoke by phone and explained ourselves to each other. He had an ear and the ability to talk rationally and allow you to be heard. I truly respect and appreciate that part of his being the commissioner.

MORE RAIN, FOR PETE'S SAKE!

Coach Pete Zell recalls how it turned out to try weather-delaying tactics on me.

WOW, when I was asked to remember a few stories about our time together on the baseball field, I took it as a complete honor. However, it is hard to remember a lot of stories about Jim as an umpire because most of the time you never knew he was on the field, except at the home plate conference.

If he was on the plate, he set his strike zone early, and you knew what you were going to get the rest of the day. Questioning or complaining would not do you any good, as he was not going to change. If he was on the bases, he would let you come out and have your say, but seldom if ever would he change his call.

As an umpire, Jim's best attribute was his ability to talk and connect with the people of the game. As coaches, no matter how terrible the call was that Jim had just made (smile, Jim) we loved having him work our games. He seemed to handle any and all situations with class and conviction. As good a guy as Jim is, he also was not someone that was pushed around or manipulated. He was able to make his calls, stand his ground, and take the tough road of umpiring out of the list of things that could be wrong on any given day.

I recall one of the most memorable games Jim umpired. Jim remembers it just like it was yesterday. Rain was threatening, and we were up by one slim run, so I was trying to slow the game down in every way I could. I did not want the other team to get a chance to bat in the top of the sixth inning and end up losing the game. So I used up my offensive conference and available substitutes in the bottom of the fifth inning and talked to everyone who would listen to me. Both the other coach and I were what the umpires called "Human Rain Delays" (umpires' terms for those moving the games along at a slow pace). Jim knew that I was stalling, so he called time, went to the backstop, and told all the parents. We were going to finish this game, one way or the other, so he might be calling on them to go get their cars, park them out in center field, and cut their headlights on so we could finish the game. Both coaches laughed and then started trying to move the game along. Of course, the rains came, and we ended up losing in the sixth inning.

SCOTT STUBBE RECOLLECTIONS

Former catcher and now longtime local high school coach Scott Stubbe wisely comments on the value of a catcher and umpire getting along.

I first remember meeting Jim Smith around 1988, when I was a catcher at Bayside High School in Virginia Beach. I was probably a sophomore at the time, and I am sure I was nervous early in the season. It's sorta funny...I remember him having a tough strike zone at the time, and as I progressed into coaching, that was how he stayed. I remember him being complimentary when I was receiving well that day, and as a result of my work or the pitcher's work, my team would often reap the benefits. On the other hand, I also remember him trying to encourage me when my pitcher or I were not having a good day. Even though he remained fair, his comments were always helpful for a young catcher playing varsity baseball in a very competitive area.

As I went into the coaching realm, I already knew that building a good relationship between the plate umpire and my pitchers and catchers could help my team. The battery has to work well with the umpire if they were going to have their best day possible. My players hear this from me all the time. Jim Smith helped me learn this important lesson both as a player and as a coach. That was about thirty years ago, and I remember it like it was yesterday Jim made a lasting impression on a young player that day, and it has never been forgotten.

THE EYES HAVE IT

Coach Chris Dotolo was intense as a high school coach. Umpires knew this and gave him their best game every time. He recalls the following day and his animated conversation with me.

So it was a game at Norfolk Academy. We were hitting, and I was coaching third base. You were the umpire in the field. One of my players hit a ball into right center and was stretching a single into a double. It was a bang-bang play, and I thought he was safe at second. You called him out, and I walked onto the field up to you and said, "Jim, let me ask you a question. Did you really see the play?"

You responded to me yes, you saw the whole thing.

I said, "Jim, are you sure you saw the play? Because I'm standing there in the coaching box, and I had a great angle."

You said, "Oh Chris I had a pretty good angle too."

I said, "Hmm, really, you had a good angle and you saw the entire play?"

You responded that you had.

Just about then, a commercial jet descending on its approach to Norfolk Airport flew over the Norfolk Academy ball field. I said, "Jim, let me tell you something that you don't know about me. Look up at the sky. See that plane? I've got really, really, really good eyesight."

You said, "I've got good eyesight too, Chris."

I said, "My eyesight is so good that I could be flying jets right now. I could be flying jets right now. The only problem is I'm afraid of heights."

And you looked at me and said again, "Well. Chris, I've got pretty good eyesight too."

I said, "Really, good enough to fly jets?" Before you could respond, I said, "You know what. Jim, when this game's over how about you and me head down to the Walmart down the street, and we'll both take an eye exam."

You started to smile.

I said, "No, seriously, Jim, we will go down and we'll take an eye exam side by side, and I guarantee you that my eyesight is going to be better than yours. And when you find out how good my eyesight is, I think you are going to realize that you didn't really see the play and you missed the call."

Needless to say, Jim did not go with me to Walmart that night. Traffic on Military Highway would have been brutal. Too bad, my guy was still called out, no matter how good my eyesight might be.

UMPIRES DON'T WORK IN CONCERT

Kevin Rooks, a player for Kellam High School in the late 1980s and early '90s, shares a good story.

Jim Smith, umpire and commissioner, was a very fair man on the baseball field and one of the best umpires to ever work my games. The strongest memory that I have of Jim goes back to September 25, 1990. It was a cold, fall ball game at Trant Field. I was catching, and Jim was behind the plate. He was an umpire you could talk to during the game, and he would respond the way a catcher would want him to respond. If I said, "Jim, was that off the plate?" he would respond with something like "Yes, Rooksy. Bring it in a few inches and you got it." He usually had a reasonable strike zone, and he would call it fairly.

The reason that this game is memorable to me is the fact that I was only tossed (ejected) from three games in my long career as a player. This night was one of them. I had given up a chance to go to a concert at the Hampton Coliseum with several of my friends. It was in the later innings, and I was at the plate. I was a very good contact hitter with two strikes, and I always gave myself a chance to make contact. If it was close, I was swinging. While catching the game up to this point, Jim was not calling strikes on anything two inches or so off the outside part of the plate. He was very consistent up to this point, and I recognized the zone he was calling.

During my final at-bat of the evening, Jim rings me up on a called third strike about four or five inches off the outside part of the plate. I turned around to question his decision face to face, and I said, "Jim, you haven't called that a strike all night!"

Jim told me it was there, and in frustration, I proceeded to tell him "that is bull$#*&!!" I was on the way back to the dugout cussing when... I turned to face him one more time for good measure, and I got the heave-ho. EJECTED. Jim was very good at handling people on the field and would usually talk to you before getting to the ejection zone. That night, something was in the air and arguing balls and strikes got me an early ticket to the showers.

The only thing I could think of as I packed my bag in the dugout was, Do I still have time to make it to the Coliseum to catch the show? NO. Jim, why couldn't you have been more considerate and tossed me in the second inning?

A TENNIS BALL?

Somewhere in the mid-'90s I was umpiring a game in Norfolk (teams and names are being left out intentionally). In the bottom of the sixth inning, down one run, the cleanup hitter for the home team came up to bat with runners on second and third and two outs. He laced one up the middle, bringing in both runners and putting them up by one run. The only problem was, the end of the bat flew toward the first baseman and a tennis ball likewise flew toward the shortstop. Equipment malfunction and a major oops.

By rule I was supposed to eject both the player and the coach, but as I was thinking the rule through, I heard a mother near the backstop yelling at her husband, "I told you something like this might happen. Now our son is in trouble." Of course, then I knew the parents and especially the father were involved in the caper.

So instead of ejecting the coach and player I called for the athletic director to escort the father off the grounds, called the batter out, restricted him to the dugout, threw the bat out of the game, and, not being able to put the runners back on second and third, ruled the inning over, as that would make it three outs.

The seventh inning was uneventful, three up and three down. So instead of going ahead and likely winning by one run, the home team lost by one run. To borrow tennis terms, "Advantage visitors" and this was not a "love set."

There was no rule to cover my how I handled this, but the AD and even the coach who lost really appreciated my decision. The school ended up suspending the player for the next two games, as they knew he was aware of his dad loading the bat. The father was also banned from the field for his son's junior and senior years.

GONE BUT NOT FORGOTTEN

One year I was selected for the VISAA baseball state championship game. Nothing excites umpires more than being chosen to work a championship. When you walk on the field, everyone knows you were among the best that year and can be trusted to work the most meaningful game of the year for the players, coaches, and fans. In this instance, the local team had won multiple state championships.

When I came home, my wife, Lou, asked me the normal question after a big game, "How did things go?" I told her I'd had one of the toughest calls that I had ever had to make in a big tournament game but knew I had gotten it right.

The next morning, she was the first one to see the newspaper.

The reporter blasted us, mainly me, and made it look like I had deliberately cost the local team the game. That really hurt me. I am sure it hurt Lou also, but she never let on to that. No matter what level or stage of the season, I always poured my heart and soul into every game I umpired. I did nothing different in this game, and for the reporter to suggest publicly that I may have cheated quite frankly left me in tears and depressed for months. All umpires miss close calls, but this sports report went beyond merely claiming that I missed a call.

To make matters worse, the next day my commissioner, Bob Kyle, received a letter from the school. It started off by saying how much they loved having me in their games and thought I was a very good umpire. The tone changed, however, and instead of recognizing that the team just lost the game, the letter insinuated that I had taken the game from them. The most hurtful part of the letter, and the part that I remember the most went, "How do you explain to the team how an umpire's call took an unprecedented eighth straight state championship game away from them?" It continued on with many other comments, faulting me for their loss and suggesting they would rather not have me back for any more of their games.

Again, this really struck me hard. As the play developed, I had known the call was going to be a tough one, but I had made the right one. Had I not made the call, my plate umpire, any neutral fan or scout, and, most importantly, I would have known that I had favored the home team, a team for whom I frequently umpire. That just cannot happen.

This incident did not go away quickly. The team also played during one of our summer leagues. One of the assistant coaches was the head coach for this team during the summer. Any time I had their game, he treated me like dirt. He refused to bring out my game fee, to talk to me, or to shake my hand. He would send my money via a player. At that point, I asked my commissioner to scratch me from any of their summer or scholastic season games for a couple of years. In the end, this was a good choice, as when I went back to their field quite some time later, things had settled down, and they again welcomed me there. Yet to this day, we still never talk about "the championship call."

WHEN EVERYTHING GOES AGAINST YOU

In 1986, the Beach District decided to play a night game at Plaza Little League. The reason it had to be played there was that none of the beach schools had lights. Both my partner Jim Stuck and I wanted the plate, so we ended up flipping a coin. I lost and had to work the bases.

The two teams were Cox High School and Bayside High School. Jim was fairly new to the varsity ranks, so Coach Ingram from Cox pulled me aside and asked me who my partner was and if we would be okay. I told him he would be fine, and Jim was a great umpire.

Talk about a tough night: Jim came to me on eight check swings and all went against Bayside. The most crucial one was the last out of the game. You can imagine the response from the Bayside crowd. To top it off, I also had six double play calls that night in seven innings, and as luck would have it, all went against Bayside.

To end the game in the bottom of the seventh, I had a double play to go against Bayside for the first two outs, and the final out of the game (check swing) also to go against Bayside. As we walked off the field, my partner could not stop apologizing for having to come to me for so many check swings and especially with the game-ending call. Umpires are taught to try and take charge on check swings and make the call themselves, but on this night, he needed to come to me, as many of the check swings were on pitches either in the dirt or up and in. Bayside Coach Terry Gowen and I still laugh about it today. He came out on several of the plays, but always walked away saying he agreed with the call.

BOOKER ME AN EARLY DEPARTURE

For those who have never worked or attended a game at Booker T. Washington High School, trust me, they have the strangest ground rules of any school you will ever work. Students and locals are constantly walking across the field in center and right fields and sometimes in front of the fielders. Now, these folks don't care much about the ball game and, just for fun, will pick up a live ball in a heartbeat and throw it in the parking lot. Hence, you need a ground rule. The coach emphatically said, "Here is the rule: any ball picked up and thrown would be a ground rule single." If you are not a baseball guru, let me tell you, there is no such thing as a ground-rule single.

As for the fences that run behind the dugout and extend down the line, they seem to make up a new ground rule each year. Let me give you one in a game I umpired back in the early '90s. This was hard to believe, but true.

We had a runner on first and a fair ground ball hit down the third baseline. The ball was hit with such a hook on it that it crossed the imaginary out-of-play line that extended past the third base dugout, roughly three hundred feet from home plate. I killed the play, called it a ground-rule double, and put the runners on second and third. The home-team coach, who was down 9-0, came out and told me the ball was hit too hard and too far to only be a double. I told him the distance had nothing to do with it. He said he wanted to be fair and not cheat the other team, so he asked me to please change the ruling. Again, I tried to explain the rule to him. No go, so I made him happy and scored the runner from first.

Here is the irony. The requested action gave the other team a 10-0 lead. Under high school rules, if one team has a ten-run lead after the trailing team has batted five times, it's game over. My partner and I placed the runners as the coach suggested and were immediately on our way to our cars. I've wondered since if the Bookers' coach had seen enough for one day and knew exactly what he was doing.

FENCING CAN CAUSE A NICK

Pete Cartwright and I were working a game at First Colonial High in early 2003. Pete was one of our better umpires and had the plate. The point of this story is to show you need to have total concentration throughout the entire game. We had a foul pop-up on the first-base side that just nicked the fence before the catcher trapped the ball against it. Pete must have been unable to "find the ball," because he never moved from behind the plate. This made it impossible for him to see the ball's change of direction or hear contact with the fence.

There was no one on base, so I ran over from my position behind first base and had a perfect look at the play. Coach Wilson came out to argue the call, but he never asked Pete to go for help. The opposing coach looked at me and both of us knew it should not have been an out, but it was not my place to say anything. Two innings later, Coach Wilson came out to make a pitching change and asked me if I saw the play. I said yes.

He said, "Why didn't you overrule him?"

I said, "Why didn't you tell him to ask for help?"

All he said was, "Gosh darn it," one of his favorite expressions, "that one is on me."

I said, "Yes, it is."

GIMME TWO WITH EXTRA ONIONS

Now on occasion, people may challenge an umpire's eyesight or even imply he is leaning a bit toward one team or another. There's one thing such doubters should never question, and that's our pre-game preparation. Here's a story I can really relish telling you. There were times when I would be working a game with a coach who was known to be particularly argumentative, especially those who like to get up right in the umpire's face, cap to cap. Now a good umpire never backs off, but some umpires turn slightly away to make the coach reposition, and some will stand their ground and argue right back. Let me share that I had a very effective technique. Anticipating such days, I would go to one of my favorite lunch spots, Jimmy's Hot Dogs, and load up on onions and chili. When an angry coach got too close, all I had to do was exhale right in his face. You know what? It took the breath right out of his argument. Hot dog, situation solved.

CHAPTER 6

COLLEGIATE UMPIRING

Now it is time to shift gears and go into my college stories. It was a long journey getting there, but again, being fortunate enough to be around some of the top instructors in both the collegiate and professional ranks, along with listening to them, I was able to break into the college ranks. The thrill of finally getting there made me feel on top of the world.

But could I stay there? Now the real work started. The expectation of perfection and the resulting stress made you feel like you were in a pressure cooker for every game. Missing a call here had much greater consequences than if you missed one in a recreation or high school game.

One of the hardest parts of the college game was the rules. Even though most were the same as the ones used in the pros, there were important differences. Depending on the rule, you could call a play one way in high school, a different way in college, and a yet different way in professional baseball.

During my career, our association was considered the top association in the state and one of the best in the Mid-Atlantic area. We were consistently sending twenty-five of our guys out to work college games every weekend. I did not want to let them down. Hopefully, I didn't.

MY FIRST COLLEGE GAME

My first collegiate assignment was on March 25, 1983. Virginia Wesleyan College was playing Frostburg State. Virginia Wesleyan won 12-3. What a miserable day to have your first game. It was twenty-eight degrees outside, with a wind chill factor of 18, and it snowed the entire game. I was so thankful that I was assigned the plate. For those who don't know, on cold days, you stay much warmer with all of your plate gear on.

I will never forget the comments from the players and coaches. One of the funniest comments was ironically from a Frostburg player, "I can't believe we came south to avoid the snow, and yet we are still playing in it."

Conditions were tough, yet we didn't cancel the game because this was the only day open on the teams' schedules. As you can imagine, the players were having a tough day catching and throwing, and my partner was also having a tough day on a couple of calls. The visiting coach, very politely and discreetly, came up to me between innings. He said, "I appreciate the job you are doing, and I am not trying to be critical, but is this your partner's first game? I know the conditions are terrible, but he seems to be having a rough day. Every close call seems to be an out, just to get the game over with."

I said, "No sir, I am the rookie. This is my first college game ever, but we cannot discuss my partner."

He said he respected that and walked back to his dugout. Maybe he just wanted to go back to the hotel? On that day, the resort city of Virginia Beach, yes, the place with over eighty blocks of boardwalk and beachfront, was actually better referred to as Frostburg.

MY FIRST DIVISION 1 COLLEGE GAME

My first Division 1 college game was at Old Dominion University back in the early 1980s. Mark Newman, who is now with the Yankees, was the head coach, and Nick Boothe, who would later become the head baseball coach at Virginia Wesleyan, was his number-one catcher. Coach Newman was a fantastic coach, but he was also known as a yeller at the slightest little imperfection.

Coach Newman, then and now, has the greatest respect for Nick. Likewise, Nick still has the greatest respect for Coach Newman, and they still see each other and talk often. I think their mutual respect helped the umpires, as Coach Newman knew Nick was one of the best catchers to ever attend ODU and knew which pitches were strikes and which ones weren't. Coach Newman always kept everyone on their toes, especially the umpires. It didn't make any difference whether it was a player or umpire: he expected perfection from everyone on the field. I appreciated his comments, as they helped me to become a better umpire.

One thing for sure: umpires and Nick generally always stuck up for each other on close pitches. ODU was having a rough game, and Coach Newman was yelling on almost every pitch. Where was that pitch? It wasn't low or high. We soon learned to say it was a ball because if we said up or down, he would still disagree and that ball was not low.

It may have been a strike, but Nick would say, "Coach, the ball was outside."

I would say, "Thanks, Nick."

Then he would turn around and yell at Nick on the very next pitch, "What was that pitch?"

Nick would say, "A slider."

Then he would yell at me, "Jim, what was that pitch?"

My response: "A slider."

Coach Newman's usual response was, "It didn't look that way from here."

Trust me, with his vast knowledge of pitching and the game of baseball in general, it was usually the umpire he was getting on.

Nick and I always stuck up for each other and remain friends thirty-plus years later. After over thirty years of collegiate coaching, most of it at Virginia Wesleyan University, like me, he decided to retire in 2014.

RECORD-SETTING GAME AT ODU

On March 21, 1985, I was fortunate or probably unfortunate enough to plate a game at Old Dominion University that lasted three hours and twenty-five minutes. It was also a record-setting game for four different ODU stats categories.

The score ended up ODU 34 and Central Connecticut State 4. Here are the first three records set: most hits in a game (twenty-eight), most runs in a game (thirty-four), most runs in one inning (the sixth inning). ODU sent twenty hitters to the plate and scored fourteen runs in that sixth inning.

The fourth record tied a record set back in 1981. Sean O'Hare drove in eight runs for the game. Some records still stand. The game was a blowout in the third inning, so I started opening up the strike zone in the fifth inning when the subs were coming in. After the game, Bullet Alexander, my mentor (observing in the stands as he always did if he was not umpiring), told me to set my zone in the first inning and keep the same zone all game. When the subs get a chance to play, this is a rare chance to show their coaches what they can do with the bat. In a blowout, if you open the zone up, it takes the bat out of subs' hands. Great lesson learned, especially at the collegiate level. There may be some recreation games where a larger strike zone benefits everyone involved.

OH, YES, MY MAIN JOB

Two things were real tough on my collegiate umpiring schedule. The first was my job. Being a teacher made it hard to get out of school to travel or do a local 1:00 PM game. I had three great administrators or principals who worked with me on the 1:00 starts. However, our school system did not approve of teachers taking sick or personal leave to go do another job during school hours. This was tricky if we had a conference series with a Friday 1:00 start time.

The other problem was both of my daughters attended schools in one of the conferences I worked, the Colonial Athletic Association (CAA). One went to William and Mary and the other to Old Dominion University. I notified my commissioner, and he got the clearance from all the CAA schools. They all had no problem with me doing any conference or non-conference games. I was very appreciative, since without their approval, my college schedule would have been next to nothing.

THE NATIONAL JUNIOR COLLEGE REGIONAL CHAMPIONSHIPS

1986 LOUISBURG JUCO TOURNAMENT—
BOB HOOD, ME, BOB CAMPBELL, AND MANNY UPTON

On May 3, 1986, two weeks prior to the tournament, our commissioner was called and asked if we would like to work the National Junior College Tournament. Even though none of our umpires had ever worked the junior college level, we said yes. Each of us was assigned to work two plate jobs, but due to the bad luck of one of our crew, as you will see below, I got to work three plates including the championship game. So on May 14, 1986, we were off to Louisburg College in Louisburg, North Carolina.

To show you how some coaches try to get an advantage, during our pre-tournament meeting with the home team's coach, we were told the strike zone was a little bit different than in Division 1 baseball. They wanted the strikes called just under the armpits to just below the knees. He also told us all the coaches were great guys, and we wouldn't hear a word from him as he never left his dugout to argue anything. He ended our meeting with "Guys, we really appreciate you coming down." Right!

Halfway into game one and after the first couple of innings in the second game, we started to hear a lot of chirping about balls and strikes. At that point we went back to our normal top of the strike zone, calling strikes below the hands and a ball just below the knees. It seemed like we were being asked to adjust the zone for only one team. Once we went back to the way we normally called the strike zone, we didn't hear a word from any team. If you remember, we were also told we would not hear a word from the home coach and that he supposedly never left his dugout to argue a call. Wrong.

In the fourth inning of game two one of my partners, Manny Upton, yes, father of *those* Uptons, had a tough call at second base or the final out of the inning. He started back out to his normal in-between-innings position in left field. He turned around, and here came the coach. So to really have some fun, Manny walked all the way out to the left fielder so the coach had an extra ninety feet to go. Over dinner we asked each other, what was going to be the next piece of misinformation?

On May 16, the day before the championship game we were out playing golf, and my roommate, Umpire Bob Hood, came into contact with some honeysuckle. He was highly allergic to it. He was supposed to work the plate in the finals, but his eyes became so swollen we put him on third. Of course, we all gave him grief about not wanting to work the plate and how that excuse really sucked.

On May 17, I was fortunate enough to get to the plate in the championship game. Late in the game, we had a hard shot hit down the third baseline that was at least a foot fair. Bob called it foul. Yikes. The coach of the team at bat, who knew about Bob and the honeysuckle, came to me and laughingly said, "I know your partner cannot see due to his love for honeysuckle, but can you overrule him?"

I told him "No."

He said he didn't have the heart to go down and make him feel more miserable. What really helped was they were up by six runs.

Another memorable part of this game was it was the first time my father had seen me work a post-season college baseball game. It was so hot that day (101 degrees) that they had thought about moving the game back from 11 AM to 2 PM to make it cooler. Shows what they knew about weather. I thought my crew was playing a joke on me when they told me to wear long underwear underneath my pants and shirt. We didn't have Under Armour in those days. I asked them if they were crazy, but they told me that after I got wet, it would act as air

1987 NATIONAL JUCO TOURNAMENT—
RESTING BETWEEN 96 DEGREE DOUBLEHEADER

1987 NATIONAL JUCO TOURNAMENT

conditioning. They were right. In the fourth inning, I started cooling down.

The last part of this memorable day was the constant chanting of "Home job" from certain fans of the visiting team and the questioning of my strike zone. Of course, that was prior to them taking the lead. The funny thing about it was my dad was sitting right there with them, egging them on, and said nothing about who he was. Yet he was talking to them all game. After the game, as we were going out the gate, he wanted to introduce me to them since their team came back and won the game. I told one of the families I had no idea who this guy was, and we needed to leave. They came to our cars and apologized for their behavior and for the gentleman claiming to be my father. I finally owned up to it and told them he really was my father. Dad and I had a laugh about this for years.

Spartanburg Methodist ended up beating Louisburg 9-4 and advanced to Denver, Colorado, site of the World Series. After the game we were extended an invitation to Denver to work the World Series. Since we had to pay for our own transportation, lodging and food, we had to decline. What a great trip it would have been to work a collegiate World Series Tournament.

FORCE PLAY SLIDE RULE GAME

On April 17, 1988, I was assigned to work a game at Virginia Wesleyan College. They were playing Virginia Commonwealth University, coached by my longtime friend, Tony Guzzo, who had just moved from Hampton Roads to VCU to coach. He came down to play his old buddy Nick Boothe, who had just taken over the VWC job. So to make sure we have the scenario correct, Coach Guzzo was the VWC coach the previous year and now was taking over the VCU job. His former assistant was now inheriting the VWC job. With two great friends playing each other that day, it was standing room only and the largest crowd ever at VWC.

The NCAA had just put in a new Force Play Slide Rule that really tied the umpire's hands. It was put in for safety reasons, and the idea behind it was good. However, when it first came out, it required the runner to slide directly into the base and stop within its confines. You could not slide to either side of the base, overslide the base, or pop up into the fielder. On this one play, the runner going into second to try and break up the double play overslid the base by a mere six inches. I called nothing. Here came Coach Boothe arguing the call and quoting the rule. I told him I agreed that he overslid the base, but, trying to get him to take a reasonable view, I asked him how much time he spent at practice each day getting his players to slide into second and stop right on top of the base.

He said, "I know, we don't do that, but that is the rule."

I told him if I called a double play on that call, I would have to end up throwing out his best buddy. I asked him which coach he thought I ought to throw out.

He laughed and finally agreed with me. He then asked me if he could ask one more question that was unnecessary, but I guess it made Nick feel better.

I said yes.

His question was, "Will I get it called the same way for me?"

I said absolutely. He turned around and went back to the dugout.

The rule has since been modified and made much easier for the umpires to call. There is, of course, an art to umpiring, and the rules are certainly important, but an umpire who does not apply some common sense to the application of the rules will not advance in his craft.

FOOD POISONING GAME

On May 10-13, 1988, we were invited back to Louisburg, North Carolina to do the National Junior College Regional Championships, which were being held a second time at Louisburg College. Our crew the time consisted of Bob Hood, Pat Mileur, Bullet Alexander, and yours truly. The night before the championship game we (teams and umpires) all ate at the same place. Everyone ate chicken but us. The next morning when we were packing to leave the hotel and go to the game, we were informed that half the Spartanburg team had food poisoning, with four or five already in the hospital.

They decided to put the game off several hours to see if anymore else was going to be sent to the hospital. Sure enough, four more were. They could have put the game off until Monday, as the winning team did not have to be in Denver until Thursday or Friday. However, the team in the winner's bracket insisted on playing that Sunday, since their opponent still had twelve players. Of the twelve, only three were starting position players, and the rest were relief pitchers or substitutes. Their All-American shortstop, centerfielder, first baseman, and catcher were four of the sickest and in the hospital.

Several times the game had to be stopped so the players could go behind the dugout to throw up. Spartanburg, the team with all the sick players, had to win two games to head back to the World Series. They only had three semi-healthy starting pitchers, and all had thrown the day before. The other starters were in the hospital. The starter in the first game went all nine innings and forced the second game. He went six innings in the second before running out of gas. Spartanburg held the lead until the seventh or eighth inning and then lost to Louisburg, 9-4. They had to use substitute position players to pitch as they had used up all their available pitchers.

This was one of the few times as an umpire you ever wanted to see one team win. It was also sad to look over between innings when they were at bat and see all the players lying down on the bench, trying to conserve energy. The fair thing to do would have been to wait a day to play one or both games, but we had to go by the ruling from the league office.

There was one additional note for this exciting tournament. In one room next to us, at the hotel, was the Yankees scout. On the other side was the Mets scout. Every day they rode with us to and from the hotel and ballpark. We also went out for dinner several nights and shared war stories.

PERFECT GAME, JUST A LITTLE BIT OUTSIDE

As mentioned earlier, I was lucky enough to have been able to umpire three perfect games in my umpiring career. My second and without a doubt most memorable perfect game occurred on April 16, 1989. We were working a conference series at the old William and Mary ballpark with James Madison University in town. I worked the plate and set the strike zone in the first inning. I was calling pitches three to four inches off the plate all day long. I didn't hear a single word from either team all day, and both teams came up swinging the bat. Since the scoreboard was not working that day, no one recognized that Brian Kimmel for James Madison University was throwing a perfect game. With the score 5-0 in the bottom of the ninth inning and a three-two count on the batter and two outs, I called a pitch four inches off the plate a strike to ring the batter up. All of a sudden, the catcher and everybody else on the team run out to the mound and jump on the pitcher.

I looked at Coach Farr and said, "What did he do, throw a no-hitter?"

Coach Farr said, "No-hitter, my ass. He just threw a perfect game."

Looking back at it, had I called that pitch a ball, he would've lost his perfect game, even if the next batter got out. What a thrill to have no clue that you were working a perfect game. Tony Dilbeck and Hank Hartz were my partners and hadn't had a clue either. Tony had had a couple of real close calls at first base that could also have resulted in a different outcome. Even if Brian Kimmel had not been throwing a perfect game, I still thought Tony got them right, but the "what ifs" do come into play.

MY FIRST SUN BELT CONFERENCE GAME

On April 15, 1990, I worked my first Division 1 Sun Belt Conference game. It was also my mother's birthday and Easter Sunday. What a beautiful, sunny day it was, a great day for a baseball game. Old Dominion University was hosting Jacksonville University.

My biggest fear was not that this was my first Sun Belt Conference game; it was what I had heard about the coach for Jacksonville, Tom Bradley. He was supposed to be a terror on umpires. My worst fear seemed to be just over the horizon as

Jacksonville got down early. I had a whacker, as we called them, or a close play at the plate. It went against Jacksonville and here came Coach Bradley. He said, "Jim, what did you have on the play? Did you have a good look at it, and do you think you were in the correct position?"

I said yes to both questions.

He said, "I agree, I just came out for the team because we are playing like bleep." You fill it in.

Their pitcher could not find the strike zone if the zone was four feet wide and four feet tall. Coach Bradley came up to me to make a pitching change in the third. I thought, *Here it comes.* All he did was give me the change and walk back to the dugout.

Two or three pitchers later, in the sixth inning, here he came again. Since they were getting beat even worse, this had to be the time he unloads on my strike zone. All he said was "Kid, keep up the good work, great timing and zone, you are doing a great job, sorry my pitching is so bad today."

I could not believe what he was saying, yet I responded, "I appreciate it."

Coach Bradley came up to me after losing and asked how long I had been doing Sun Belt Conference games. When I told him this was my first, he was floored. That game helped me mature as an umpire.

A STITCH IN TIME SAVES BOTH NINES

Somewhere in the early 1990s, Old Dominion University was playing in the Sun Belt Conference. Even though we had never had a problem in this area, the conference somehow decided the games were moving too slowly and implemented a few rules to speed up the game. It just so happened that my crew had the first game with the new rules. I had the plate, and Bullet Alexander was one of my partners.

What the conference had decided to do was put up clocks, one on the outfield fence and one in each dugout. The outfield clock started at one minute and thirty seconds as soon as the last out was recorded. What they wanted was for the first pitch of the next inning to be thrown before the clock hit zero. This contradicted the one-minute rule in the rulebook. If the batter was not in the box, a strike was to be called. As for the clock in each dugout, if the pitcher did not throw the next pitch within twenty seconds after getting it back from the catcher, a buzzer would go off and the plate umpire was supposed to call time and award a ball on the count to the batter.

What made this so tough was that we had just received the new rulings when we walked in our dressing room. No prior notice. During our pre-game discussion we knew we were going to have a problem. How to handle it was the question. Sure enough, in the second inning with a three-two count on the batter, the dugout clock hit zero, meaning ball four and awarding the batter first base. As soon as I called time, here came the coach saying, "Jim, this is ridiculous, he was just getting ready to throw the ball."

I immediately got with my partner, and we decided we were cutting the clocks off and let the conference office handle our situation on Monday. Neither of the coaches had a problem with our ruling, and the game continued with no further problem. The conference very shortly did away with the clocks.

FOUL PLAY

As a rule, umpires are very loyal to each other and can become close friends. After all, they are working as a team of two to four guys who are expected to be perfect from the moment they walk on a field. That kind of pressure and expectation can help to create close bonds. Sometimes, however, umpiring can be a cutthroat business.

Somewhere in the early 2000s, I was assigned a doubleheader at Old Dominion University. The Monarchs were playing Rutgers. The Rutgers coach at the time was on the NCAA postseason umpire selection committee. The games were scheduled to be played on a Saturday at 1:00 PM with rain in the forecast. Late the night before, the coaches had decided to start the games early at noon.

One of my partners, who really did not care for me (can you imagine that), was the one who should have called me to let me know of the time change. Well, he didn't call, so at 11:30, when I was still about fifteen minutes from the ballpark, I got a call from my local commissioner, asking where I was. When I told him I would be there in plenty of time, his response was "Are you aware the game starts in thirty minutes?"

Boy, was I angry. Knowing the time was moved up, and neither one of my partners calling me made me look like the bad guy. Frankly, I now feel that was deliberate.

I pulled into "The Bud," ODU's stadium named after our local legendary major leaguer Bud Metheny, about fifteen minutes before game time. I saw my partners, one of whom was the crew chief, and the coaches standing at home plate. I got dressed quickly and was at home plate before the plate conference was over.

I need to mention my two partners hoped to impress the Rutgers coach, possibly getting them his vote for a postseason slot. One was the crew chief, and he was also a friend of the conference assigner. My gut feeling was that the umpire who didn't care for me knew the crew chief would probably put my late arrival in my written evaluation, and this would hurt my chances in the future.

Later, in a roundabout way, I found out a bad evaluation was written on me. I called the conference assigner and told him I must be losing it as a college umpire and was probably going to quit college baseball. He said everyone has a bad game and not to let it worry me. I asked him which game he was talking about, and he said the one for which I showed up late. The eval said that I had a rough day on the bases, missing a couple of calls.

At this point I blew a gasket and asked him to do me one favor: to call both coaches and ask for their opinions. I was not about to throw one of my partners under the bus, but under these circumstances, I didn't mind letting the coaches do it. The assigner ended up calling both the Old Dominion and Rutgers coach and got the real story. To sum up, this gambit backfired on both of my partners. Neither got postseason assignments, and the conference assigner called me back and said the coaches were very impressed with me that day. The assigner took the time to get the facts, and of course I made my own mental notes of what my "friends and partners" tried but failed to accomplish that day.

Now, the ending of this foul-weather day did turn out to be funny. It had been raining all day, and we must have used eighty bags of Diamond Dry on the field. With the time change, we got the first game in and started the second. We probably should have never started the second, but we did. We used another twenty or thirty bags of the drying agent. As umpires, we could not stand in our normal spots, as there was standing water everywhere. We decided the fifth inning was going to be it. As luck would have it, I would have a whacker to end the game. It was on a swinging bunt back to the pitcher. I slipped on a water puddle and did not see a tag. I called the batter-runner safe. Freddie, the coach for Rutgers, asked me if I would go for help. I said yes. The plate umpire said he was one hundred percent sure there was a tag, so I reversed the call and got the out. Here came Coach Guzzo rumbling out from Old Dominion, asking how could I overturn it. He got that out of his system and then laughed, saying he saw the tag, and had I not called an out to get that darn rain-soaked game over, he would have drowned me.

TRIPLE PLAY AROUND THE HORN

In 1994 I was assigned a Seton Hall and Virginia Commonwealth University game. We had a play that very few umpires get to experience in their umpiring career, especially in a college game. We had runners on first and second, and a ground ball was hit to third. The third baseman steps on the bag at third for the first out, throws to second for the second out and on to first for the third out. Keeps the game moving and gets the umpires home.

A LITTLE BIT OF EVERYTHING

This game occurred on March 21, 1995. Let's just say it was a game played between two powerhouse teams from two really strong baseball conferences. The story is the main part, so I will just call them home and visiting team, coach and player. The visiting team was ranked in the top five college teams in the nation. In fact, I think they were number one at the time. The leadoff hitter for the visiting team, as we had heard, was supposed to be the possible number one MLB draft pick that year or at least one of the top ten picks. His first time up to bat he questioned a strike I called. He looked down at the plate saying, "That is not a bleeping strike."

The home team catcher hearing him moved about two more inches inside, and the pitcher hit the spot. I called strike two.

Again, the batter looked down saying, "That is not a bleeping strike."

The catcher, being smart, moved two more inches inside, and on the next pitch we rang him up. The next time he came up to the plate, the catcher said to me, "I am going outside this time."

I just said, "Okay, if it is a strike, we will get it."

We got the same scenario, the F-bomb on all three pitches. I rang him up on three pitches, all hittable, but in his mind off the plate. The third time he came up, his comment as he stepped in the box was, "You mother-bleeper won't get me this time."

I kept my mask on, swept the plate off and said, "Keep it up, Big Boy, you have a lot of scouts back there, looking at you making an ass out of yourself."

By the way, if the plate umpire needs to get a message to a batter or catcher, there is no better way than to do so while brushing the plate. So when the umpire calls time and brushes a completely clean plate, you know he had an ulterior motive. The foul-mouthed batter ended up getting on with a fielder's choice this time and later scored on an easy safe call at the plate. He got up chest to chest with the catcher, with both having their hands on the other's chest. I said "Drop them," and the catcher did. The batter-runner ended up pushing the catcher, so I immediately tossed him out of the game. This game ended the batter's twenty-three game hitting streak, so justice, umpire style, really was served that day. Justice delayed perhaps, but justice just the same.

In the fifth inning, we had a trouble ball down in the right-field corner. The home coach argued it for what seemed like forever and ended up getting tossed out of the game by the first-

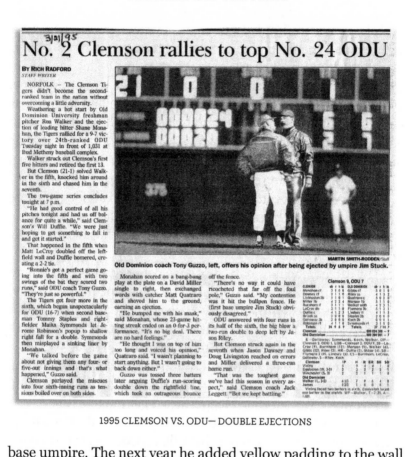

1995 CLEMSON VS. ODU— DOUBLE EJECTIONS

base umpire. The next year he added yellow padding to the wall making what we had as a fair ball now a foul ball. If you can't change the call, change the ballpark.

After the game, the visiting team's coach came to our locker room to see if his player was ejected for fighting, which would result in his having to sit out several games, or if it was for another reason, which meant just for that game. I told him it was for that game only. I said the teacher in me said it was not a fight since no punches were thrown, but more of a pushing match. I told him the reason he was tossed is that he pushed the catcher after I had told both of them to drop their hands. He said he had no problem with the ejection. The next year the NCAA changed the fighting rule to include open hands as grounds for ejection.

Thinking back about this batter's treatment, at no time were the pitches unhittable, they were just not where he wanted them. Did I stretch the zone a little due to his attitude? Maybe. Could he have been tossed out of the game earlier? Absolutely. Did I enjoy all three of his at-bats? You bet.

A few of my friends who were also scouts approached us after the game and asked if he was running his mouth in the batter's box, and if so, what he was saying. I just said that for professional courtesy to all, I preferred not to say anything. I told them to go on what they observed and that should give them a clue. When the draft was held that year, we had a hard time finding the player's name. I suppose character matters.

HEADS, HE'S SAFE; TAILS, HE'S OUT

On Tuesday, April 10, 1995 I got a call asking if I could work the next day. Since that was my anniversary, I figured I had better call my wife. She was okay with it and told me to have fun. The game was NC State at Old Dominion.

What a way to start the game off. I had a real close play at first in the first inning. Coach Elliot Avent for NC State came out and asked what I saw. I admitted to him that my timing was "Horse_____." He knew it; I knew it, and any good umpire would know it. I told him I was not one hundred percent sure of the call. He asked if I would go for help and I told him no, it was my call all the way.

I told him I was going to turn him to face the outfield, and he could call me everything in the book, but could not kick the grass unless he wanted to hurt his foot. I then told him when I felt it was time to end the argument I was going to turn around and head back to my position, and I would appreciate him going back to the dugout. We argued a little bit and then, to throw some humor into the situation before he left, I asked him if he had a coin. He asked why.

I said, "Heads, he is safe; tails, he is out."

He threw his hands up, laughed and said, "How can I argue with a statement like that." He walked away and said, "Well, you missed it."

As good umpires are taught, when a coach is walking away, you just let him go, especially if you are not one hundred percent sure you got the call right.

What I must interject is I had known and umpired Coach Avent's games for at least four years. This is the only way I could have said the things I said in trying to defuse or handle the situation as I did. Two innings later, I asked my third-base umpire what he saw or thought about my play at first. He told me he thought I had kicked it. The very next inning I told the first baseman (the very same player I had called out) to go tell his skipper, "Heads."

After listening to the first baseman regarding my information, Coach Avent stepped out of the dugout and tipped his cap toward me in appreciation for my acknowledging I kicked the play. However, the first baseman, who still didn't care for me, came back out the next inning and said his coach forgot whether "heads" was safe or out. I told him when he went back in to let his skipper know I forgot too. Again, Coach Avent tipped his hat to me again and laughed. The very next inning. I told him to tell Coach Avent I missed the call.

Two innings later, the right fielder and second baseman for NC State wanted to know who threw out the player from the game at ODU in early March. (This player was the player mentioned in the previous story.) They said they heard the umpire was at the park and would love to meet him. I said, "Be careful what you wish for" and left it at that.

They kept on me for several innings, but I would not give in. Somehow, they found out from a spectator that it was the first-base umpire. I hesitated to own up to it and finally told them, yes, it was the same umpire who kicked the play in the first inning of the game tonight, but I could not talk about it.

Now the first baseman and I were on good speaking terms. He said anybody who had the [guts] to throw that guy out, could call him out anytime. He said he was one of the most disliked players in their conference because of his attitude. I did not respond, knowing that if I agreed, it could get me in hot water.

At the end of the next inning, I took my normal position in the outfield grass behind the second baseman. I was facing the outfield fence when I noticed several players taking throws near me. When I turned around, they started asking me questions about the ejection. I told them I could not discuss it. All of a sudden, Coach Avent came out on the top step of the dugout and wanted to know what was up.

The shortstop, who was also the captain, yelled in "Coach, I got it" and told everyone to take their normal throws. At the end of the inning, when the team was entering the dugout, the shortstop went over to Coach Avent and told him what was going on.

Coach Avent stepped out of the dugout, tipped his hat toward me for the third time, and said, "HEADS, I got it." Smiles all around.

HOMECOMING

On March 14 and 15, 1997, I was scheduled to work a Colonial Athletic Association Conference Series at East Carolina University in Greenville, NC. ECU, as you may remember, is the school I attended and played baseball. All the coaches in the conference knew I went there. They also knew I played baseball there but had no problem with me umpiring at any

ECU VS WILLIAM & MARY IN 1972; MY FIRST CONFERENCE GAME, AND MY PARENTS, TWO FANS PULLING FOR THE HOME PLATE UMP

site in the CAA. I took that as a compliment, as I never wanted anyone to think I would make calls in their favor just because I had played there.

This was my first game back after neck surgery. Two months earlier, while on bus duty, three men had gone on one of our school buses to beat up one of our students. What you might need to know is I taught in one of the rougher areas of our school system, and the assault had been the result of a neighborhood problem spilling over to the school grounds. I called for help, but as I was pulling the bad guys off or trying to get between them and the student, I got hit pretty hard in the back of my neck. I ended up with two ruptured disks.

Since Greenville was also my hometown, I thought I would take my five-year-old son Ryan with me. This way he could spend one night with his grandparents and one night with me in the hotel.

ME IN MY UNIFORM—
FIRST CAA CONFERENCE GAME

The first thing my son asked me on the night he stayed with me was, "Do they have a breakfast buffet?"

When I said yes, he was happy. As soon as he asked me, the lady at the front desk started to explain where the buffet was, but Ryan interrupted her and proudly proclaimed he had already found out where it was. This coming from a five-year-old was priceless, and although Ryan is in good physical shape, I don't think he has missed the location of a buffet ever since.

As mentioned earlier, I had worked for the newspaper office and still had a great relationship with them. Hearing that I was coming to do the game, Woody Peele, the sports editor for *The Daily Reflector*, wanted to do an article on me, showing how I had gone from being a player at the local high school to playing for the local college (ECU) to moving to Virginia to teach, to now becoming a Division 1 college umpire. I told them no, because if anything controversial happened in the game, it would come back to bite me in the rear. They promised not to publish it until Monday, the day after the conference series was over. I finally gave in and said yes, but only under those conditions. They agreed, but as you will see, they published it Sunday morning, getaway day. I still keep that article in my desk.

I had the plate for Saturday's game and was the most nervous I had ever been. Tons of former classmates, family, and friends were there. Thank goodness Saturday was over, and now to our last game. I was working first base and called a balk on the William and Mary pitcher. Coach Farr calmly walked out and said, "Nice newspaper article. Now, Hometown Hero, what did you see?"

With equal calm I told Coach Farr it was a move I had never seen and what I thought I saw I must not have seen. I told him I might have missed the play.

Very quietly, he said, "You missed it, but I will not embarrass you in front of a lot of people who came to see you umpire today. I have you at home in two weeks, and I will show what he did and why you missed it."

For those who do not know, Coach Farr was a pitcher in college and played professional ball. He also served as a pitching coach for many years under some top coaches before getting a head coaching job at William and Mary. He is now a scout for the Kansas City Royals organization and is still someone with whom I still keep in touch. That kind of graciousness is rare in college coaching and very much worthy of mention.

Two weeks later that day came. Jeff Doy and I were working a game at W&M. Normally we ride to college games together, but on this day, Jeff and I drove separately. I got there first, and Coach Farr showed me the move. He showed me how deceptive it can be and how they pick off so many runners with it. I was very appreciative, as it gave me an edge in case I saw it again. He then asked me who had the plate that day. I told him we had not decided, but I would get back to him as soon as I talked to Jeff.

I called Jeff who was about fifteen minutes away. I asked him what he wanted to do, and he said he did not care. I told him I would dish it since my gear was already in the umpire's dressing room. I went back to Coach Farr and told him I had the plate.

As I was walking back to our dressing room, which was right behind the dugout, Coach Farr got on his walkie-talkie and told his pitching coach, "Smith has the plate, and he will give you down and away but not up or in."

I went back to Coach Farr and asked what that was about. He said he had a book on all the umpires. I asked him about Jeff.

He said, "Jeff will go up and away, sometimes down, but not in."

I told him, "I am not that predictable, and I was going to call strikes up and in today."

In the fourth inning, he came up to me to make a pitching change and said, "You just can't do it, can you."

I said, "What do you mean?"

He said, "You just can't call that up and in pitch even when you want to."

He was right, darn it, but it is probably for the best because in college ball a plate umpire can get in a world of trouble for calling high strikes.

THREE FINGERS

This is another great Coach Farr story. Somewhere in the 90s, I was assigned to work a non-conference game at William and Mary. For non-conference games, they only used two umpires. I was working the bases and had numerous tough calls that day. Keep in mind that because this was a non-conference game I was the only one on the bases. Earlier in the game I had had three tough calls that Coach Farr came out on. He told me he appreciated my hustle, but still thought I missed them. He and I ended up agreeing to disagree.

On the fourth close call, here came Coach Farr again. As he was about thirty feet away from me, I held up three fingers. When he got up to me he asked what that meant.

I said, "Coach if we had three umpires, we could have gotten a better look at that one and the others that you disagreed with." I told him my partner and I were doing the best we could do in a two-man system. He argued a little more, told me about their budget, agreed about needing the third man, and walked away.

I had the plate about two weeks later and had a shot hit down the third baseline. It was hit so hard the batter was still in the batter's box and both the catcher and I were still in a crouch. The ball was three feet beyond the third-base bag before either of us had a chance to move. I called the ball foul as I had never saw it hit fair in front of the bag, just two-three inches foul beyond the bag. The ball was hit so hard that the third-base coach, Ryan Wheeler, was even bailing on the play.

Coach Farr came out of the dugout to question the call and saw me put three fingers down beside me. As he was walking toward me, he said, "I see the three fingers, but I had a clear view, straight down the line and that ball hit just in front of the bag before going foul."

I said, "Coach, if you had a view straight down the line, that means you were not where you were supposed to be—in the dugout—right?"

The logic of that must have been inescapable, because he just turned around and went back from where he had come. Score one for the umpire in just another professional disagreement with a coach for whom I have great admiration.

TWO FOR ONE

Having my daughter attend William and Mary offered me the opportunity to visit her quite often when I was assigned a game there. All the coaches in the conference knew where she was going and let my assigner know they had no problem with me doing games at William and Mary. So I got to go do two things I loved, visit my daughter and work a baseball game. Of course, working the game also afforded me the opportunity to make money to help pay for her tuition. Maybe that's three for one?

RARE OPPORTUNITY FOR MY SISTER AND HER HUSBAND

On April 4 and 5, 1998, Jim Stuck, Ron Sebastian, and I drove to the University of North Carolina at Wilmington to work a conference series with George Mason University. I was working the plate the second day. Due to the distance factor and their jobs not allowing them to travel, this was the only time my oldest sister and her husband ever got to see me umpire. My mother and father also drove down from Greenville, so I was hoping not to screw up the game. This park, at the time, had some very strange ground rules, and it seemed like every time a ball was hit we had to make a judgment call as to fair or foul, or in play or out of play. Nothing was simple that day. To make matters worse it was cold, very windy, and rainy and neither pitcher could find the plate.

The game ended on a very tough call. We had two outs and a runner on third with the home team, up by one run. The ball was hit to the left fielder. It started off clearly in fair territory. I would say at least ten feet fair. However, by the time he caught up to the ball, the wind had taken it about twenty feet foul, right at the dead ball-live ball line. We didn't have a fence, just a line, which meant you had better hustle to get a good look at the play. If you didn't, you could bet the first thing out of the coach's mouth would be "How can you call it fair or foul standing at home plate or on the third baseline?"

The left fielder caught it running at full speed in foul territory, took it into dead ball territory and then fell down. Our first determination was to rule on whether the ball was fair or foul when he first caught it, and then whether he had control of the ball when he fell to the ground. We ruled it a legal catch and, lucky for us, he had held on to the ball and there were already two outs. Otherwise, the tumble into the dead ball area would have meant the runner on third would have scored, and we would have gone into extra innings. As bad as the weather was, I think everyone was glad it was over, and we didn't get any arguments.

SNOW DELAY

I had umpired in many a game with snow or snow flurries, but never had a game delayed by snow and then played. Normally they would just cancel the game. However, in Richmond, Virginia on February 13, 2000, opening day of the 2000 Season, our game was delayed for three hours due to snow and sleet and then played. When they finally decided the game was on, the grounds crew had to clear about an inch of snow off the infield. The outfield, normally green, was now white.

We ended up playing with the temperature reading 34 degrees at game time and 32 degrees when we called the game after four-and-a-half innings. The sleet changed to all snow. We figured both teams wanted to get an official game in, as visiting St. Peters was heading farther south the next day. These were probably the most miserable game conditions in which I ever worked. Virginia Commonwealth University ended up beating St. Peters 11-8.

One last part to this game. Due to the terrible weather conditions, all of us wanted the plate, as we would stay warmer wearing all our gear. Jim Stuck won the coin toss and got the plate. Then Robert Turner and I flipped for third. He won the toss and got third. For those who do not know, when working third, you run more. So on this day, I got the coldest spot. Baseball in February is for the birds, or maybe for the penguins.

UMPIRING WITH HALF A BRAIN

On March 5, 2000, I was assigned the NY Tech at William and Mary game. In the seventh inning, I got hit in the back of the head on a batter's backswing. I went to the ground, and the trainer came out. He was checking for a concussion and asking me all sorts of questions. I guess I answered him okay as he cleared me to continue. However, I never remembered the game from the seventh inning on. Not sure how I did it, but I am sure many said it was one of my better plate jobs. After the game, the trainer did some more tests. He told me it was definitely a concussion, and he apologized for letting me continue. He wanted me to go to the hospital to get it checked out, but I told him I would have it checked when I got home. When I got home, it was confirmed, and I has to sit out a week as a safety precaution. My partner and everyone else must have thought I had finally gotten some sense knocked into me.

QUICKEST EJECTION OF A PITCHER AND HEAD COACH

On March 10, 2001, Old Dominion was playing UNC Charlotte. We had just started the game, and out of nowhere, in the top of the first, the pitcher and head coach were ejected by the plate umpire, Rich Humphrey, for throwing at a batter's head. It kind of floored everyone, as we had no prior knowledge of any bad blood between the teams, but there was no doubt he was throwing at him. A heated debate followed, but after order was restored, the game was played with no further problems. What a way to start a game!

BLAME IT ON THE UMPIRES

On March 11, 2000, Ducky Davis and I were assigned to work a doubleheader at William and Mary. They were playing the University of Delaware. Here are the stats for my game so you can see where the umpiring really had nothing to do with the game. W&M had 23/22/4 (runs, hits errors); Univ. of Delaware had 19/20/5. For the game that's forty-two runs, forty-two hits, and nine errors. Seems like lack of pitching or defense were the problems. Add to that four controversial plays at the plate, one broken ankle, one torn ACL, three hit batters, ten home runs, the wind blowing a gale, and the scoreboard not working correctly. Other than that, it was routine!

I plated the first game and Ducky had fun on the bases. Actually, the game was fun to do as no one knew what was going to happen next. I had three very close plays at home plate that all went against the University of Delaware. The coach came out to argue on all three plays and said, "I cannot believe you guys, who are supposed to be that good, have missed all of them."

On the last play, he said, "You're going to have to throw me out of the game."

I told him no, because as cold as it was, he was going to have to stay here with us and freeze.

Again, he said, "I cannot believe you missed all three of them."

I told him that if he thought that I had missed them, he might consider not sending his runners home if he thought it was going to be close. I told him I respected him coming out, but we were going to have to agree to disagree. He also whined to Ducky all day long about his calls at the bases. He went out on Ducky at least a dozen times.

In the second game of the doubleheader, Ducky had the plate, and I had the bases. The coach hated Ducky's strike zone all game and continually chirped from the dugout. Again, we were not going to throw him out. He was going to stay there and suffer with us. He came out to me several times on the bases about pickoffs. He had two players picked off and swore that the pitcher balked both times. When it happened the third time, he came out and said, "Are you going to get even one right today?"

My comment was I had gotten every one of them right, and if he thought that I was missing them, he should have his players shorten up their lead. There was no way that coach was getting to a warm place before Ducky and me.

TERRIBLE TERP TROUBLE

On March 12, 2000, Virginia Commonwealth University, ranked in the top twenty in the Nation had the University of Maryland in town. Thinking this was going to be a blowout in favor of VCU, the assigner gave Keith Buttolph his first collegiate plate job. Ducky Davis worked first, and I was on third. To show you how the game of baseball is determined by the play on the field and not who should win, Maryland ended up beating VCU 12-4. This was a major upset, as Maryland then had seventeen players suspended for hazing or underage drinking. When we walked through the tunnel to the field, we only saw three or four players in the dugout and four or five in the outfield grass warming up. When Maryland took the field, there were only five or six players in the dugout.

I asked the shortstop what was going on. He told us about the suspensions and that half the players were being suspended for one game and the other half for another game. He also said had this been basketball or football players, probably nothing would have happened or at least they would not have had to sit out a game. He said since baseball, at that time, was not considered a major sport at the University of Maryland, they felt they were being made an example.

The call that I will now try to share with you is probably one of the toughest calls I ever had to make in my umpiring career. I had to eject a friend and one of the coaches for whom I had the utmost respect. I knew the reason he was coming out there was more to fire up his team than to complain, as they were losing to a team whom they should be killing.

We had a runner on first and I was positioned behind and slightly to the third-base side of the pitcher's mound, in what umpires call the C position. A ball was hit to the second baseman who tossed the ball to the shortstop for the start of a double play.

However, the toss was inaccurate, and the shortstop had to turn his back to me and dropped the ball. I ruled the play a no catch. All of a sudden, like a lightning bolt, here came Coach Keys from the VCU dugout. The F-bombs were coming out of his mouth left and right. He kept yelling, "Jim, there is no bleeping way he dropped the ball, it was on the exchange."

I told Coach Keys it was not on the exchange and he had dropped it, meaning no catch. Now I turn around and see his hat on the ground, but I had no idea how it got there. I found out later he had thrown it as I was originally turning to walk away, hoping to give him two or three more steps to cool down before getting to me.

We are still going at it and now he gets chest to chest with me. I said, "Paul, if you bump me, you are done. You know the penalties that go along with bumping an umpire."

Sure enough, he bumps me, and it may have been accidental, but he gave me no choice, I had to dump him. Two innings later I asked the left and center fielder, who saw the play clearly, along with the shortstop, what they really had. Again, it was such a screwed-up play because the shortstop was forced to turn his back to me. All three said, "Please do not say anything to Coach, or he will kill us; you got it right, the ball was dropped."

We were later told that VCU had been playing lousy the last two games, and this may just have been the straw that broke the camel's back, as the saying goes. They were a top twenty team playing a team with only thirteen or fourteen players, so it should have been an easy win over the Terps, but that's why we play the game.

CERTIFICATE RENEWAL

Every five years, teachers have to renew their teaching certificates. This can be done either during the school year or summer. Being both a teacher and a sports official during the school year, I choose to take some classes in the summer. During the summer following the previously mentioned ejection, I decided to take two of the coaching classes being offered at Hampton University. Coach Keys was teaching one of the classes.

He looked me up and apologized for his actions. AWKWARD!

I told him I had considered us friends until that day, but with the abuse and embarrassment he threw out, I never wanted to do another one of his games. He asked me to please give him one more chance. Being a softy, I gave in.

I also ended up going to the class he was teaching, which further helped to mend our fences. I continued working his games until March 20, 2004. On that day, he heard I was having surgery on Tuesday, March 24. He called his secretary and asked her to come out to the ballpark to type up a letter for me, wishing me a speedy recovery and to hurry back to The Diamond, where VCU's home games are played. He also had the coaching staff and team sign a ball for me. He also coached first base one inning to talk to me. Coach Keys was a coach that always coached from the dugout and never the bases. He let his coaches take care of first and third base. This was the last college game I worked before surgery, Rutgers at VCU on March 20, 2004. No one knew that almost on the four-year anniversary of "The Ejection Game," doctors would blow the call on my operating table and this would be my last time on the collegiate field. Sometimes I wish I could have ejected the doctors.

GAME BALL FOR DAD'S EIGHTIETH BIRTHDAY

On April 10, 2001, I was assigned to work NC State at VCU. Even though my dad's birthday was several weeks off, I wanted to do something special for him. I asked Coach Best, the assistant coach for NC State as well as the son of one of my mom and dad's best friends, if he could get a ball signed by the team for my dad for an eightieth birthday present. I knew this would be something special, since my father had attended NC State and been a guard on the football team for four years. Coach Avent and Coach Best had the entire NC State team sign a ball for my dad. They also signed an individual one for him. Both balls had the NC State logo on them, and that meant the world to my dad. The balls stayed on the table next to his chair until he passed away. Today they are among the treasures in my curio.

ODU'S PRICE[LESS] TAG

On March 27, 2002, I was assigned with two other seasoned umpires to work the NC State at Old Dominion game. It was a raw and damp 38 degrees at game time with the temperature dropping and a stiff breeze blowing in. I forget the inning, but we had a pickoff and then a resulting rundown play between first and second. Both base umpires were boxing the runner in as they should have been doing, but both on the outfield side, which did not give them the best angle. After several throws, on the way back toward first, my partner called the runner out on the tag. However, the fielder kept running after the runner, suggesting that he missed him. In reality he had. He missed him by at least twelve inches, but not my call.

Then, Coach Avent came flying out to me at the plate, saying, "Jim, you have got to help them. The fielder told you he missed the tag when he kept chasing him."

I told him to go talk to the two umpires who had the play.

Before leaving to go out there to discuss the call, he said, "Every time I come here I get bleeped and tossed."

I told him, "Not tonight. It is 38 degrees, a great night for a game, and you are going to enjoy or suffer the night in the dugout with us."

"Jim, I like you, but your partners . . ."

"Stop right there, or I am going to have to toss you. Coach, you are going to have to agree to disagree with them, but I am not going to overrule them from ninety feet away."

He finally went out and talked to them, and they stuck with their call. Both also knew if they came to me for help, someone was going to have to be tossed. So for Coach Avent, the night just kept getting colder.

Both my partners did ask me after the game what I had. We always preached honesty, so I told them the player missed the tag by a foot, but I was very appreciative they hadn't come to me. Someone was going to have to dump the ODU coach if I overruled the call.

In the bottom of the eighth inning, tie ball game, with two outs, a three-two count on the batter, and a runner on third, not even thinking about trying to steal home, and really no possibility of a squeeze play, the third-base umpire calls a balk on the NC State pitcher.

Coach Avent came flying out of the dugout, asking me "Jim, what the F-bomb is going on? That is two he has kicked tonight. With a three-two count and two outs, why the F-bomb would our guy want to pay any attention to the runner on third?"

After a little more profanity, I said, "Elliott, how is the family? Where are you guys going for dinner?"

"What?" I said, "I'm just trying to calm you down so you can stay around. Now go talk to my partner."

This was another mess that would result in an ejection if it was reversed. While Coach Avent was arguing with the third-base umpire, I spent that time trying to calm the NC State pitcher. Because the pitcher and I had been on the same page all night, he listened to me. When Coach Avent took him out of the game in the ninth, the pitcher thanked me for keeping him in the game and complimented me on my strike zone.

After the game, as an umpiring team, we talked about the rundown and balk calls. I told my partners what I saw on the rundown, and they both agreed they hadn't boxed in the play correctly. When we got to the balk call conversation, one partner and I both said we saw nothing. Our other partner apologized for getting us into that mess and said he probably kicked it. Of course, in that situation, with no thought of the runner on third advancing other than on a ball in play, a balk call should be very obvious, really calling itself. In all fairness to that partner, he hadn't worked a lot that year and was filling in as a last-minute replacement. He was a great umpire, and we all do miss them once in a while. I would still go on the field with him any day.

THE BOBBLE SCREWUP

On March 29-31, 2002, Robert Turner, Tony Carilli, and I were assigned to a Colonial Athletic Association Conference Series at Virginia Commonwealth University. The Rams were hosting Drexel. What a game my plate turned out to be, especially with Drexel just joining the CAA and this being their first CAA

Series. At one point, we had a runner on first who was stealing on the play. The batter hit a rather hard ground ball to the second baseman, who first bobbled and then dropped the ball. At this point the runner was almost to second base. The second baseman picked the ball up again and dropped it a second time. Now the runner was approximately three steps past second on the third-base side of the bag. The second baseman finally picked up the elusive ball on the third try, and with the batter-runner about ten feet from first, threw the ball into the first base dugout.

Now came the awarding of bases, which was my responsibility, as the crew chief for this game, not to botch. Inconspicuously, I pointed down to the ground to my partners to make sure we were all on the same page for awarding bases. I was awarding the runner who was on first home, since he had attained second at the time of the throw and put the batter-runner on second. No problems from anyone, and my partners agreed.

Screwing up the time of the pitch rule is what got me in trouble. A bobble and drop is not considered an attempt to record an out, and so the dead ball related back to runner's location at the time of the pitch. At the end of the inning, not when the rule was screwed up, the Drexel coach politely came out and said that was the screwiest thing he had ever seen. He asked me to explain the rule to him. I told him the runner on first had actually attained second when the throw was finally made, and the runner was awarded two bases. He bought it. After the game, all three of us, not being sure we had it right, pulled out the rulebook. We came to suspect we had missed the call. We got dressed and went to Hooters and did some more research and now knew we, or more precisely I, had blown the call. Yes, there were other research observations done as well.

We went back for game two of the series the next day, and no one said anything or even questioned the call. We went back for game three of the series on Sunday and again, nothing from anyone. However, on Monday, we all got calls from the conference assigner. He said the coach wanted to know how three Division 1 conference umpires could miss a rule like that in a conference series. I told our assigner that I had the plate so it all fell on me. However, had the coach really known the rule, why didn't he question me or us then or prior to the start of the next two games? We surmised he got back home and was explaining it to someone and that person told him the runners should have been on second and third. That made our work done at the aforementioned restaurant just not worth a hoot.

JUSTIN VERLANDER'S SLIDER

In 2002 and 2003, when Justin Verlander was playing at Old Dominion, I had the privilege of being assigned to work several of his games. He was one of the two toughest pitchers I ever worked. The other was another ODU pitcher by the name of Jeff Ware who spent some time with the Toronto Blue Jays back in the '80s. Both had nasty sliders during which the bottom would just drop out if you didn't follow the ball all the way into the catcher's glove.

With Justin, I found out rather quickly, I better never relax and concentrate on every single pitch. You see, he had a nasty slider and then he also had a really NASTY slider. You never knew when the really NASTY slider was coming. Again, if you relaxed and didn't follow the ball all the way in, you would do what I did on three separate occasions. The ball looked great three feet in front of the plate, and then the bottom dropped out. Umpires call that timing: let the pitch or play finish and then call it. Each time, I had it in my mind that the pitch was going to be a strike, right at the knees, and called all three strikes. Boy did my strike mechanic look great. Then as your right arm is going out calling it a strike you would see the catcher picking it out of the dirt. You knew you were getting ready to get a dirty look from the hitter and comments from the dugout like "Get helmets for the earthworms or get a sand wedge out, we must be playing golf today."

CATCHER IN THE FRY

For the most part, catchers and umpires get along great. In my thirty-eight years of umpiring, there is only one catcher who I did not like, and that was because he was two-faced. He would agree with us on pitches and then signal or tell his coach something different. Not a good move.

If you read the rulebook, umpires are supposed to have the same strike zone as the umpire who worked the day before and the day after. Yet we all know that is not the case. However, all the coaches and catchers want to know is how far out, in, down, or up you are going to call strikes that day. Once they know, they can let everyone on their teams know what today's zone is going to be like. What gets you in trouble is when your zone bounces around or is all over the place.

The College of William and Mary had a catcher named Mike DeCarlo, somewhere around 2002, who earned a very bad reputation among all umpires. He was a transfer from a northern school. Again, when on defense, he would tell you he agreed with you, but then he would tell the coach the complete opposite. If the coach asked where a pitch was, and I said off the plate, he would vocalize to the coach that the pitch was away. However, we soon found out he had a signal to the coach when he thought we kicked one. I was the sixth guy from our association to have him that year, so his reputation had already spread prior to my game. I was warned about him, but I still tried to go in with an open mind. It didn't take long to find out everything I heard was true.

In my game he kept wanting pitches four inches off the plate to be called a strike. I told him if his pitcher could consistently hit the spot, I would start giving it to him. By the third inning he proved he could hit it, so I started giving it to him. He was happy, even though I knew he had been shoving it up my rear for the first three innings by giving the signal to his coach telling him I was missing the corner.

He came up to bat in the sixth inning, and now it was my chance to see his true colors. I told the opposing catcher to set up four inches off the plate and throw gas. His pitcher had great control all game and hit the spot all three times. I rang him up. As he walked away he started running his mouth. His coach came out to save him. He kept yelling that ball was four inches off the plate.

I responded back so he, the coach and the other team could hear. "So you want me to call the pitch four inches off the plate a strike when you're catching, but not when you are hitting, is that correct?"

His head coach and I had a very quiet conversation between innings, and I told him all umpires knew when he went to his mask, he was giving you the signal that he thought we missed the pitch. I told him I had seen him go to his mask at least six times already but hadn't said anything.

I just said, "If he wants us to give him that pitch on defense, then we're going to call it the same for both teams, including when he's at bat."

The coach agreed.

Years later we talked about him, and we agreed this was one of his more challenging catchers. With the exception of this year, Coach Farr always had very professional and polite catchers. They kept the ball off of the umpires and always worked with us.

THE TORNADO GAME

On May 9, 2003, Jeff Doy, Jack Horner, and myself were sent to The College of William and Mary to work a game with The University of Delaware. This was one of the scariest games I ever umpired. The sky was nasty and ominous, but no rain. Game time was 5:00 PM, yet it was so dark it seemed like it was midnight, so we started with the lights on. The coach or trainer received information, we think from a parent or fan, that there was a tornado warning in the area. We held up the game until he got a weather update, and we were safe to play. As soon as we got the go-ahead, we finished the game.

After the game and prior to our leaving, the coach got a weather update for us. We are glad he did, as the worst of the weather was south of the ball field and in the direction we were heading. We stopped and got something to eat and waited until the storms had moved out of the area. Whatever twisters may have spun up had passed, but we couldn't head home until somewhere around midnight.

FAIR OR FOUL POLL, UMPIRE GETS THE ONLY VOTE

If you like controversy, you will enjoy this story. John Thomas, a former minor league umpire, had the plate, and I was on third. This was a conference game at Virginia Commonwealth University. They were playing James Madison University. The game was being played at The Diamond, former home of the Atlanta Braves AAA team, the Richmond Braves. This was a great park in which to umpire a game, but you did need to know how the fences came into play.

Somewhere in the middle of the game, with no one on, the JMU pitcher splits the middle of the plate with a low-nineties fastball on an oh-two count. The batter connects, sending the ball it seemed like three hundred feet high and five hundred feet deep. The ball, unlucky for me, just had to be one that was either just fair or just foul. The foul pole, no matter what the average height is for professional baseball was not high enough and made it a very difficult call. The ball was at least fifty feet over it. I locked in and gave it the best look I could. I called it a home run.

Here came Coach McFarland from JMU, flying out of the dugout. "Jim, how can you call that ball fair? I am looking straight down the line, and that ball was easily three-six feet foul."

I told him if he was looking straight down the line that he was not in his dugout, but rather in the on-deck circle.

He said, "No, I was in the dugout, but still had it foul."

Please know that I had umpired several of Coach McFarland's games in the past, so we both knew how far to push each other and had great respect for each other. I also knew this was a big conference game for him, and knew he had to argue the call. Again, he asked how I could have that ball fair.

I told him "Coach, from your angle in the dugout, with the ball clearly fifty feet over the top of the foul pole, how could you tell that the ball was three-six feet fair or foul?"

Very professionally, he said, "You are correct." He asked me one more time. "With you looking straight at it, are you one hundred percent sure with no doubt in your mind it was fair?"

I told him, "Great question." I told him I gave it the best look I could, and the one he should be mad at was his pitcher for throwing the ball down the middle of the plate on an 0-2 count.

He said, "So now you are telling me how to call pitches."

I told him "No, but the play is over."

Before leaving me, he gave it one more shot and asked if I would go for help.

I told him no, it was my call. What he didn't know was that my plate guy and I had both communicated on Coach McFarland's way out. We both thought it was fair.

As he got ready to go to the mound, he said, "I agree with you, but I had to come out and stick up for the team."

I told him I appreciated his honesty.

Coach McFarland then proceeded to the mound, had some highly pitched words for his pitcher and then proceeded to take him out of the game. He probably told his pitcher the same thing I had said about the location of the pitch.

After the game, the plate umpire said that call was one of the toughest calls he had ever seen in either his professional or collegiate career. This situation proves one particular point. Like it or not the umpire gets to be the one that's right—or wrong, not the coach.

FIGHT AT NORFOLK STATE

One weekend in 1995, we had several major league umpires up from Florida putting on a weekend clinic for our local umpire association. Mike Perez and I were assigned the last game of the MEAC Conference Series between Norfolk State University and Bethune Cookman University. It was also the last game of the regular season. That morning, we started off at the clinic and then left for our game around 11:00 AM.

The previous day's umpires, Billy King and his partner, were also at the clinic. They let us know about the problems and bad blood they had noticed during their Saturday games. They told us one of the NSU players, "Country" as he was called, had thrown a ball in the Bethune Cookman dugout while warming up between innings. Words had been exchanged and players had started out of the dugouts, but nothing more had happened.

We were advised by our assigner and given further advice

from one of the major league umpires who were putting on the clinic to treat the game like any other game and not say anything at home plate or warn either team. We were told just to be aware of what had happened, and if problems arose to just sit back and take down numbers and facts. During our pregame, I decided to take the home team and my partner would take the visitors if anything happened. After the game was over, I would be glad we each took a team.

It was in the fourth or fifth inning when we started to see things heat up. We had a batter-runner run on the inside of the first baseline and step on the foot of the first baseman. We nipped it in the bud right then. Even though we couldn't prove it was intentional, there was little doubt in our minds it was.

The next inning, the other team's pitcher retaliated and hit a batter in the small of his back. Both teams stepped to the top lip of their dugout, and I immediately ripped my mask off and warned both coaches and teams.

In the seventh inning, we had a player go hard into second in an attempt to break up a double play. The slide was borderline dirty. Both players got up chest to chest, but my partner stepped in between them and defused the situation. We got both coaches together and told them we were going to start throwing out players but would give them the opportunity to take care of it prior to us doing so. They were appreciative, got their teams together, and let them know we were going to throw out the next player who in our mind was out to hurt someone. The last two innings were played without any further problems, just two good teams battling it out.

At the end of the game, we got the key from the equipment manager to get back in our dressing room. However, as soon as we stepped five feet outside the gate, we decided we would just shower at our homes, since we only lived ten minutes from the ballpark. As soon as we stepped back in to return the key, we noticed the players starting to shake hands, but then, out of nowhere, players started throwing punches at each other. They were being thrown against the fence and through the gate. Jerseys were ripped off of chests, and there was quite a bit of blood on faces and uniforms. One player was even thrown on top of a drainage cover and had a big gash in his head. It was the worst fight I had ever personally witnessed in a baseball game.

We just stepped back and started taking numbers and writing down the best description we could of what we observed. As soon as the coaches got it under control, we got both coaches together. They felt our responsibility ended when we stepped through the gate and told us they would handle it. They told us there was no need to send in a report to the conference office.

I told them I understood, but the report was still going into the conference office, and they could make decisions about suspensions. I told them I was not going to have the office calling me Monday morning asking what went on, and why they weren't notified. We ended up giving them the numbers of sixteen players whom we could identify as the ones throwing punches. As stated earlier, this was the last game of the conference series and last game of the season. What made it so bad for both teams is the conference tournament started the next week.

BULLET ALEXANDER

Time for another Bullet story. Because Bullet, a local umpiring mentor and legend, loved the profession of umpiring so much, what he liked to do if he was not umpiring was to go out and observe umpires. He might be sitting in the stands or lounging in his truck with a chew.

After the game, he would always come up to you and let you know what you needed to work on. The conversation may last ten minutes or an hour. Whatever you did wrong, he wanted you to correct. He never let you know what you did right. As he said, "You already know what you're doing right. You still need to know what you're doing wrong." That is an expression I continue to use with the umpires whom I go out and observe.

How did Bullet earn his nickname? I could tell you he tossed coaches so quickly that he was faster than a speeding bullet, but that's not exactly correct or true. Bullet would let a coach show his bad behavior before earning the early exit, but once that occurred, the coach was on his way. Actually, Bullet was playing football for Wilson High school and was quite a talented player on the unbeaten state champions. He even won the Browning Award for the best player that year. He played blocking back, which called for protection of the quarterback on certain plays. In one game, he blocked a player on the opposing team, taking him off his feet so that he landed on his hind parts feet up in the air. The player apparently had some respect for the hit, because he remarked afterward that he went down so fast and so hard that he felt like he had been hit by a bullet. That nickname stuck forever.

THREE COLLEGIATE COACH EJECTIONS

In my collegiate umpiring career, I was fortunate enough to have worked 315 games. In those, for whatever reason, I only had to eject three college coaches. Call it luck, game management skills learned from mentors, not ejecting some who should have been ejected, using the teacher skills in knowing how to defuse the situation or whatever the reason was, I am glad I only had to do the paperwork three times. Filling out those reports is time-consuming.

My first collegiate ejection of a coach happened in 1990 and had a very funny twist to it. New York Tech was playing a day game at Old Dominion University. It was near freezing outside, with the temperature hovering around 36 degrees. The wind coming off the water made it feel like it was minus 36. My partners were Bullet Alexander on first and Jim Stuck on the plate. It was another one of those days where both Bullet and I lost out on getting the plate.

We had an overthrow at first on a ground ball to the shortstop. No runners were on base at the time, so I was coming in from third with the throw in case we had something goofy happen and there was a play at second. The New York Tech batter-runner ran through first and made an effort toward second when he saw the overthrow heading toward the fence. They threw back to first and a tag was applied. He was called safe. The problem is both the first-base umpire and the plate umpire went with the ball to make sure it did not go into dead ball territory, and no one saw the effort but me. The ODU Coach, Pat McMahon, who is now with the New York Yankees, came out and asked Bullet if he would go for help. He said yes and went to the plate guy. Jim told Bullet he had also gone with the ball. Bullet told Coach McMahon what Jim had, which was, of course, still not what he wanted. Coach McMahon then asked Bullet if he would come to me and see if I saw the turn. He told him yes. Bullet then came to me, and I remember it like it was yesterday.

I said, "Big Dog," as we occasionally called him, "after all the schooling you have given me, how could the two of you failed to communicate and both go with the ball and not see the play?"

He said, "I know, but have you got anything?"

"Yes, one hundred percent effort and an out."

The three of us got together, and I told Bullet and Jim to let the NY Tech coach come out to me to argue. I also told them we were definitely not going to toss him and have him go to a warm locker room. He was going to stay out there and freeze with us.

Sure enough, here he came and asked how I could make that call. I told him on that play I only had two responsibilities: 1) to come in if the ball stayed in the infield, which it did, and 2) to watch the runner and take him into second if he came.

He kept yelling and said, "You are going to have to throw me out, as there is no way he made an effort toward second."

I said, "Coach, you are going to stay out here and freeze with the rest of us. The only way you are going to get tossed is if you bump me, and I know you want to do that, but you won't."

For the next five or six innings, the coach complained about balls and strikes, normally an automatic ejection, and questioned any close safe or out call. Finally, in the top of the ninth, his last time at bat, with two outs, Jim called a close pitch a strike. The coach went crazy.

I said, "Alright, that is enough, you are done."

"I thought you weren't going to toss me."

"I guess I lied."

One side note to this story. Anyone who umpired any of ODU's games when Coach McMahon was there knows that he never went down to the bullpen. However, on this day, right after I reversed the call, he went down to the bullpen and very quietly whispered on the way "By doggies, Jim, I know it took a lot of guts to make that call, but I appreciate your seeing and calling it." *By doggies* was one of his favorite sayings.

One other thing I would like to mention about Coach McMahon was that at the end of every season, he would send a personalized letter to every umpire who worked a game at ODU during the season. Somehow, he found out something about every umpire's family and made sure it was in the letter. He never used a generic letter.

The second ejection occurred on April 29, 1997, when the University of Virginia was playing a game at Virginia Commonwealth University. It happened on the first play of the game. I had a whacker at first and called the UVA player out. The head coach came out to discuss the call with me. Very professional, very quiet.

During our discussion I kept hearing someone complaining/ chirping from the top step of the dugout. I took a step back, saw who it was, and told him to knock it off. He continued, so again, I told him to knock it off. When he wouldn't stop, I asked the head coach if he wanted to take care of it or have me do it.

He said, "By all means, go ahead."

I stepped aside and tossed him out. The coach said he appreciated my listening to him and understood my ejection. He said he still thought his runner was safe.

As the assistant coach was getting his coat to leave the dugout, he walked by me, saying "Wow, that was fast, especially on the opening play."

He wanted to know if he could go sit in the bullpen. I told him he knew the rules, but if he stayed quiet I was not going to go looking for him. He went to the bullpen, sat there quietly, and about every two innings we would chat long distance.

The third ejection was the ejection of Coach Keys, mentioned previously in the "Terrible Terp Trouble Game."

MICKEY IRVING—EASY AS ONE, TWO, THREE

The next story is probably best told by the umpire who sent it to me, as he remembers the details. His name is Mickey Irving. Mickey worked for our local umpire association, EVOA, for a couple of years and then went to umpires' school. He was fortunate enough to be picked up by professional baseball and then worked in the minors for several years. After getting out of that, he came back to EVOA, and this is where the story now picks up, as told through Mickey's eyes.

As an umpire Jim always carried himself as a professional. From the shined shoes to the perfectly clean and neat uniform, that is the way he always went on the field. He never seemed to get rattled during the games. The best example of this was on the field at The Diamond in Richmond for a college game between VCU and the University of Virginia quite a few years ago. I had the plate, and I had recently completed umpires' school and had a few years in professional baseball under my belt. I felt I was ready for anything that could possibly happen on the baseball field. The first-base umpire was also a recent graduate of professional umpire school. Jim, the senior umpire on the crew, had third base. I knew as we traveled up to Richmond that day it would be an enjoyable game with such a great crew to work with.

The game started routinely as any other game. It was still close in the middle innings. With a UVA runner on first, they decided to steal. The hitter took a violent swing at the pitch, missed, and fell toward the plate, bumping into the catcher as he made his throw. The ball flew into center field. The VCU second baseman and runner from first collided in front of the base and decided to push and shove one another as they untangled. The runner retreated to first as the centerfielder threw the ball in. Unexpectedly, the throw went wild, and the runner decided to head toward second. He failed to touch second as he advanced to third base. While advancing to third he collided with the shortstop. As the ball was fielded and thrown into third, the runner backtracked and went back into second base.

It might have been one of the craziest plays in the history of the game. Everybody was screaming and yelling and pointing fingers at each other. It was mass confusion and chaos. Possible interferences and obstructions, even possible ejections for the shoving match around second base.

I pointed and called the runner out about the same time the first-base umpire awarded the same runner third base. It was the worst nightmare an umpire could have. It was as if an explosion went off in both dugouts. The arguments from UVA were directed at me, while VCU decided to argue with the first-base umpire. This went on for a good amount of time.

As the arguments are going forward, I glance over my shoulder at Jim standing at third. He is standing on the outfield grass looking serenely around at the beautiful ballpark we were fortunate to work that day. Jim seemed unfazed by the screaming and finger-pointing that was going on. The first-base umpire told VCU one thing, and I told UVA another, causing both sides to go crazy. Glancing over at Jim again, I could notice the unexpected smile on his face as he stood out on the outfield grass. This argument might have gone on for at least ten minutes.

Finally we were able to get both teams back in their dugouts, barely avoiding a disaster. The first-base umpire and I get together in the middle of the infield to figure out what to do, after battling with both teams for what seemed like an hour. Jim strolls into the infield to meet with us and help figure out the mess we have created.

As only he could do, he smiled and deadpanned, "That looked like fun." He paused and looked at the scoreboard and said, "I think we are going to be fine. I just wanted to see how long that mess would go on. I think I can fix this pretty quick."

He looked at me and asked what the count was when the batter had swung and missed. Then he asked how many outs we had had before the pitch. The batter had two strikes already and there were two outs. Jim had immediately stepped in and solved the problem. The swing made it strike three and that made it the third out. All the other events and possible rulings never really happened since it was the third out.

We two young, up-and-coming umpires had worried about obstructions, interferences, rundowns, and ejections. Jim enjoyed watching us trying to make sense of it all and gave us a valuable lesson that I carried throughout my umpiring career. Keep it simple, use common sense, work the game, enjoy the game. He worked that way as an umpire and as our commissioner, but most importantly, he was the only person on the field who could count to three!

A LION HAT TRICK

William and Mary was moving into its new park, Plumeri Park, in the spring of 1999. It was supposed to open up on Saturday, but got rained out, so Rich Humphrey and I had the opening games on Sunday. Coach Farr had scheduled Penn State as the team against which they would open up. He picked Penn State as his opponent, since that is where he played his college baseball.

The wind was very gusty and swirling all day. We must have had seven or eight balls hit hard enough to leave the yard in right or right center, but none ever did. They ended up as the proverbial cans of corn. Every time I communicated with Rich that I was going out, the wind caught the ball and kept it in the park.

For those who do not know two-man mechanics, anytime the base guy goes out on fly balls, the plate umpire, with all the heavy plate gear on, must take the batter-runner into first, second, third, and home. On routine fly balls, which these ended up being, the base umpire should give ball responsibility to the plate umpire and take the runner into third.

Even though I wasn't doing it intentionally, it seemed like I was running my plate guy to death. I couldn't seem to read a routine fly ball all day long. Around the fourth inning, I tried to go in to apologize to him for running him to death and all my bad reads. However, when he saw me coming, he went to the third base foul line. I did this again in the fifth and sixth innings, and he did the same thing. This was all being done to mess with me.

So in the seventh inning, the new nine-man/ten-man offensive/defensive DH rule came into play. The coach came up to give Rich the changes, and he had no clue where to put the subs. He was signaling for me to come in and help him with the new rule, but I just kind of looked off in left field like I didn't see him. My time to get him back.

I finally went in and we both agreed, even though we had our cheat-sheet laminated cards with all the explanations on it, we had no clue.

Coach Farr, seeing we were struggling, came up laughing and said, "You are not sure who goes where, are you?"

Rich said, "Correct."

Joe, the Penn State Head Coach, was also lost, so we all got together. The next inning, the first base coach asked me how we kept track of the new changes, and I showed him our laminated cheat sheet. He asked how to get one, and we told him our association made them up for us. When the game was over, the head coach came over and thanked me for giving him one of the cards and asked if he could do anything for us. I told him my neighbor was a diehard Penn State alum, and I would love to get him an authentic Penn State baseball hat.

He said, "It will be in the mail to you tomorrow."

It was, along with one for me.

THE INFAMOUS AREA CALL

The following two stories were written by the late Bob Campbell, who was perhaps the most influential member who ever served with the Eastern Officials Association. Bob mentored hundreds of umpires in his fifty years in the game and experienced just about everything.

In May 1986, four officials (Bob Campbell, Bob Hood, Jim Smith, and Manny Upton) from EVOA went to Louisburg, NC to work the Regional JUCO Baseball Tournament. Each game was to be worked by three officials, and the final game worked with all four. Three of the officials had many years' experience, and the fourth member, Manny Upton, was fairly new to the college level.

The scheduled assignments for the entire tournament were preset. The new official was scheduled to work third base for the opening game. Prior to the start of the game he was told to try and not be nervous and that Coach Fraiser never came out to argue calls. In the second inning he had

a play at second base which was referred to as an "area call."
An "area call" is one where the fielder does not touch the base
and is normally seen during the front end of a double play.
It was quite obvious that the fielder did not touch the base
however the umpire called the runner out. He had no sooner
got it out of his mouth when Coach Fraiser came charging
out of the dugout and made a beeline toward him. After
several minutes of berating the umpire, Coach Fraiser turned
and headed toward his dugout with a smile on his face. The
umpire just stood there during the tirade with that "deer in
the headlights" look, staring at the other umpires, wondering
what went wrong. We all were laughing under our breath as
we never thought Coach Fraiser would come out. We busted
Manny's chops all night at dinner. Just for an FYI, Manny
is the father of BJ and Justin Upton, both with successful
careers in the big leagues, but not of Kate, or as we now know
her, Mrs. Justin Verlander.

THAT CALL REALLY SUCKED

Prior to the beginning of the same tournament, each
official was assigned to his game and the position he would
work. On the morning of the final day, we all went golfing. On
the seventh hole, one of the golfers hit his drive near the fence
on the left side of the fairway. As he approached his drive, he
started hollering at his partner to get him out of the area.
His face started to immediately swell up and his eyes started
to water. He indicated he was allergic to honeysuckle, which
was covering the out-of-bounds fence. We immediately got
him to a doctor who gave him medication to take care of the
problem. He was scheduled to work the plate that night but
could not do it, so we put him on third base, and talk about
missing a call down the third baseline. The ball was at least a
foot fair, and in the college tournament final he called it foul.
The coach came out to argue with the home-plate umpire,
who happened to be Jim Smith. Jim told the coach our third-
base umpire was struggling and sick as a dog. He said the
guy sucked too much honeysuckle and had an attack. It was

so funny that the coach just ended up leaving the call alone and went back to his dugout, leaving his team wondering why he was laughing so hard.

NEW SYSTEM USED FOR STRIKEOUTS AND RETIRING THE SIDE

Somewhere in the late '80s, I was working a college game at one of our local universities. It was a cold, rainy and just nasty day to umpire. The score was something like 16-0 in the third or fourth inning. We had two outs and an oh-one count on the batter for the team that was down. The next pitch, I called a strike. The count was now oh-two. However, the batter walked away, thinking it was strike three. I told him no, it was only strike two.

He continued walking to the dugout, and his own coach said, "Jim, I think you missed a pitch."

I said, "No that is only the second pitch." He asked me to check with my partner.

To appease him, I did, and he agreed with me.

But the coach still disagreed, so I let him have his way. Who am I to argue if he only wants to give his batters two strikes?

Fast forward to the eighth inning, and now the score is something like 25–0. We have one out, and the next batter for the team that is behind pops up for the second out. Everyone grabs their gloves and starts heading out to the field. Not only is the team who is ahead confused, so are we.

I walked over and said, "Coach, that is only two outs."

He wryly smiled at me and quietly said, "As bad as we are playing, we only deserve two, and please, let's get this game over."

BUT IT'S OUR ANNIVERSARY

I'd like to end this chapter with a loving wish and recognition of my wife, Lou. At the peak of my on-field career, and with baseball season in the month of April, it seemed like, even though I had April 11 blocked for my anniversary, I was always assigned a big college game on that day. Lou was always supportive and told me to go work the game, as we could go out for our anniversary dinner another night. It was I, not Lou, who would say, "But it's our anniversary." Many wives would get upset and say, "You owe me this night, not baseball," but not mine. Lou knew the college opportunities were special and would not come along that often or for too many seasons. She was always supportive, no matter the reason, but most of the time it was just for me. During these seasons I had not reached my silver or golden anniversary, but I had and have an umpire's bride far more precious than silver or gold could ever be.

CHAPTER 7

BASEBALL COMMISSIONER

Taking the job of assigning commissioner for a large association like EOA is like asking for a sentence of community service without committing any crime. The incumbent is sentenced to high-pressure, crisis situations. They need to exhibit world-class political skills, and even then, often can't please even some of the people some of the time. The following is an explanation of the events that led me to decide to become baseball commissioner. I leave it to you to decide whether I needed to have my head examined.

In April 2005, all the minor league umpires went out on strike. Three weeks prior to the start of the season, I received a call from a college assigner I knew, asking if I would be interested in assigning the minor league replacement umpires. I told him no, as I was retired. I further told him he needed to call our association's commissioner, who was then on vacation in Europe, and seek permission from him.

At 2:00 AM that morning, I received an overseas call from our commissioner asking me to assign the replacement umpires for the Norfolk Tides AAA minor league games. I let him know

I had just received another call asking me to do the same thing and wanted to make sure this was legitimate and supported by our association. He replied that it was.

I did not realize until about three weeks later that it was possible the umpires who really knew me would soon find out that I had no idea what was going on behind the scenes. However, they told me I needed to see it through until the strike was settled. My uneasiness grew when I made phone calls to our umpires, asking if they wanted to work the games; their response was no. When I asked why, they said that we had several of our former association umpires working single-A baseball, and they felt like this would be offensive to them. They also said they were under the impression the association had voted against us working the games. When I told them the commissioner said it had been cleared, eight umpires asked me to assign them to the games.

In July of 2005, when the strike ended, a number of veteran umpires in our association cornered me in one of the minor league ballparks and asked me if I would take over the association as they didn't think our present commissioner was going to stay on.

He decided not to, and so I had to make a call, to run or not to run. Well, I have been making calls all of my life, most of them even good calls. This one I was not so sure about, and I sure as heck wouldn't get the benefit of instant replay. I decided to run for baseball commissioner and was elected. It was upsetting to many that the previous commissioner chose to leave several boxes on my front porch, rang the doorbell, got in his car quickly, and left before I could get to the door. I tried calling and emailing him, but he would not answer. I had to start nearly from scratch in rebuilding the association.

As is evident, I did not take over in the best of conditions. No one really knew exactly why, but many of the schools and leagues that contract for our services had lost faith in our association and wanted to part ways. My jobs were now to rebuild that trust; keep our association financially sound; and oh yes, recruit, train, and assign highly qualified, professional umpires. With the help of many new and veteran umpires, in numerous face-to-face meetings with all of our customers, we asked them for a chance to show we could return to the days of old and meet their expectations.

I started by forming a very strong baseball committee, instruction team, and a mentorship team as well as opening communication lines to all. I also came up with a meeting schedule under which all umpires were required to attend. Meetings would not be optional as in the past. We also increased the amount of instructional time. These changes were difficult, but they projected a positive and professional demeanor for the association as well as our goals. We got everyone to buy into what we were doing, and progress became evident. We again began throwing a well-pitched game.

Now for a closer look at what transpired during those eight-and-a-half years and my job as the commissioner of baseball for the Eastern Officials Association. When I took over as commissioner in September of 2006 we had ninety umpires, worked roughly three thousand games a year, and put approximately $300,000 in the umpires' pockets. In my years, we built the association into 150 umpires at our highest point, worked seven thousand games a year and earned nearly $750,000 for umpires and the association. Trust me, when I first took over, success required that I sell as oceanfront property something in the middle of a swamp. I needed umpires, whether seasoned or just ones who were willing to support me and the association. Eight and a half years later I fully credit the umpires' support and dedication to the growth of the association. Maybe I did inherit some oceanfront property, and maybe I found some more. As of 2014, in baseball alone, over an eight-and-a-half-year period I assigned right at fifty-four thousand games and helped the umpires earn over $3,648,549. Wish more of that was mine.

I tried to step down from the commissioner's job in 2010, but the umpires talked me into staying on for two more years and then an additional two more years. I ended my service as the longest-tenured commissioner to date. It has always been very heartwarming to know how much the guys thought of my leadership. Even after my fourth term (think FDR), many tried to get me to stay on for at least a few more years, but at age 66, I had handled quite enough rainouts, mediated enough ejections, and corrected more than enough blown calls, and it was time to pass the phone and the keyboard.

The friendships I built with many of those with whom I came in contact will last a lifetime. We were both a team and a family from the first day I took over until the day I retired. I can honestly say I thoroughly enjoyed my tenure, except of course for the rainy days.

THE BATTING ORDER

For the history buffs who wonder about the longevity of a baseball commissioner, I offer the following. During my membership in EOA, Hollis Drake started off as our commissioner and served for six years, followed by Bullet Alexander for two years, followed by Pat Mileur for three years, followed by Billy King for two years, followed by Bob Campbell for two years, followed by Tim Francis for six years, followed by Bob Kyle for three years, followed by Tyree Brown and again Pat Mileur for two years, followed by Tyree Brown again for three and one-half years, ending up with me for a little over eight years. That's just about forty years' assignments.

HOT DOGS AND STEAKS

As commissioner I served on the Rules and Protest Committee for all the postseason regional playoff games that were held at Old Dominion University (2006 until 2013). During the four-day tournament, my day would begin at 8:00 in the morning and often end around midnight. I got tired of eating hot dogs all the time! I guess you say with that schedule and limited meal choices that I was dog-tired.

A fellow umpire, Chris Burton, and I decided one year to cook steaks on the grill outside the concession stand. All I had to do was bring the steak. Each morning I would get there with a cooler in one hand and my scheduling book and lawn chair in the other hand. In the cooler were five one-pound ribeye steaks, a couple of salads, some fruit, and a lap tray—enough to carry me through the day, and it sure beat those hot dogs. Talk about having some fun: all the scouts and fans sitting around me wanted to know where they could buy the steaks. I told them down the street and to the left, there was a Food Lion. The steak tradition lasted for five years, until they changed the tournament format, realigning the entire state. That took the steaks and tournament away from ODU.

WHEN BEING CALLED OUT IS GOOD

One playoff game that will always stand out in my mind as baseball commissioner is a game that occurred during the regional high school playoffs at Old Dominion University (2009 finals). It was very evident that our hard work in teaching rules and mechanics had paid off, especially with the guys working the playoffs.

Robert Turner was working the plate. We had a runner who happened to be the potential winning run on third base. The batter hit a slow ground ball to the second baseman who threw to first for the out. However, we had catcher's interference. Robert, called time and sent the batter-runner to first base and the runner who scored back to third.

Coach Roland Wright of Western Branch came out of the dugout slowly scratching his head. He asked Robert about the play. "Can I take the out at first and have the run score?"

Robert said yes. He then called the runner out at first, scored the run and the game was over. The visiting coach, from out of town, knew the rule and knew that it had been applied correctly. No argument from him.

SUMMER AND FALL LEAGUE

One accomplishment of which I am most proud is working on something new with the same Coach Wright of Western Branch High School. We developed a summer and fall league where the JV and varsity players could play ball without having to spend a fortune to play on all the travel teams. The parents also loved it, as it reduced travel, kept them home for chores and saved them hotel money.

The scholastic coaches in our state were allowed to coach in the offseason, but they could not schedule their own games. To get around this, we named the league the Eastern Virginia Officials Association Summer/Fall League, after our association. This made it one hundred percent legal. All we had to do was make sure we were not playing games during the mandatory dead parts of the season.

We started in the summer or 2011 with four JV teams and an invoice of approximately $3,000. Four years later, we were up to forty-eight teams (JV and varsity combined) with an invoice in the neighborhood of $60,000. Because of my contacts, our great rapport with all the local coaches, and Coach Wright's willingness to do the scheduling, all the upper-age players now had a place to play at a reduced cost.

WORKING WITH MANY DIFFERENT PERSONALITIES

As you can imagine, 150 umpires and 200 non-umpire contacts meant there were many different personalities. I often felt that was one of the hardest parts of the job. Maybe a degree in psychology would have been of great assistance. The most common questions umpires ask each other are "How many games did you get?" or "Where are your games?"

They may also wonder whether someone has a better schedule or game than they do. Many think they should always be in the top game, every day. I was a firm believer in making sure the big games were spread around evenly. When it came to scholastic games, I took a spreadsheet at the beginning of the year and made sure all the top umpires got the same number of top games.

Some umpires came up with a variety of different excuses if they got a game at a site to which they would rather not go. You can't imagine how many, but here are some of the most popular.

1. "I have to work late and I forgot."
2. "My wife made plans without telling me."
3. "I just lost one of my close relatives." No disrespect meant, but this was sometimes the same person they

lost two or three years prior to that. (I thought only cats had nine lives.)

4. "Do you have anything closer; that is a long ways to drive." If this happened I always gave them a great closer game after they accepted. In most cases, I usually took the game back and then sent them right back to the same site on their next schedule. They soon got the message.

PROMOTIONS AND RANKINGS

As much as I loved and depended on them, umpires are rarely pleased with their schedule and their ranking in our association. Ranking determines the quality of games assigned, which in turn determines game fees. When it comes to all-important promotions and rankings, many umpires speak out of both sides of their mouths. They will tell a fellow umpire they can't understand why that

ONE CRITERIA FOR ADVANCEMENT IN THE ASSOCIATION IN PROFESSIONALISM. (L-R:) STEVE KANTER #8, BOB BARRY #9, AND BRET STEWART #10

partner didn't get promoted, but the next day they will call me or an evaluator and tell us that their partner that day was horrible, and they can't believe they were in that game. Keeping my thoughts to myself, I understood that there is competition among our umpires for promotions.

Every year, each umpire gets at least four evaluation assignments. After the game both the umpire and the evaluator go over what they observed that day. The evaluator writes up the report and sends it to the evaluation chair. It is reviewed for accuracy and then posted on our website so the umpire can correct his mistakes. We found this system to be very beneficial. Many veteran umpires coming in from other associations said they wished their former association had a similar system. We appreciated their compliments.

We have a system in place, in which if an umpire did not get promoted, he could come before the Baseball Committee to see what he needed to improve to get promoted next year. Achieving level three was a watershed moment for many of our umpires. At level three an umpire would be assigned high school varsity contests, the backbone of our spring schedule. We also awarded a uniform number to those attaining this level. Above level three, promotion became very difficult, with the possibility of college assignments as a reward.

PITCHING OUR WEBSITE

In April 2013, Great Bridge High School had one of the best pitchers, Connor Jones, to come out of the area in a long time. He was going to be a very high draft pick but ended up not signing a pro contract, instead going to the University of Virginia. This year and month, in particular, also happened to be one of our rainiest seasons ever. After a solid week of rain, we finally got some sun, so I decided to go to Great Bridge and watch the game.

In May, Connor pitched and won the AAA state semifinal. Had he been eligible for the finals, he would have probably brought home the state championship, but the Great Bridge coach did what most good coaches would do, which is decide, *Why save him for the finals if you lose in the semis?*

While at the game, I saw a good friend of mine, Billy Best, a scout for the Atlanta Braves. He was telling me this was the third day in a row he had driven from Raleigh to Chesapeake to see this pitcher. I told him he should have called me or used our website. As games get rained out, I posted them on the web. Billy told me he had lost my business card. I pulled out another one and gave it to him.

All of a sudden, I bet you twelve heads, all scouts, turned around and started looking at Billy and me. To make a long story short, I gave all of them business cards and told them to call me any time they were coming to see a player, especially if there was a threat of rain at any site. I also gave them our web address and again explained that as soon as a game cancellation was called in, I posted it on our website.

Our website was designed by Robert Turner, the treasurer of our association and one of our very best umpires. On a rainy day, umpires go to the website to check the status of games. This greatly reduced the number of phone calls I had to make or receive. It was also a very valuable resource or recruiting tool for umpires moving into our area. During my tenure, I had two umpires join our association, one each from Australia and Japan. They used our website to find out about us.

NO PRICE TAG

One of the greatest rewards of this job was meeting and building relationships with so many professional players, scouts, athletic directors, high school and college coaches, league directors, and general managers. It is my hope that our organization plays a small part in teaching positive life lessons to the youths playing baseball. I still keep in touch with many of them. Although our profession offers modest financial compensation to umpires, there can be no price tag on the relationships we create and the professionalism we model. Those who do not meet those expectations do not stay long in our association.

MY REWARD TIME

When it came time for postseason assignments, I made sure I traveled with as many of our crews as I could. Not only does it show the crew that you care about them, but it also shows the state office a special interest in the umpires you sent to represent your association. It also gives you a chance to see some great baseball.

The hardest part about leaving town to go with your crews is knowing that you still have games going on back home for which you are always on call. For those days, you pray there is no rain in the forecast and no umpires have to cancel. If you do get rain or emergencies back home, you are locked to the phone and not able to enjoy the game.

CHARITIES

A very rewarding part of the job that I began in 2006 was giving to many local charities. Some, but not all, were the Wounded Warriors, the American Cancer Society, the American Heart Association, the MS and MD Societies, Breast Cancer Awareness, Volunteer Rescue Squads, missionary work, scholarship donations to one of our local high schools and many others.

We also held a raffle at each of our general meetings. We had guys brings in gifts like gift certificates to local restaurants, power tools, golf balls and free rounds of golf, movie tickets, golf shirts, and so on. Participating members would buy raffle tickets and then, at the beginning and end of each meeting, we would draw tickets for the prizes. The proceeds would go to local charities. Of course, we would also work a game without a fee for a good cause.

SKY BOX RECOGNITION

Bill Holloran, among many others, was a great supporter to me and for the association. Bill's company leases a Sky Box at our local AAA ballpark. Bill graciously offered it to me for four nights during the summer. I invited evaluators and committee members to the Sky Box to watch the games. They were the ones who did so much volunteer work for the association. We would all enjoy a night out at the ballpark. The ladies seemed to really enjoy the night, as it was a way for them to have a night out with their significant other, yet not talk baseball all night. What made this so special is these umpires didn't receive any extra benefits, and I didn't give them extra or better games for their contribution. Their schedules were no different than any of the other umpires. My only unfulfilled wish is that I could have invited all the umpires out for a night at the park.

OFFICIATING AND OPPORTUNITIES

When you put in almost forty years on the baseball fields and basketball courts of Hampton Roads, you get to meet a lot of people. More times than not, you run into them in the least likely spots. This happened quite often when our family went on a vacation. My children, as they were growing up, always laughed and joked with me about seeing someone I knew every time we went on a vacation. It never failed. To this day they continue to say, "Dad, no matter where we go, you always run into someone you know."

Some of the places I thought we would never run into anyone were the Dallas-Fort Worth Airport, Disney World, Sesame Place, and Hawaii. Sure enough, whether it was McDonald's on the way to Sesame Place or seeing one of my NBA friends at DFW or Chicago's O'Hare airport on the way to Hawaii, it happened. I would just tell them I was fortunate enough, despite my only average officiating skills, to have been in the right place at the right time and trained by and working with some of the best umpires or referees in the country. Getting out in public and meeting people was something I loved to do.

As commissioner, I have had the privilege to help mentor more than four hundred umpires. I have also had the honor to umpire, meet, and get to know many of the present big-league players like BJ and Justin Upton, David Wright, Ryan Zimmerman, Michael Cuddyer, and Mark Reynolds. I also met and was able to spend time with many MLB scouts. As mentioned earlier, getting to meet John Smoltz, Joe Morgan, and Ozzie Smith was a thrill of a lifetime. In addition to the abovementioned relationships, I also developed great working relationships with our present 110 athletic directors and numerous recreation league liaisons. I feel extraordinarily lucky to have met so many wonderful people. I will always cherish those memories.

EJECTIONS ARE NO FUN

Earlier I covered the three college ejections I had as an umpire. Those were much simpler than it is now, as after the ejection or game, the umpire would write up the report and it was finished. When you are commissioner, ejections can be straightforward and quick, but others can take days to be completed. The ejection for Bethel HS, which I will cover, took two and a half days with continual phone calls from the principal and athletic director. The following four ejections are most memorable to me.

The first was in April 2006. The game was Kempsville versus Cox, and I was in attendance for it. The VHSL and National Federation had just put in a new rule pertaining to malicious contact. The way the rule was written was very confusing. It was meant as a safety rule and mainly applied to protecting the defensive player fielding a ball or throw. On this play, we had a single to right field and the right fielder came up throwing to home. As the runner rounded third and started home, the throw veered off, ending up fifteen feet up the line toward third base and head-high. The runner put his hands up in a defensive manner as he saw the catcher's glove coming toward his face. The runner slightly extended his hands, which to me was a normal reaction; however, a collision occurred. By rule, he should have been ejected from the game, because he did not try to avoid the catcher. Even though the player was ejected, common sense and baseball knowledge were applied, and it was later reversed by both schools, the VHSL, and our association.

The next ejection occurred at Old Dominion University during the high school regional playoffs. Bethel High School (from the Peninsula) was playing Western Branch from Chesapeake. In the fourth inning of the ballgame, a player from Bethel hit a ball down the left-field line that seemed to leave the ballpark. The third-base umpire signaled a home run. The left fielder then went and pulled out the ball, which had wedged behind the 325-foot sign. The Western Branch coach came out to discuss the call. It was reversed and called a double, as it should have been.

Now Brett Wheeler, the coach from Bethel, came out to argue with the third-base umpire, as it was his call. What started off in a normal tone soon escalated, and he started getting very upset. When he couldn't get anywhere with the third-base umpire, he came to the home-plate umpire, Randy Jones. Randy tried to calm him down, but Brett was incensed with Randy, as well. After several warnings and attempts to calm him down, Randy had to throw him out of the game. One of the ironies of the situation was that Randy and many of us had umpired Brett's games when he played college ball. We all had a great umpire-to-player relationship. Since this was a one-run game and two of the top teams in the area playing, I am sure emotions took over.

As soon as play was resumed, there was a pickoff attempt at second base. The runner thought the second baseman applied a hard tag and intentionally put his knee in his back. He immediately jumped up and got in the second baseman's face, ready to fight. Pete Michaud, the radio voice of the local AAA baseball and hockey teams, was the umpire whom I had assigned to work second base in that game. He got in between them real quick, and all seemed fine.

Suddenly, the entire Bethel bench starts charging the field, with the exception of number 13. They all seemed to want to join in. The home-plate umpire immediately went to the mound and let the entire Bethel team know that anyone who passed him would be thrown out of the game. He repeated this loud enough to be heard a hundred feet away, where I was sitting.

Both the pitcher and catcher for Bethel continued charging toward second base and ended up getting thrown out. I spent the next two days on the phone with both the principal and athletic director for Bethel, who requested that both ejected players be allowed to play in the next game. They both argued that the players never threw a punch. I told them that we would not rescind the ejection, and the only way that they would be allowed to play is if the VHSL office put them back in the game. The ejections were upheld, and neither of the players nor the coach was allowed to be involved in the next game. The rule was very simple to apply, as it clearly states that any player leaving the bench to join in or participate in a fight is ejected.

The third ejection occurred in April 2012. We were working a three-man crew at Grassfield High School. It was a real big game, so the school requested three umpires, versus the normal two-man crew. There was a short flyball to center field that neither of our base umpires went out on. Both are really good umpires, but what got them in trouble was the lack of communication as to who was taking flyball responsibility, and neither went out. No one knew whether it was trapped or caught. Not only was there confusion on our side, but there was also confusion among the base runners. The problem was the delay in making a catch or no catch call. We ended up with an inning-ending double play that should not have happened. The coach from Grassfield High School was very upset and came out to argue the call. He ended up getting ejected. The coach, umpires, and I all had and still have a great working relationship, and to my knowledge, this was his first and only scholastic ejection.

In the "old days," umpires would both hear and use language that was not appropriate but was still deemed part of the profession and was overlooked. These statements would be a normal part of an argument with no ejection. Those days have changed in the scholastic game. We didn't do a great job on this play, and during the argument/discussion with the coach, one of our umpires, very softly, made a comment that we may have _____ up the call (using an inappropriate word). This was when the coach's voice escalated, and he ended up getting tossed.

That night, around eleven o'clock, my phone started ringing. The athletic director and I talked for over an hour. The next morning, we used a three-way conference call between me, the athletic director, and the principal. They had no problem with the ejection of their coach. However, they didn't think it was right that the umpire would not be reprimanded for using profanity toward the coach.

I talked to both of the administrators, the athletic directors and the umpires the next morning. I felt that since both sides could have handled the situation differently, the ejection could be rescinded. I felt I had done the right thing. An hour later I got a call from the VHSL office, chewing me out for not following the correct protocol. The correct protocol is for both schools to appeal and send it to the VHSL office. If the officials' association wants to agree with the appeal, they can. The position held by the VHSL was that I did not have the right as the commissioner to make that ruling on my own. I must say I disagreed, but I was told in no uncertain terms that I had not followed the correct protocol.

The fourth ejection was a collegiate ejection in the spring of 2012. The game was Rappahannock Community College, coached by Coach Jack Morris, versus the Apprentice School, coached by Bryan Cave. There was a runner on first and a fair ball hit to right field. The wind was blowing rather briskly and carried the ball into the tarp along the right-field foul line. The player threw his hands up, signaling the ball was out of play. The base umpire also threw his hands up, killing the ball, instead of just going out to check on it. Suddenly, the right fielder picked the ball up from behind the tarp and threw it home. Things became chaotic as we had killed the play, which meant putting runners back at second and third. The only problem was the offensive coach wanted the runner who was on first, who scored on the play, to count.

The defensive coach (Cave) argued, "No, you killed the ball."

The umpires got together. They determined that since the ball was killed, the runners had to be placed back at second and third. The offensive coach (Morris) ran back out and basically delayed putting his runner who scored back on third. Coach Morris was ejected because he continued to tell the umpires in a sarcastic tone how great they had been all day and didn't put the runners back until he got ejected. The hardest part of this ejection was the coach who got tossed was right in saying we should not have killed the ball and just gone out and looked at it. Both umpires involved are great, and a great lesson was learned that day.

Both the coach and athletic director called me the next day and apologized. Coach Morris and I still talk and laugh about this play every time we see each other. He always says, "I am just too old-school and sometimes don't know when to stop."

That night I immediately put out an email to all umpires reminding them not to kill the ball on that type of play. Umpires are always taught that we can always move runners back, not forward, so the coaches know to keep them running and let us move them back. Wouldn't you know it, the very next day we do the same thing in a high school game. We kicked the very same mechanic. Throw goes to third and gets by the third baseman ending up in/behind/under the tarp. Our plate umpire kills the ball. The left fielder then picks up the ball and throws home. After that day, I just wanted to quit.

There were several other collegiate ejections, but they all dealt with Division 3 northern teams coming down to at the beginning of the season. Most of their ejections, I felt, were due to the frustration of being cooped up in the snow and just getting outside for the first time. All were for arguing safes and outs. Enough about that, let's move on to "rain days."

RAIN DAYS

I would say that the hardest thing for a baseball commissioner is rain days. We cover close to a seventy-five-mile radius, therefore it may be raining at my house and sunny and dry two miles away. Bryan Cave, the coach at the Apprentice School, covers that very nicely in his reflection he sent me. He said, "I keep radar minimized at the bottom of my screen, but that only helps if a big storm is coming that is going to cover our entire assigning area."

We used a great scheduling program called Arbiter to assign and cancel games. As mentioned earlier, in addition to Arbiter, we also had our association website. It let the umpires know as soon as the game is canceled. Once I put the cancellation on one of those two sites, it sent a message out to the umpire. That saved any umpire who has internet access from having to call me.

Those who were not near a computer to see cancellations, they called me and all I wanted them

RAIN DAYS AS COMMISSIONER
COURTESY OF *THE VIRGINIAN PILOT*–
RAIN WILL ALWAYS GET YOU ON TV/NEWSPAPER

to say is, "Jim (name on the school like Kempsville, Maury, Cape Henry, Western Branch, etc.) on or off." If they said something like it is raining in Norfolk and their game is in Chesapeake or Virginia Beach, I just hung up the phone. It did not take long for them to learn my system.

The college coaches, athletic directors, student activities coordinators, league, and travel teams were great to work with. We had a great system for cancellation calls. A typical goes like this. "Jim, Mark Harrison Salem, we are canceling our game for today, would like to make it up tomorrow, will follow up with an email, have a great day."

Coach Harrison was always the first person to call me, usually around 7 AM. He intentionally did this because he knew I did not get up until around 8 AM. He would end his call by singing me a lullaby. What a great way to start what would be a very tiring and busy day.

After the 150 rain emails and seventy-five-plus rain phone calls, I went into our scheduling program, entered the new games replacing the rained-out games, assigned the umpires, notified them, and then responded to the email request, saying "You are good to go for tomorrow." This had to be done before I went to bed.

WORLD SERIES TRIPS WITH OUR UMPIRING CREW

In 2011, we were asked if we wanted to go to Chesterfield, Virginia to do the U11 Bronco World Series. I said yes and put Arron Ashford in charge of getting all the resumes. We put a four-man crew together. All games were worked with four umpires, except the finals, which used six umpires.

To make sure we were on top of our game and prepared to the best of our ability, everyone going worked at least six four-man games to make sure they were prepared. We pooled the money from those games, so we could have a steak dinner one night and enough money for laundry. The first two years, we worked one field and a crew from North Carolina worked the other field. After our second year, the North Carolina crew did not return, and we were not given a reason why.

The first year, many of the tournament officials did not associate with me. My feeling was they thought I was just a friend of the Virginia crew and along for the ride. Toward the end of the tournament, two of our local PONY directors shared with the gentleman running the tournament that I used to be a pretty good umpire but was now out on disability. They also let him know I ran the Officials Association down in the Tidewater area and knew a little about umpiring. For whatever reason and to my astonishment, the tournament director asked me to select the crew for the semis and finals. I took that as an honor. I am pleased to say we have developed a very close relationship since then.

The director was curious and one day asked me what I was doing with all the note-taking and switching of fields. I told him I was doing recon. He asked me to clarify. I told him I wanted to see who had the best team and was looking for their strengths and weaknesses. I told him I was also doing the same thing with the other umpiring crew, since we would be combined for the finals. He asked me who I thought had the best team in year one, and I told him I thought it was Miami. Miami ended up winning the championship.

He then asked me to rank our umpires and also the crew from NC. I told him I preferred not to do that but would give him my top three from the NC crew. We both agreed. He asked if I would, off the record, allow him to sit down with me and see what I saw with all eight umpires. I said yes, but it had to stay confidential.

For the NC crew, I told him to watch the plate umpire. Two of them used the scissors and set up too far back, so they would never be able to see a hard slider on the outside corner.

Then I pointed out one of the other umpires. I said, "Look at his back pockets." He had two empty water bottles in his pockets. I told him for a World Series or any other game, it looked unprofessional.

As for the fourth member of their crew, I told him to watch his hands. "He is showing up his crew by trying to get them in the right position. This is not the place to learn four-man umpiring mechanics."

I explained to him how we prepared. I guess we were doing a pretty good job as they continued to invite us back (2012, 2013, 2014,

2014 BRONCO 11U WORLD SERIES AT CHESTERFIELD

2015, and 2016). We were also assured that we would be invited back as long as the tournament was hosted at its present site. The President of PONY Baseball also asked us if we would be interested in doing the Pony and Colt World Series. We would love to do all three, but we would have to pay for our travel, lodging, and food. Right now, all we get is a minimal game fee, and many of our guys just can't afford to take off for three to four weeks. Pony Baseball knew that I was retiring, but they asked if I would continue to come and give them my input. I told them I appreciated the offer and would be honored if circumstances would allow it.

SUNDAY SELECT GROUPS

One of the enjoyable parts of the job was working with the Sunday Select teams. In the old days, these teams played under the AAU umbrella. Over my eight-and-a-half-year term, I had the pleasure to build our Sunday Select customer list to 110 customers. By contract, they were supposed to get their schedules to me at least two weeks in advance. They seldom did. Scheduling then became a nightmare. However, I always was able to find umpires for their games. We just did not believe in hosting travel tournaments and not having enough umpires for our everyday scholastic and recreation customers.

Here is where the problem came from. Another umpire group only assigned umpires for travel ball tournaments on the weekends. Quite often they didn't have enough teams to sign up, so they ended up canceling the tournament at the last minute. That is when my phone would ring, late on Friday or Saturday night, asking for umpires for Sunday just so the available kids could play. Back in the late '50s and early '60s, our association started off with the recreation games only. We didn't start branching out into the high school and college arena until the late '60s. To this day, we have always taken care of our recreation and scholastic customers first. To do so would be a disservice to them and, in our opinion, be very damaging to the game to baseball. Not every player is a superstar, but they all need umpires.

One of our Sunday Select customers, Jason McEwen, had this to say about me and the association, "It was certainly a pleasure to work with you for so many seasons. You assisted coaches to orchestrate game times and were always a liaison to the game. You were someone with whom we could discuss game situations/calls/rules made on the field. A lot of people forget umpires are human, and I know this comes as a surprise, but they are not perfect. We all know that a lot of times an umpire may not admit he got the call wrong, but your guys would. You would allow us to talk about controversial plays. As a coach, you helped teach us the rules of the game, so we could pass that on to the players. It was always a great feeling every time your guys stepped out on field. There is nothing worse than being in the heat of a battle and suffering questionable calls made due to lack of knowledge and experience. Most of the players in Hampton Roads have no idea or knowledge of who you are, but I can assure you, you have had a great impact on them and the game at all levels. Jim, with you stepping away from the game, I would just like to say I have the greatest respect for you and consider you to be a great friend. The Tidewater area is a better place to play baseball, and one of the main reasons is because of you."

Another of our Sunday Select customers, Channing Williams, has this to say about our association.

"I first met Jim Smith back in 2005, when I was coaching for the first time over at Green Run Little League. Jim had come over to observe some of the umpires that day, and everybody seemed to know who he was. He struck me as a friendly guy who enjoyed what he was doing, but I really didn't understand what he or EOA was all about, and so the awe I saw in others' eyes was lost on me. That changed, however, over the next several years as I got to work more and more with Jim and got to know him not just as an umpire but as a friend.

"During the last decade, the landscape of youth baseball has changed dramatically. What was once a sport dominated by 'rec leagues' with just a few travel teams has morphed into an explosion of travel teams offering kids more and more opportunities to play baseball year-round. Somehow, Jim seemed to see this change coming, and when I made the decision to start a travel team of my own, Jim was one of the first people I called.

"'Sure, I can help you,' he said, 'just tell me what you need.'

"What I've come to learn over time is that's just how Jim is. Certainly, he takes personal pride in running a first-class organization of officials, but that's only part of the story. What I've come to learn is the bigger reason was simply that Jim believed the kids deserved the best he had to offer. He knew the kids were looking forward to playing baseball, and he didn't want to see them disappointed.

"When I look back over the time I've known Jim, it's astounding the lengths he would go to in order to make sure the kids got to play ball that day. I can't count the number of times I've called Jim late on a Saturday to see if he could squeeze me in for Sunday. The answer, always, was 'I'll figure it out.' Rainouts are always problematic in baseball, especially in Hampton Roads where the weather can change in five minutes, and I can't imagine what it took for Jim to somehow juggle dozens of games and hundreds of umpires in numerous locations when there was a storm. If you needed to delay the start, start early, or change venues, the answer was still the same, 'I'll figure it out.' And if you're field's too wet to play? 'Let me make a phone call for you . . . I might be able to find you one.' I've seen him empty trash, rake the fields, work the scoreboard, whatever it took. All because the kids were looking forward to playing ball that day, and Jim didn't want to let them down."

SOME COACHES REALLY DO UNDERSTAND

Clay Dills, a Sunday Select coach, relates a story about how coaches may really understand and work with a commissioner, at least once in a while.

> About a year into our friendship, one day behind the backstop, Jim Smith is hugging my wife. Holding her off the ground. She's giggling while her feet are dangling. Jim from the top down: ball cap, sunglasses, Bluetooth in ear, mustache, baseball polo shirt, schedule in hand and French fries. I'm not sure what Jim actually looks like except for this description. He just loves being around baseball folks.
>
> There's a game going on that I'm coaching. The umpire

behind the plate (in my opinion) could do a better job if he was just guessing balls and strikes. Between innings, I go say hi to Jim which ends up taking the whole next inning, no surprise there. This means the kids are running the game. I'm a little frustrated and ask Jim about the umpire. Jim then tells me he's new, learning the craft, but is a recent retiree from the police department. He then tells me how many kids he has, where his kids played, what lunch he likes, where he grew up, and how much he cares about the sport and about all the boys playing.

After giving up five runs while the kids are coaching each other and I am talking with Jim, the calls behind the plate seem better. Better because the guy behind the plate was learning the same way the players were learning, Jim knew this. It changed the way I related to Jim, and how I worked with every umpire he sent. There were some more experienced than others, but all came with the same reason for being there—they care about the sport.

We would always have to reschedule games and umpires. I would send a schedule to Jim, a perfect season in a spreadsheet. Then the masterpiece fell apart about one week into the season. Rainy weather comes, and we cancel, we reschedule, we cancel again, repeat. We would repeat this sixty times a year, just for our league alone. Each time I say "I'm sorry to do this . . . " and each time he repeats, "It's okay, we're all doing this for the kids."

An eleven-year-old kid trying to learn how to be a catcher is painful for an umpire. The kid is small, can't block a ball, and is somewhat tentative in general. This means the umpire behind him takes a few direct hits each game. Jim knows this better than anyone, since he was a catcher and an umpire. There's a whole generation of young, would-be catchers from our league who have had a talk from Jim or one of his umpires, including my own son.

After the game, everyone's hanging around and wants to talk to Jim. Quite often it is the catchers and coaches who have questions or concerns about the game. Jim tells them things that will help them understand what goes into umpiring and helps to make sure everyone is on the same page. They soon learn he has a great understanding of the catching position and umpiring and has much to offer to anyone who wants to improve themselves. My son tells me it's about being tough, protecting YOUR umpire, and making him YOUR umpire in every game.

One day, my son asks me, "Who's that guy who just gave me a clinic on catching?"

I tell him, "He's the head umpire for all of our area . . . but really he's was a catcher and an umpire prior to being the guy who is in charge of the umpires. He's one of the cornerstones of baseball in this area."

Enough said.

RECREATION LIAISONS

As I said earlier, the association's foundation was built on our recreation leagues. Since this part of the book deals with my time as commissioner, I would like to share with you a kind comment sent to me from the liaison of our longest standing customer Kempsville Pony Baseball as told by the longest-tenured liaison, Bernie Kozuch.

Jim Smith has been a valued and respected member of the Kempsville Pony Baseball family for over twenty years. First as a father watching his son play baseball, then as an umpire doing games on our old ball fields, and finally as the baseball commissioner of Eastern Officials Association (EOA). In each of these roles, Jim has always understood that it is the young boys and girls entrusted to us who must come first, and Jim could always be counted on to do the things necessary to allow them the fun and positive baseball experience that they deserve.

On a personal note, I am proud to call Jim Smith a true professional colleague and, more importantly, a friend. As most people familiar with the sport of baseball can attest, the viewpoints of coaches, fans, and umpires can sometimes differ. As EOA baseball commissioner, Jim shared the goal of Kempsville Pony Baseball: that umpires, managers, coaches, players, parents, and fans be held to the highest standards of conduct. The ability to communicate freely and openly with Jim was instrumental in pursuing that goal.

Finally, every recreation league, middle school, high school, and college baseball player in Tidewater owes Jim Smith a debt of gratitude for the quality of baseball played in our area. Kempsville Pony Baseball wishes Jim all the best and looks forward to seeing him as a fan at our games.

WHAT I WILL NOT MISS

One of the things I will not miss is the 150-plus emails I seemed to get each day—plus all the phone calls and schedule changes. However, they are all parts of the job, and I knew this when I accepted the position. Ignoring any of them meant losing business. Another thing I can live without is trouble with a league. I have two stories to share on that subject. One deals with kids and a darker one with adults.

Kids first. One of the toughest decisions I ever had to make as commissioner was taking a recreation league to court. The thing that made it tough was that you never want to hurt the kids because of the actions of adults. During the spring of 2010, I received numerous phone calls from this league that the schedule was on the way. After four weeks of promises and no schedule, I started to worry. Two weeks later I found out that even though they were under contract with us, they had decided to go with another umpire association and had already started their season two weeks earlier.

I called the president of the league to discuss the situation, and he failed to respond to any of my phone calls or emails. After three more weeks, our executive board decided to file court papers to help recoup the lost damages. As you can imagine, as soon as the league president got the court papers, he called me saying he never received my phone calls or emails and was not going to pay anything. He said he would be in touch with his board of directors and Little League Baseball. As you might imagine, both his board and Little League Baseball told him that since he made the change unilaterally when he knew he was under contract with us, they would not help with legal counsel or monetary damages.

To keep from going to court, we offered him a $1,000 buyout clause, and he refused it. When we got to court, he came there without legal counsel, hoping to get off. Our lawyer, Bob Barry, who also happens to be a life member umpire in our association, knew just what to do. We put on our case, and the judge ruled in our favor. The judge hit the league with a $5,500 judgment. As we left the courtroom our lawyer asked the league president if he would like to go in a room and have a private talk. Having just experienced the equivalent of a taking a high hard one just under the chin, the guy had little choice.

Knowing the court's decision would probably shut down their league, we made an offer the president couldn't refuse. Instead of the $5,500 judgment we had just gotten, we offered him the $1,000 amount one more time. He said he was strapped for money but asked if we would settle for $250 every two weeks. We agreed because although we went to court as a matter of principle, first and last, Little League is for the kids. Even though he had breached our contract and was behind on his payments, we found a way to make our point and keep the bats swinging and the balls flying. The debt was settled promptly after court.

As mentioned, the good thing that came out of this was the league played their regular season games and the kids did not lose their season. The bad thing was the president was replaced. Maybe, on second thought, that was not such a bad thing after all.

I'll turn now to an adult baseball story in more ways than one. During my eight-and-a-half years as commissioner, I can honestly say that for the most part every league president, liaison, coach, or athletic director was great to work with and always professional on the phone. There was one exception, and I share this story because sometimes one sees a side of a person that you didn't know existed.

It was a beautiful summer night in 2013. I received a call from one of our collegiate summer league liaisons. Thank goodness my cell phone was on silent, and I did not hear the call. When out observing umpires, I always had my cell phone with me and checked it every ten to fifteen minutes for possible missed calls. I listened to this guy's message later.

This profanity-laced call lasted for about two minutes, and the F-bomb and BS words were used at least ten or eleven times. This liaison served in dual roles, both as a scheduler and an assistant coach. What shocked me was that we had known each other for over twenty-five years, and he was someone I considered to be a friend.

On this night, when a crucial call went against him, he had been told by the other coach (a great friend of his), "Do not call Jim." However, his temper got the best of him, and he called anyway. He was yelling at the top of his lungs.

One of the things that made him look so bad in this situation, other than his profanity, was that he knows all our umpires assigned to his games by name and face, and that they are top-level college umpires. When he was describing the play, he had the names backward, and he accused the wrong person of making the call he thought we missed. He also started quoting an umpire's mechanic on which he was one hundred percent wrong. For those who umpire, in two-man mechanics with a runner on third and a fly ball to left field going toward the line, the plate umpire has both the catch and tag up at third. He swore one umpire had the catch and the other umpire had the tag at third.

I waited until the next day to call him, and I told him that he had better never ever use that language with me again, or I would pull his umpires. I also told him he had the names backward and the mistake he had made on umpiring mechanics about.

He started explaining with I thought this and I thought that.

I told him to stop right there so he didn't make himself look any worse. Nothing would explain or excuse the previous night's phone message. To defuse the situation and for a little humor I sent him a picture of both umpires. It's amazing what a little time to cool down will do. He laughed and said, "I know, I just had them mixed up!"

I drove ninety miles later in the week to see him in person. He apologized for his behavior and said his wife had taken him away from the field right after he made the phone call. I had saved the call, so I asked him if he wanted me to play it for her. He said, "Please don't."

I thought to myself, *Wow, have I ever got this guy over a barrel.*

That was not the case, however, as she was standing right there, and said she had already heard it!

NO MORE EXTRA INNINGS

I'll share some of my thoughts after serving so many terms in the association's toughest job. I feel it is most important to use a personal touch if you want to run a successful business, and I hope I was able to give that to all of my customers. Yes, umpiring is a business, and those who use our services are our customers. It was my policy to make sure all emails were answered and all requested schedule changes were made before I went to bed, even if that meant staying up until the early hours of the morning.

Everyone who knows me knows I can talk forever about baseball. It is a big joke among all the umpires, customers, and most of my friends that they have to come up with an excuse to get me off the phone. However as several of my closest friends have said, that passion is also one of my strengths. When you are dealing with bringing in new business or umpires into the association, you need to be a good PR guy and make sure your customers or new umpires get as much information as they can before committing to you.

When I first took over in 2005, the sport of baseball in our area used to be a four-month-a-year job at around $30,000 a year. In 2018, it has grown into a seven-days-a-week, ten-months-a-year and $60,000-a-year job. Yes, the salary was a good one and helped to put our three children through college. For me, though, it was never about the money, or I would have stopped one or two years earlier. This job was always about the game of baseball, helping umpires develop their talents, and giving them a place to work.

The first two years were the toughest part of my tenure. During the offseason, which is only about two months, I spent most of my time trying to collect unpaid invoices and getting things ready for the start of the next year. Those long hours will not be missed for the most part. It was difficult not having vacations, juggling appointments, and canceling previous commitments. That part of the job could really wear on you.

A commissioner's job meant being on call twenty-four hours a day if you wanted to keep all of your business. I could not ignore calls or emails as this could cost us business. If it rained on a Saturday or Sunday, I would start getting phone calls at 6 AM. To keep from waking up my wife, I would sleep on the sofa with my cell and home phone right next to me. As soon as the first phone call came in, I was at the computer sending out cancellation communications to the umpires. As mentioned earlier, my wonderful wife was one hundred percent behind my decision to continue or to give it up, and left it up to me as to what would make me happy. Knowing that the association was in a strong place, I knew it was my time to step down and pass the phone, keyboard, and the headaches to the next commissioner.

REPORTING BY RECKLING

WAVY-TV 10 and later Fox 43 reporter Chris Reckling took an interest in me as a player and then later as a reporter. He described his observations one day with vivid memories as told below.

> With my view clouded by the dust in the air, I looked up at home-plate umpire Jim Smith, and he calmly called me out, but what happened moments later almost got out of hand.
>
> It was early spring of 1981, and my Princess Anne Cavaliers were playing our rivals from First Colonial High School. It was late in the game, and we were down one run. I was on third base with one out, and nothing was going to stop me from scoring. The moment the ball left the bat I started home. Never mind that it was a hard-hit grounder to the shortstop; I had already made up my mind. The throw was well ahead of me, but high. The catcher came down and blocked the plate. I lowered my shoulder and took him out. The both of us were

sprawled out on the ground looking up at Jim. I was out, and I knew it.

That was the moment First Colonial head coach Norbie Wilson came screaming onto the field. "Throw him out... throw him out," yelled Wilson. He stood tall in the late evening sun pointing at me with venom and veins popping. "Throw him out," he demanded. This irate coach with fire in his eyes could be heard screaming all the way to the oceanfront.

But Jim, always the voice of calm and reason, quickly defused the moment, walking Wilson back to the dugout.

Jim Smith has always had that type of presence on the baseball diamond. While three highly emotional and competitive players and coach awaited the outcome, Jim, ever calm and poised, quickly changed a potentially ugly situation.

As a player or as a coach, you want to know who is calling your game behind the plate and in the field. Jim Smith behind the dish was always a welcome sight for coaches and players. You knew, regardless of what would happen in that game that you were going to get an honest and fair ball game. Thankfully I was not thrown out. This was before the rule change prohibiting forceful contact with catchers. A stickler for the rules, no doubt Jim would have sent me to the parking lot if that were the case back then.

As an umpire and later longtime commissioner, Jim Smith commanded respect from the entire baseball community. He would always find the time to talk to you if you had a question.

On a couple different occasions, I was fortunate to see his operation and how he worked. He allowed me to film and air days that would have most people pulling their hair out. Rainouts are a pain for all involved, but no one dealt with it quite like Jim. From deep inside his home fortress, he would weave a delicate balance between coaches, athletic directors, and umpires on a daily basis. Juggling schedules from high school, college, and recreational leagues is no easy task, but Jim made it look so. And he it did with a professional approach. He was like an artist at work.

Some of the best umpires in the nation came through

his program. His workshops developed the next generation of umps, and they would not advance if they did not fully understand the rules and the mechanics of calling a baseball game. This hands-on approach from some of Jim's more accomplished umpires made sure that umpires at every level showed up on game day ready to call an honest and fair game.

From calling his first game to mentoring dozens of new umpires, Jim Smith left his mark on the game of baseball in Hampton Roads, a mark of professionalism, fairness, and honesty. I'm glad he didn't throw me out of the game that day back in 1981. But then, Jim Smith always let the players decide the outcome of games. He got it right that day and most days after.

ROLAND WRIGHT, HEAD BASEBALL COACH, WESTERN BRANCH HIGH SCHOOL

The state champion Western Branch baseball program has been one of the most successful in all of Hampton Roads. Coach Wright has been in the dugout, and yes, occasionally out of it, during the Bruins' best years. He comments as follows.

I first met Jim in the spring of 1997 when I was an assistant at Great Bridge High School. We were playing Salem High, and one of our other assistants kept fussing with Jim about balls and strikes. That assistant made it until the fourth inning, when Jim cordially told him his day was over, and he could watch the rest of the game from the parking lot. I have had the extreme pleasure from that day until now to know Jim and develop an extremely important friendship.

Jim has always been gracious with my requests for game changes, times of games, and dates. He was known for going out of the way to help all the local coaches get their games moved.

In the summer of 2006 Jim and I decided to provide student-athletes with an alternative league during the summer, and thus we created the EOA JV Wooden Bat Summer League. That summer we started with four teams;

since then we have grown to over thirty-five teams each summer. Baseball in the Tidewater area is among the most talented across the Mid-Atlantic region, and one of the reasons why is that we have people like Jim giving these student-athletes alternative options to play baseball.

I also have the extreme privilege each year to assist Jim in several umpire clinics at my facility. I think this is where you get to see Jim at his best, teaching new umpires the correct technique to be successful on the field. Jim holds these umpires to high expectations, as he does himself, and will quickly tell one to get off the field if he/she is not hustling or doing the correct mechanics. I think Jim has never looked at being an umpire or the commissioner as a burden or job, because he truly has had a passion for both and has put his heart and soul in it.

In my eleven years as a head coach and sixteen as an assistant, my relationship has grown tremendously with Jim and is one that I cherish every day. As Jim will surely be missed as our commissioner, I am grateful for all the contributions he has given baseball in the Tidewater area.

UMPIRES LEARNING ON THE JOB

EOA umpire Dave Roach shares what it's like to transition from a newbie to a veteran.

My first contact with Jim Smith was via a phone call, in which he really got me mad and almost made me not want to pursue a career in officiating.

Let me explain. I was given his name and phone number by my local Bennett's Creek Little League (northern Suffolk recreation league) president. This person told me over a phone conversation that Bennett's Creek Little League contracted its baseball umpires through a very professional organization (EVOA) headed by Commissioner Jim Smith.

When I called Jim, he told me I could not join the association because I had missed a majority of the "New

Umpire Class" training sessions, that unknown to me had occurred over the winter months. I was astonished that this commissioner of a professional organization, did not want to accept me in its ranks. After all, I was a lifelong baseball player and had six years of Virginia high school league coaching experience at two different Portsmouth public high schools.

A week had passed since our first phone conversation when Jim called and invited me to attend an on-the-field scrimmage, where newly trained baseball umpires were fully dressed in uniform and officiated a local recreational league's early spring scrimmage. Jim flat-out told me that I would not be participating in the live scrimmage, but I could show up and get a feel for what a properly trained baseball umpire should be able to perform during a "live game situation." I swallowed my pride (for not being admitted into the current training class) and attended the scrimmage.

After watching Jim interact with the umpires on the field for those two hours, I knew I had contacted the right association to begin my officiating career. In the succeeding weeks of the high school baseball season, Jim would notify me of game times and locations in which I could attend and interact with game officials before and after the games. I simply found the guys in the parking lots who were undressing and dressing into uniforms, walked up, introduced myself and said, "Jim Smith said you would welcome me and entertain all of my questions."

To a man, every EVOA umpire whom I blindly met in the parking lot "dressing room" said, "If Jim Smith sent you, then we're here for any and all questions you have of us."

I soon found I wanted to be trained under Jim. I found myself enrolled in the next available "New Umpire" training class EVOA and Jim offered, which was in the late summer of 2012.

One of the best, if not the best, Jim Smith quotes I can share about attending and participating in an EVOA "New Umpire" training session was when Jim stood before my brand new class of fifteen want-to-be baseball umpires and said, "Be the very best baseball umpire you can be, no matter what the level (recreation, middle/high school, college or beyond) because the kids/players deserve a fair/unbiased official to enforce the rules of the GREATEST game ever invented."

I knew from that night on that the reason I wasn't able to join the association earlier that year was because I wasn't educated/trained well enough to officiate a game that was being played by young boys/men who deserved nothing but the best from me as an official.

I have been fortunate with Jim as the commissioner to have been given the opportunity to challenge myself and my abilities as a learning baseball umpire by working some upper-level games. Jim realized that I was willing to learn . . . by mistakes and by working with more veteran umpires. My proudest personal moments to date happened post-game when after plating two separate league championship games I found myself in conversations with Jim and league directors in the concession stand. When the league directors questioned my appointment to such games, Jim simply stated he would not have put me in charge of the game if he didn't feel I could handle it. From those games forward, I've come to realize I am a representative of EVOA and a product of Jim's training. God bless Jim for the thousands of lives he's affected in such a positive manner.

NO BATS ABOUT IT

In the spring of 2014, one of my umpires reported to me that in his game that afternoon, one of the teams had fifteen bats, one for every player, and the other team had two bats, one cracked and not usable and one good bat. He told me how bad he felt for the home team with only one bat.

So I called up a good friend of mine at a sporting goods store and asked if he could help me out. He told me he had five used but good aluminum bats that he would give me for $100. I jumped right on it.

The next day I drove to the school and met with the principal and coach and shared the opportunity to help them out. They made it happen. What makes this story more rewarding is they had not won a game in two years, but with the new bats they finished the season nine-two.

COMMUNITY CONNECTIONS

Ed Timlin, who was a former EVOA umpire and a great friend of mine, asked if I needed a place to hold the clinics. He knew I wanted a much larger place and a place we could call home for the training of new EVOA umpires, so he offered us his school, Point O' View Elementary.

Two years into my term, Ed asked me if I would have the association become a partner in education with them. I said yes knowing this was not only good for us, but good for the school. Every year I go over and help with the opening of school and the state-mandated Standards of Learning testing. A bonus for them is the free publicity they get when the TV stations come over to do specials on the association. Community service and visibility are an important part of what we strive to do.

COACHES HELPING UMPIRES

Just like players in the big leagues, we have our own form of spring training. In fact, we get busy each year in January. We hold six required clinics for all umpires, and we run two new umpire sessions, one in the fall and one in the spring, each lasting eight weeks. We also hold one mandatory, on-field clinic for all umpires just prior to the start of high school season.

Now, you might observe that coaches try to "help" us umpires all the time. That's the kind of help we really don't want or need. We are fortunate, however, to have a lot of coaches in the Tidewater area that really care about the game, especially Coach Roland Wright at Western Branch. Roland is a coach who really does help out, at least in the pre-season. Not only does he let us use his field for our preseason training, he brings out twenty or thirty players to run drills for us. All I had to do was pick up the phone, and he says "Jim, when and how many players do we need?" St. Clair Jones at Kellam High School is another coach who is always there for us. By no means are these the only two who offer their support for umpiring, just the two who started with me.

BULLDOGS USE THEIR JAWS

Not sure of the exact date, but as with many of the other stories in the book, the date or names do not matter. The events or actions during the game are what make it worthy of including.

It happened to be a beautiful Thursday night in early May. Since all games were already started, I didn't have to worry about rain or phone calls about umpires not showing up for a game. I decided to head out to one of our independent high school semifinal tournament games. I got to the field, pulled out my chair, and put it down in a roped-off area, hopefully where no one would see or bother me. As you will see that didn't happen.

All was going good until around the third inning, when the home team started to pull away. Frustration started to set in for the visiting team coach, who was known to be rather a bulldog, and he started barking about balls and strikes. Instead of telling the coach he had heard enough, our normal way of handling that situation, the plate umpire went to the opposite foul line and started staring him down. Not what we teach, so as you can guess, the coach now yelled, "Are you trying to big-league me and stare me down?"

The home-plate umpire yelled back, "Are you talking to me?"

It wasn't really a question, and as you can guess, fifteen seconds later they were chest to chest in a very heated conversation. The first-base umpire finally had to come in and separate them.

Just as the head coach got near the dugout, there asw a throwing of bats and helmets in the dugout. Thinking it was the head coach, the plate umpire blasted the coach and said, "One more word out of you, and you are done."

Here we go again. The coach yells, "What are you accusing me of? Did you see me throw anything, Rabbit Ears?"

Now this is something that should have gotten him tossed. They went at it for several minutes, and luckily, the first-base umpire again came back in and separated them with no one getting tossed.

The game resumed, and about two minutes later the visiting athletic director came down and asked me if I knew what was going on. I summarized it for him and told him both your coach and our umpire had not handled their action in the way they should have for a postseason game. I also informed him it was their assistant coach who was throwing the equipment and not the head coach. He was the one who should have been tossed.

Three days later, on a Sunday night, I received a phone message from the headmaster of the coach's school asking if I would return his call. When I did, what I found was one of the most polite and professional gentlemen I had ever spoken to. The first thing he did was apologize for taking up my valuable time, but he said he had heard good things about the way I ran the association and would appreciate it if I could give him a couple of minutes to talk about the game and what my thoughts were about his coach's action and coaching style.

We agreed each side could have handled the situation in a more professional manner. He then told me he had several complaints from parents about his coach's way of handling his players and wanted to know what my opinion was in regards to his head coach. I told him I had known his coach for roughly twenty years, as a college player, coach, and now high school coach. I told him the expression us old timers used was that his coach was "old school," yet one of the most respected coaches by umpires throughout the coaching ranks. By "old school," I meant that umpires and coaches used to be able to say things during arguments that are now ejection offenses.

I ended the conversation with a shocking revelation to him. I said, "I bet I can tell you the names of two of the parents complaining about the coach. Please do not respond with a yes or no, so as not to violate any confidentiality."

When I gave the names, he just laughed and thanked me, but from the way he reacted I knew I had guessed right. I told him it was easy because they were also complaining at one of the recreation games I had attended.

POOR COACHING, UMPIRE HAVING A BAD DAY TOO

Deep fly ball to left field, near the foul pole that goes over the left fielder's head—the home-plate umpire goes out and rules the ball foul. The home team coach, whose team is in the field, comes out and asks the umpire if he will go for help on the call. Why, I have no idea, since the call went in his favor.

Who does the home-plate umpire go to for help? You would think his partner, who would tell him once foul, it remains foul. Wrong, he went to the left fielder. Now the left fielder, instead of saying it was foul, told the home-plate umpire it was fair. How you turn that into a home run and not have to run someone I could not understand.

Same game—The runner on third is attempting to steal home. We have a wild pitch that ends up in the umpire's ball bag. The runner slides in safely, but the umpire sends the runner back to third saying he interfered with the catcher trying to find the ball. Find that one in the rulebook if you can. You won't. I can promise you.

Same game—There were no outs and runners on first and second. We had a ground ball down the third baseline that went over the bag fair. The third baseman fielded the ball and accidentally stepped on third, then threw to second for the second out and then to first for the third out. Triple play, you would think. Wrong. The coach came out and argued that the third baseman never stepped on the bag. Easy answer is, "Coach, yes he did." Wrong answer is, "I will go check with the third baseman." Need I say any more? Now imagine trying to explain that game to the athletic director.

THERE WAS NO JOY IN MUDVILLE

During my time as commissioner, I dealt with one of the strangest and poorest umpire rulings that I have ever seen, but knowing the league director helped ease the pain for everyone. This game was contested by eleven and twelve-year-olds. The next batter was a kid who had managed only one hit in four years. No one ever expected anything of him except, like Mighty Casey, to strike out.

Well not this time, not this night. On the second pitch, to the wonderment of all, he hits a towering home run over the left fielder's head. As he is rounding third base, the dugout empties to meet him at the plate. The fans erupt with that special joy that comes when a long-suffering benchwarmer finally comes through. That is, until the umpire, my umpire, calls young Casey out because several players high fived him before he reached the plate.

For those, like my umpire-in-disbelief, who may have forgotten, the ball is dead once it leaves the park. Sure, you can throw players out for leaving the dugout if you want, but why? The one thing you can't do is call the batter out. The next day, the call was reversed, and the young man awarded a home run, along with the ball he hit. People said of that night that our young hero nearly tore the cover off the ball. Parents were still upset the next day, but not the young man. Goes to show who the adults really are.

CHAPTER 8

FORTY YEARS
OF STORIES

In the early '70s, the Yankees used to play the Mets in an exhibition game on their way back north from spring training. The game was played at the home of the AAA farm team for the New York Mets, which just happened to be the Norfolk Tides. Talk about luck and being in the right place at the right time: read further . . .

This memorable event all started with a student teacher coming to the school where I was teaching, saying I was his cooperating teacher. He introduced himself as Colin Caddell. I told him I couldn't be his cooperating or supervising teacher as I was a second-year teacher and did not have tenure. I called downtown to the School Board Office, and they said yes, I was. Sitting down eating lunch one day, he told me how he and his dad ran the clubhouses for the Norfolk Tides. He also told me about the special night when they got to work the Yankees and Mets exhibition games. He asked me if I want to help him. Dumb question, so on this night we took care of the Yankees, and his dad took care of the Mets.

I cannot remember who the pitcher was for the Yankees, but he wanted to have some fun with the bat boy. He sent him in to get his bat. We went to the pitcher's locker and gave the bat to the bat boy. Five minutes later, the bat boy came back in and said the pitcher wanted his left-handed bat, so we pulled out another one. This went on for about ten minutes and five different bats, so we ended the boy's puzzlement by writing LEFT HANDED BAT in Magic Marker on the bat and waited to see what happened next. The bat boy came back in and thanked us for covering for him.

After the game was over, we always had food and beverages for the players. In addition to beef stew, we also made some ham sandwiches with mustard on this particular night. After showering, the great Yankee Bobby Mercer made some comment to the even better-known catcher, Thurman Munson, about his throws to second base. He was poking him about throwing breaking balls to second and that he couldn't throw one straight if he wanted to. I found myself standing directly between Murcer and Munson and thought it best to move. Then Murcer told me to stay where I was, because Munson could not throw a ball straight, much less a sandwich. Both put $100 on this truly important question of whether Munson could throw a sandwich straight. I stood still, and from about thirty feet away, Munson hit me square in the chest with mustard flying everywhere. Mercer, who was ever the jokester, pulled out a $100 bill, and gave it to me rather than Munson since he had lost the bet. What did Munson do? No worries, he just went and got another sandwich. For years I remembered this unforgettable evening and said to myself, I was glad the bet wasn't about throwing the beef stew!

The great Whitey Ford was then near the end of his Hall of Fame career, and out of the kindness of his heart, gave me a new Yankees tee shirt. Being a bachelor at the time, I would stupidly ruin it one later night when I ran amuck with Easy-Off oven cleaner. We also got an autographed ball from Whitey Ford, Mel Stottlemeyer, Murcer, Munson, Mets reliever Tug McGraw, and a few more of the Yankees, but that was not the end of the story.

Before leaving the clubhouse, it is a long-time custom that all the major league players are required to tip the clubhouse guys.

After all the players had left and gotten on the bus, the Yankees' traveling secretary, the man who makes sure everything is done properly, came in to us and asked if everyone had paid up. We said we were okay.

He said, "That is not what I asked you."

We again said we were okay. He asked us to let him see the payment sheet. One guy's name was not checked off. The Yankees' officer went out to the bus, pulled the offender off the bus and made him pull out of his wallet. We got every last dollar in there, about $450, Just before the bus pulled out, we could hear the rest of the Yankees giving the guy all kinds of grief. One of them told us he would not forget again. We tried to give it back, but then a bunch of the Yankees pulled more money out of their wallets and apologized for his forgetfulness. We knew he had not done it intentionally, but I would love to have been a fly on the wall in the bus on the way back to the airport. I think all of us cleared well over $500 that night, even after paying for the food and beer.

Colin stayed in teaching for a while and then became a chiropractor. Teaching was just not what was right for him and his family. I ended up helping him about half the season and got to meet a lot of the guys who were called up to the big leagues. His mother was one of the secretaries at our school, and we still remain friends today. This is the same lady who took the phone call that got me into umpiring.

WOMEN'S LEAGUE: WHO WOULD HAVE THUNK IT

Somewhere in the late '80s, the women tried to form a Women's Adult Baseball League in the Tidewater area. Talk about some crazy rules, but they could play. They were also a lot better to look at than the men. It lasted for about two years and then died due to lack of players.

OLD TIMERS' GAME

On August 16, 1987, I was fortunate enough to be asked by Dave Rosenfield, a legend with the Tides for over fifty years, to

umpire the Braves/Mets Old Timers' game at Met Park along
with Bullet Alexander and Bob Hood. We had a lot of fun in this
game, as the pitchers would come out with nail files, vaseline,
and any other tool they could find to doctor the ball up. Bugsy
Moran even brought out a circular saw. We blew calls (staged)
so we could get into lengthy arguments with the players. Bases
and hats were thrown, and we had a blast. Several of the players
even brought money out to us to pay us off. The crowd roared. At
the end of the game, we got autographed balls from Bob Feller,
Bugsy Moran, and local big leaguer Hank Foiles.

MLB HOME RUN DERBY FUND RAISER

2007 GRASSFIELD GRIZZLIES HR DERBY.
(L-R:) MLB STARS DAVID WRIGHT, RYAN ZIMMERMAN, JUSTIN UPTON,
MICHAEL CUDDYER, B.J. UPTON, MARK REYNOLDS

In March 2007, our association was asked to umpire a
"Home Run Derby Contest" at the new Grassfield High School
in Chesapeake, Virginia. The purpose was to help raise money
for the newly built Grassfield High School baseball program. The
place was packed (sell out) with thousands of fans, and all three
local TV stations were in attendance. David Wright, Michael
Cuddyer, Ryan Zimmerman, Mark Reynolds, and BJ and Justin

Upton, all local stars now well established in the show, battled it out, and Wright finally won it. Bob Barry organized the event, and together with Bob, I came out of retirement to work with my son Ryan and Bob Campbell. What a treat, especially to work with two guys who had eighty years of experience between them and with my own son. After the contest was over, the players stood outside a trailer that had been

2007 HOME RUN DERBY CHARITY EVENT AT GRASSFIELD HIGH SCHOOL

brought in for them, and each and every one of the players signed autographs for the next two hours. What a great moment for so many, and especially for the kids. They were chasing the home runs all day long and got to keep the baseballs for autographs.

MEETING THE BIG GUYS: OLD DOMINION UNIVERSITY BASEBALL BANQUETS

Each January, Old Dominion University holds its Spring Baseball Banquet. Its primary purpose is to help raise money for the baseball program. I have had the pleasure of attending most of the banquets, but the four I have most enjoyed were the ones where the guest speakers were John Smoltz, Ozzie Smith, Joe Morgan, and Goose Gossage. Besides being great speakers, they stayed afterward and signed autographs and took pictures with anyone who wanted a picture with them. Happening to know the right people

BEING A BRAVES FAN, IT WAS GREAT TO CHAT WITH JOHN SMOTLZ AT ODU FUND RAISER

in attendance for two of those events, I was able to go up to the suites, where I got to talk baseball with Joe Morgan and Goose Gossage. Talk about a party in Goose Gossage's suite: we must have stayed there until around 3 AM, consuming whatever you wanted to drink and talking baseball. This was definitely the night for a designated driver. John Smoltz preferred to stay downstairs and socialize, but with hundreds still in line for autographs, I was able to talk with him for about five minutes. Being a Braves man and getting to meet and talk to him was the thrill of a lifetime. I have pictures of all of them framed in my office except the one of Ozzie Smith. I forgot my camera that night.

A CHRISTMAS TO REMEMBER: SHADOW BOX WITH MY JERSEY

We have a Christmas tradition around our house in which the children, even in their teens and twenties, have to wait to see what Santa brought them. My wife is in charge and has them wait until she is ready with her camera. Then they get to come in to see what Santa brought. After that, we exchange the other gifts among family members.

On the Christmas morning of 2005, I was asked to close my eyes while one gift was brought in. I saw it but had no idea what it was. When I opened it, I broke down crying. My daughter Lauren had taken the shirt I wore in the last game I ever umpired and had it placed in a three-foot-by-three-foot shadow box frame. It immediately went on a wall in my office and is positioned as to where I can see it every day. Any time I am on the computer working, there it is. It is definitely one of the greatest gifts I have ever received. The place where she had it framed is probably one of the most expensive shops in the Tidewater area, yet probably does some of the best work.

SCREENSAVER OF ALL SCREENSAVERS

While we're on the subject of framing, our commissioner at that time came out and took a picture of me umpiring the game between Princess Anne High School and First Colonial High

School. The date was March 23, 2004. At the time, we thought I would be back in two to three months. No one knew it would be the last game I ever umpired. I normally worked with my knee forward when doing the plate, but with back surgery the next day and the pain I was experiencing, I used the box stance that day.

Since I seldom worked the box, I asked the commissioner to print me off a copy to see if I was in the slot and had the proper head height. He sent me the picture, and to this day I have it in a four-by-six frame on my desk. I also use it as my screensaver. Most of us never know when a game will be our last. At least mine is preserved.

BLACK BOOK OF ALL BLACK BOOKS

I always had a hard time remembering coaches' names when I first started umpiring, so I kept a book with all their names. Not sure how the next part came about, but for a few I got the names of their wives or girlfriends. That way when they came out to argue, I would ask them how their wife/girlfriend/family was doing. If they were really upset, I might say, "Do I need to call your wife tonight and tell her that we may have missed a call but you were acting like an ass today?" Of course, you had to know which ones you could use that on and which ones you couldn't. I used it to defuse situations and try to keep anyone from getting thrown out of the game.

My most famous line was with Coach Norbie Wilson, head coach of First Colonial High School for over thirty years and one of my best friends. Off the field he was like a teddy bear, but on the field, he was one of the most intense coaches for whom I ever had the pleasure of working. Very seldom could he walk out slowly or talk quietly, so knowing him as well as I did, I would always put my arm around him as we were walking to my partner and say "Norbie, am I going to have to call Candy tonight and tell her you are acting like an ass today?"

For the rest of the game, he would always say "YES, SIR" or "NO, SIR." That was all it took. His wife seldom came to any of his baseball games because of his intensity, but she came one day just to meet me. That meant the world to me, and we still laugh about it today.

Since Coach Wilson is one of my all-time favorite coaches and a very close friend, I would like to digress back to the days before he started coaching, and I started umpiring. Before both of us moved to the Tidewater area to teach, we both played baseball against each other in college. Neither one of us knew the other when we were playing. He went to Barton College in Wilson North Carolina, and I went to East Carolina University in Greenville. We just thought of each other as two guys playing baseball at two different colleges. We really did not know each other until we moved up here. It really is a small world, and in baseball it can be really small.

Another one of the coaches I could use the wife line on was Coach Tony Guzzo. He and I played baseball together at East Carolina and developed a very close relationship. He then came back to the Tidewater area where he coached at Catholic High and then moved on to Virginia Wesleyan College, Virginia Commonwealth University and then Old Dominion University. I had a game with Coach Guzzo against Rutgers at ODU . It had been raining all day, and we must have used forty bags of drying agent to get the game In. Due to the terrible field conditions I missed a swipe tag at first. I went to my partner and reversed the call. Tony came out to argue, used role reversal and said, "Jim, do I need to call your wife and let her know you missed a call just 'cause it's raining?" Due to the torrential rains the game was ended right after that call, but I got a dose of my own medicine.

PROUD FATHER, YOU BET

Our association has a policy that you do not get to put a number on your uniform shirt or jacket until you reach the varsity level. I was lucky enough to have the honor of having my son earn varsity status and then inherit my shirt number 22. That was one of the proudest days of my life.

We had two other father-and-son combinations in the association, but with the very sad passing of Bob Campbell we are down to one. Following our tradition, Bob's number 5 has been inherited by his grandson.

RAIN GETS TV AND NEWSPAPER COVERAGE

It was an honor to have Chris Reckling with our local TV stations, WAVY-TV 10 and Fox 43 Sports, ask me on three separate occasions if he could come over to the house to interview me about what rain days were like as an outdoor commissioner and how difficult it was to reschedule with such short notice. I will always treasure those interviews and they will stay saved on my computer. My question to Chris, though, was always "Why me? I am not that important. I am just doing my job."

I will never forget the look Chris always gave me on his first question of every interview, and trust me, it was always the same question. With his head cocked to the side, as the phone would continue to ring and interrupt him, he would ask "Jim, how do you do that?"

My response was usually something like this. "Everyone knows I can be 'Chatty Cathy' and talk forever on non-rainy days. But on rainy days, I need complete silence, a special format for documenting the calls, two phones, a headset, my office door usually closed, and no one bothering me with something that does not have to do with anything other than today's rain. On those days, breakfast usually ends up coming somewhere between 6 and 7 PM."

Chris also came over to our training site, Point O' View Elementary, and did four specials on our training of officials. He was surprised at how much goes into what we do. The four pitching machines in action and the videotaping of all our umpires, in addition to the mechanics and classroom instruction, are things very few on the outside ever see. We picked up umpires from these broadcasts and many compliments from those who knew about our association but never knew how much went into umpiring.

Chris came over to the house on two other occasions to ask my opinion on hot topics at the time. The first was umpires being graded on the use of television's K Zone. My short answer to him was we always want to get the pitch right, but baseball is a game written in black and white but never called in black and white. Umpires are humans and make mistakes. The second topic was instant replay. I am against it except for HRs in the big leagues.

Part of the game fans enjoy are some of the arguments. These umpires would not be there if they didn't get most of them right.

Bruce Rader, the lead sportscaster for one of the local TV stations made it a point one day to look me up at Harbor Park and thank me for allowing him to do specials for the station. I told him I appreciated Chris coming out and taking the time to shoot the footage, but the thanks go to the umpires who come out to the clinics and learn to do things the right way. It was not about me.

Larry Rubama, one of the sports writers with our local newspaper, *The Virginian Pilot,* also asked if he could come over one morning to do an article on what it was like to be a commissioner of a spring sport, especially one that had to deal with rain. He got backlogged with work and ended up asking if he could send one of his female photographers over to follow me around for about thirty minutes. She picked a perfectly awful day, as it poured from morning till night. She was amazed at how much went on and ended up spending four hours taking pictures and watching me work. I kept that article and picture and hung it on my wall. It truly depicts what a rainy day is like. Believe me, you wouldn't want to be there when the phones start ringing.

HEAVEN AWAY FROM THE DAY-TO-DAY GRIND

As an escape mechanism or way to relax from all the daily stress while serving as the baseball commissioner, I loved going to our local AAA ballpark and seeing all the friendly faces. I also loved watching and studying the umpires. Every couple of weeks, on sunny days only, I enjoyed going by Dave Rosenfield's office to talk baseball and discuss umpiring. We always started off with the intent of a quick five or ten-minute chat and ended up having a thirty-to-forty-five-minute conversation. I am not sure if there was a more knowledgeable man in the business. Dave's book is a great read, and if you have not read it, you need to do so. I thought I knew Dave pretty well, but after reading it, I found out I knew very little. I will always be grateful to Dave and Randy Mobley (president of the International League) for sending me a season pass for two to go see all the Norfolk Tides games. I am grateful to the entire Tides staff for allowing me to sit in the section with the family members and scouts. Here you can meet nice people from all over the country, enjoy the game, and not have to deal with those who have had too much to drink or the obnoxious and rowdy fans. Meeting and talking to the scouts is something special, but I always let the scouts start up the conversation, as they are there to do a job. It seems like when they find out what I did for a living, it always generates lengthy discussions between innings and the development of lifetime friendships. Did I mention that some of the players' wives are drop-dead gorgeous?

AAA USHER OF THE YEAR

One highlight of our local AAA baseball games was seeing Elliott Atherholt (my favorite usher). We loved to harass each other, but it was always in good jest. Since I had umpired and assigned umpires for roughly forty years, my name to him became "Big Blue." My name for him was "Deputy Dog." How I came up with that name, I am not sure. It probably came about due to his usher responsibilities. His section was section 100, the top section in the ballpark, designated for the scouts and family members only. He had to make sure everyone sitting there had a ticket saying section 100. If not, he ushered them out.

Most of our games started at 7:05. Somewhere around 6:55, Elliott started looking for me. As soon as he saw me coming down the steps, he would go to the second row from the top of the section and cleans aisle seats 1, 2, and 3. He knew I put my coat in one seat, my books in another seat, and I would sit in the third seat. He then made sure I knew all the teams for whom the scouts worked and which wife was related to which player. Anytime there was a close play he would come down and ask for my opinion. It was always the same question: "Alright, Big Blue, what do you have?" I always gave him an honest answer.

Any time I had someone come sit next to me whom I really did not want to be there or who took away from my watching the game, we had a secret signal for him to come run them away. I would scratch my head with my right hand. Like clockwork, thirty seconds later, Elliott would be right down, telling them they only had one minute left, and then they had to go. Since this is a reserved section, I never wanted to take advantage of the privilege given to me by the International League and Tides office. But I also wanted to watch the game.

WORKING WITH TIDES FAMILY AND THE TOP BRASS

One of the things I will always treasure is working with the Tides' Heather McKeating in helping to organize and bring scholastic games to Harbor Park. It was a win-win situation for everyone. The schools raised some money for themselves and the Tides sold one thousand or more tickets. Anyone who has attended Tides games knows that Heather is invaluable to the organization. She has worked there her entire adult life. Her first pitch was in Harbor Park's year two, 1994, and she has dedicated her career to serving the Tides and their community. Every organization needs a can-do person like Heather who works behind the scenes but is so important to organizational success.

With my great relationship with all the schools' athletic directors I was also able to get all the schools to buy into using three umpires, just like the AAA Tides, for high school games played at Harbor Park. I received many compliments from the players, coaches, parents, and athletic directors for making them feel like they were getting the "Big-Time Treatment" when they saw three umpires working the game, just like the pros get. This may have been my idea, but the real credit goes to Heather, who made it happen.

I owe a big thank-you to Gretchen Todd for taking care of my parking spot. She made sure I had a spot to park and one that was real close to the front gate. Without her help, my walking distance would triple or quadruple, an important issue after my injuries prohibited me from working games. We also had a running joke that she would not talk to me on the game days when the scholastic teams played. When they played, usually following the Tides' day game, it meant she and the staff had to stay three hours longer. Okay, that's not really true, as they had to be there anyway. It was just her way of saying I was making her workday longer and harder. We just smile at each other on those days, but in all seriousness, she is great to work with, and the Tides are lucky to have her on staff.

Last but not least, I owe a big thank you to the general manager, Joe Gregory, for allowing me to be a part of the Tides family. Joe never sits at any of the games. He is always walking around greeting and talking to all the fans. For many years, he juggled being the general manager for both a professional ice hockey and baseball franchise at the same time. I find that amazing.

MILE HIGH TOUR OF A LIFETIME

My daughter Ashley and her husband moved out to Colorado in 2009. Lou and I have always enjoyed visiting her and experiencing new things in her part of the country. Ashley always tries to think of new things that we might enjoy, and this trip was no exception.

Early one morning, she told us to get dressed and ready to go on a short trip. Her only caveat was to wear comfortable walking shoes. We did as instructed and headed off toward Denver. When we arrived and began a short stroll toward the home of the Blake Street bombers, Ashley let us in on the secret that she had signed us up for a tour of Coors Field. I was thrilled. This was something I had never thought of doing before, and what baseball fan wouldn't love a little behind-the-scenes tour of a major league stadium?

The tour took us through the press box area, the executive suites, the players' locker rooms, and many more areas. It was a beautiful, sunny day in the Rockies, and our tour ended on the field for pictures and an opportunity to sit in the dugouts. As our group was ushered up the multiple tiers of steps and out of the stadium, I asked one of the employees if there was an elevator we might be able to take up to avoid the steps. He kindly told us to follow him and that he would take us the back way. With a wink, he whispered that we would need to hurry.

As we hustled through the maze of hallways under the stadium toward the elevators, I struck up a conversation with this older gentleman and told him about my time as a baseball

2015 TOURING THE COLORADO ROCKIES UMPIRE ROOM WITH MY GRANDCHILDREN, KATE AND CAMERON

SHOWING CAMERON WHAT A MAJOR LEAGUE FIELD LOOKS LIKE

LOU, MY WIFE, WITH THE GRANDCHILDREN

NO PLACE I WOULD RATHER BE THAN ON A BALLFIELD

player and umpire. He pulled out a set of keys from his pocket and told us he had a room I might like to see. I read the sign on the door—"Umpire Lounge"—and couldn't believe where we were. He quickly ushered us into the locker room and allowed us to look around and take as many pictures as we wanted. My grandson and I sat down and took it all in, and for a minute or so, I had visions of what it would be like to be an MLB umpire. Big screen televisions, lavish food set-ups, comfortable seating . . . it was something to behold. I profusely thanked the gentleman for the kindness he showed in letting our family view a typically unseen part of a major-league ballpark. As I was a former official, it's not surprising that this glimpse into the umpire's lounge had an impact on me and quickly became my favorite part of the stadium tour.

I'VE SEEN FIRE AND I'VE SEEN RAIN AND HAIL

After retirement, I was looking forward to visiting different major league stadiums with my family. Lucky for me, Ashley, living in a suburb of Denver, makes trips to the beautiful Colorado Rockies' stadium a favorite pastime of ours in the summers. You've just read about our stadium tour, but let me tell you about one evening when we had game tickets.

It was a few days after my grandson's fifth birthday, and like dutiful grandparents, we made plans to take him out for a birthday night of baseball. Okay, I didn't exactly have to be dragged along. Anyway, as they say, you make plans, and God laughs.

It all started out as a beautiful 92-degree day. We noticed a chance for scattered showers in the afternoon but didn't think much of it. I helped pack up the two grandkids and their mom and dad—all of us clad in our purple and black Rockies gear—and we got on the road. As we neared Coors Field, we looked to the western sky as the early evening light started to darken over the gray Rocky Mountains. We found parking and began our trek up to our mile-high seats in the stadium.

Imagine our surprise when we were stopped by an usher and told that we would not be allowed up to our seats yet. We were instructed to remain in the stairwells, and we watched as buckets of rain began to pour from the sky. The family alternated between hiding out in the stairwells of the stadium, the bathroom entrances, and finally the Rockies store. We watched as sheets of rain came in horizontally over the field and stood in awe as baseball-sized hail covered the diamond. My son-in-law snapped several pictures of the

2015 ALL SMILES AFTER A 3 HOUR HAILSTORM. JAN CHALUPKA, KATE AND CAMERON

empty stadium as the grounds crew tried desperately to protect the field for a delayed game. After all my years of dealing with the stress of rain as a commissioner, I guess I still couldn't get away from weather issues even in my retirement!

We were all looking forward to the Rockies' last game in the series versus the Toronto Blue Jays, so we weren't quite ready to pack it up and head home. We braved the downpour and found a nearby pub where we drank, ate, and waited out the storm. Ashley was glued to her phone for information regarding a possible start time for the game, and after a two-hour-twenty-minute rain delay, the game was slated to start at 9:30 PM. We headed back over, wiped off our seats, and settled in for a disappointing 14-9 loss for the Rox.

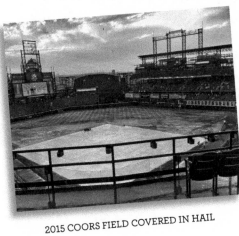

2015 COORS FIELD COVERED IN HAIL

In the end, it would be a record-setting storm, with water pouring into the dugouts and hail covering the field as though it was a snowstorm in June. Despite the rain delay, it was a fun adventure and a trip to the Rockies stadium that I will not soon forget!

HE WHO LAUGHS LAST

Time to switch sports to basketball. After all it's got to get too cold to play baseball for some of the year, and what's an official to do?

In the late '80s or early '90s, I was selected to work the Beach District Girls Championship basketball game. This was one of the few times my wife and oldest daughter, about age six at the time, ever went to one of the games I refereed. They just happened to be sitting on the side of the team that lost.

After the game, our crew took showers and had our normal post-game discussion. This evening discussion was very short as nothing really happened. The coaches were relatively quiet toward us the entire game. A few questions, but no technical fouls or warnings.

Then I went into the gym to get my wife and daughter. As luck would have it, the lady sitting in front of them happened to be the losing coach's sister and must have thought we were horrible. She started yelling at me so everyone could hear her. She refused to let my wife and daughter get by her to join me. So as not to further fuel the scene I beckoned to one of my friends, who also happened to be the police officer in charge of the event, to come over. She still refused to let them down, so he kindly escorted her out into the lobby.

As we were leaving, he asked me if I wanted to press charges. I said no. At this point she started blowing up at him. He then told her she had two choices, leave the school or be locked up. She said she would calm down and go back in the gym, to which he said, "No, you will be leaving—now!"

She started yelling at him again, saying, "If I am leaving I want my money back."

He told her that wasn't going to happen, so she stormed out the door, slamming it behind her. What happened from there I did not want to know, but even though the game was pretty routine, I sure enjoyed the post-game excitement.

ALMOST A TECHNICAL KNOCKOUT

Also, as luck would have it—or not, as may be the case—I had the very same team the following week at Phoebus High School in Hampton. My father-in-law, who had never seen me referee, went to that game with my wife. You can imagine which side they were not going to sit on. This was also a locally televised game, so it was fun for all and especially me, as they gave each official a copy of the game tape.

The team from Phoebus was one of the strongest teams around and had one of the top players in the country. They were picked to win the state championship that year. She had already signed with the University of South Carolina and lived up to all of her expectations in the game.

Phoebus also had one of the most vocal coaches in the area, Mike Talon. We would later grow to admire each other's ability and knowledge of each other's craft.

I was working with two officials from the conference in which he played, so we needed a lengthy pregame to make sure our officiating mechanics were all on the same page. To help the officiating crew, during the pregame, we traditionally shared any tendencies we had observed about the team from each officials' area. They told me the Phoebus coach was very vocal and loved to yell at or try to intimidate the official. I told both my partners, "Not tonight."

From the time we tossed the ball he started on all of us with "Three seconds," or "Where is the foul or that's a travel."

After my fifth or sixth time down the court, I told the coach I had heard enough. I said, "You coach, and I will referee." That produced no positive results, so my next statement to the coach was one more outburst, and I was going to "T" him up.

I guess he didn't believe me, so I warned him once more. The very next time down the court I heard, "You have got to call a foul on that last play."

I stuck him with a technical foul. The funny thing about it was when I turned around to give him the technical foul I was looking dead into the camera. Man, was I styling and profiling.

Coach Talon approached me and asked what the "T" was for.

I explained to him that I had given him more warnings than normal, but I was trying to give him the benefit of the doubt since this was postseason playoff time.

Later in the quarter, one of his players got injured, and he came out on the court. While attending to her, he wanted to continue giving me pointers on things I might be missing. I asked him to take care of his player so that I would not have to issue him a second and disqualifying technical foul, which would mean his removal from the gym. I told him I also did not want to write an ejection report and I was sure he didn't want to explain the ejection to his principal on Monday morning. From that point forward, I did not hear a single word.

I did see him again at the state tournament, and he complimented me on that game. He apologized to me and said he had to try me and see if he could get in my head. For the next four years, every time he came to play one of the Southside teams, I seemed to be assigned to his game. Over the next several years, we developed a very close relationship. He loved having me work his games, and I loved working his games. We are still friends today.

SHE HAD NO SHOT AT WINNING

This is a short story, but a very memorable one. Mike Lester, Deborah Brinker, and I were selected to travel to Ashland, Virginia to work a state AAA quarterfinal on March 8, 2003. We had a great, back-and-forth game with two really good teams and quite a few three-point shots. Just like today's college games, it must have taken thirty minutes to play the last two minutes of the game. After every play, there was a timeout.

What made this game tough to call was the placement of the clocks on the scoreboards. They were hidden by either the baskets or the stands. Even though each official has certain responsibilities on shots, in this game, we had to come up with our own mechanics.

With twenty seconds to go, the home team was ahead by two points. The visiting team brought the ball up the court and put up a shot from the top of the key with five seconds to go. It missed and bounded into the corner. A player from the visiting team picked it up and threw up a last-second shot that didn't get out of her hands as the buzzer went off. SWISH, of course.

Since the shot was put up in front of the visitors' bench, they had a good look and, of course, thought the shot was good. They came running out on the court, thinking they had pulled off an upset. However, my partners, the scorer's table, and the home team saw me signaling the shot did not get off in time. Based on our positioning on the court, the last person who should have had clock responsibility was me, but somebody had to make the call. Oh, to have had instant replay in those days. But it was great that we had discussed this exact scenario in our pregame.

The coach argued briefly, but then said, "Great call." After an argument he needed to make, he said he also thought the horn came first. I knew he had to argue, at least for a moment, and he knew I had gotten the call right. We both did our jobs.

CON ARTIST REFS

Somewhere around the late '90s, Dennis Nixon and I were assigned to referee a game involving the top girls' team in the state, Lake Taylor in Norfolk.

As with every game, you get hecklers, just boo-birds or someone screaming at almost every single close call that goes against their team. Lake Taylor had one of the best teams that I ever experienced in my entire basketball officiating career. Anyway, there was this one guy who ranted nonstop all game, and for reasons unknown, always got there an hour and a half early. He was always in time to see the officials walk in.

One night, Nix and I decided to have some fun with him. The same police officers were usually assigned to work every home game, so on our next visit, prior to entering the gym, we asked two of the officers if they would go along with our prank. After explaining it to them, they were more than happy to oblige. They walked us in, conspicuously looking around like something important was going on.

As soon as we passed our mark he started in: "Not you two bums again. Oh, well, I will let you know if you get one right tonight, but I doubt it. Either way I paid good money to yell at you and I am going to get my money's worth."

After escorting us to the dressing room, the officers stationed themselves at each end of the gym, boxing things in, if you would.

About three minutes into the game I had an inbounds play right in front of him. No profanity, but he started calling me and my partner everything else in the book. The time was right to get our fun started. I edged closer to him, only two feet away, and told him softly that it was okay to yell at me, but my partner was on work release from Eastern State, the mental institution in Williamsburg, and even I never knew how he would react to someone yelling at him.

The fan half-whispered back saying, "I ought to tell the cops if he was that crazy."

Leaning over one more time, and even delaying the game slightly, I told the guy, "Hey, we're way ahead of you. See those police officers? They serve as his court-ordered escorts to and from the game."

To make it realistic, the police officers waited and escorted us out of the gym after the game. They always walk us to the door as a common courtesy, but the fan didn't know that. Just to sell the con even better, we had them walk us to our vehicle in the back of the school. We were the only ones allowed to park back there, so the guy had to think we were provided secure and separate parking.

Two weeks later, Nix and I were back at Lake Taylor, same officers, same deliberate walking into the gym with both officers at our shoulders. Two minutes into the game, I had a controversial foul call on a steal play. The coach called time and was more upset with his team than my call. But once the game stopped, my favorite fan started laying into me and didn't stop throughout the entire timeout. This time, my partner had to inbounds the ball and guess where it was? Right in front of the fan.

While waiting to inbounds the ball after the timeout, my partner pulled a role reversal. Just like I had two weeks before, he leaned over to the guy, who noticeably backed away. Even so, Nix told the fan he had been around a long time and he didn't mind him yelling at the officials, "But please don't yell at my partner over there across the floor." He told him I had just finished serving hard time for malicious wounding, that I carried a knife everywhere I went, and that I had violent tendencies when someone yelled at me.

The fan looked apoplectic, but Nix could sell you oceanfront property twenty miles offshore, so the fan now thought I was the crazy one. Silence finally prevailed, as the fan just didn't know which of us was more likely to go off. Finally, just as before, after the game we made sure the fan saw we again had the police escort us to the private parking area. I kept reaching in and out of my pocket, fingering what was supposed to be my blade, just for effect.

One week later, Nix and I had them one more time. This time, it was in the playoffs. On the way in, and this time without the police, we purposefully diverted from our usual path to the locker room and quickly walked right over to the fan. Again, this time the police were nowhere in sight. The look on the guy's face was absolutely priceless. As I reached out my closed hand he froze. I then opened my hand to shake his as we introduced ourselves and the police officers who made their entrance right on cue. We told him the whole truth and the look on his face changed from shock to embarrassment to, finally, fun.

True story, and it was all so good to play out. We talked for a few minutes, and then went in and got dressed. From that game on, he loved seeing us. He still yelled at us, but always told us "good game" on the way out.

AWARDS

During my thirty-nine years in the Eastern Officials Association I received six association awards that I will always treasure, plus one scholarship renaming.

The Bob Hood Award is for exceptional spirit and dedication to EOA baseball and the continual development of future umpires. I received that award on March 7, 1995.

The Lifetime Membership Award is in "Recognition of Outstanding and Meritorious Service." This award includes all sports, baseball, softball, football, swimming, and volleyball. In addition to the service and contribution components, one of the main criteria for this award is a minimum of thirty years of service to the association without any negative marks against you. This award was presented on March 1, 2003.

2003 LIFETIME MEMBER AWARD
WITH TYREE BROWN AND REN COLLIER

The Bullet Alexander Award, presented on March 1, 2009, is for exemplary contribution to EOA baseball and fellow umpires. This, along with the EOA Hall of Fame Award, are the two highest individual awards in the association. Bullet's award is probably my favorite, as very few have received it and because he was the one most responsible for mentoring and molding me into the umpire I became. It is also special for what he did for my son and all the other umpires in the Tidewater area.

On August 16, 2015, I was inducted into the EOA Officials Hall of Fame. The presentation was rewarding as it was given by "my guys." My successor as EOA commissioner, Chad Foltz, presented the award. The text of the presentation appears below.

Good evening. This evening it is my distinct pleasure to present the newest member of the EOA Hall of Fame. Election to the Hall of Fame is the zenith for recognition in our association. This evening's honoree has dedicated his officiating career to the advancement of EOA and its members for over five decades. The honor of his enshrinement should come as no surprise to the members of EOA and the baseball community.

Tonight's honoree began officiating baseball here in the Tidewater area as a member of the Virginia Beach Officials Association in 1972.

During this tenure with VBOA and EVOA this official umpired close to 5,500 total games, including 289 college, 756 scholastic, and over 4000 recreation.

Our honoree was selected to work eleven state playoff games, including one state AAA championship and one AA state championship game.

As a baseball member of EOA, tonight's honoree served as a Baseball Committee member from 1988-2004 and 2006–2014, an evaluator from 1989–2004 and again in 2015, as the baseball delegate for eight years, as baseball commissioner for another eight years, and on the EOA board of directors for a total of sixteen years.

As an umpire this individual has been honored with the Bob Hood Award in 1995, Lifetime Membership in 2003, and the Bullet Alexander Award in 2009.

During our honoree's term as commissioner, EOA Baseball saw dramatic increases in multiple areas. The number of officials increased from approximately ninety to more than 130; the number of games from approximately three thousand to almost seven thousand a year, and total officials' fees from roughly $300,000 to close to $750,000 a year.

Over his eight years as commissioner, our honoree assigned approximately fifty-four thousand games for the association, earning its umpires over $3.5 million in game fees.

In my fifteen years with the association, I have met no other individual with a love and dedication for EOA equal to that of our newest Hall of Famer.

Congratulations to the newest EOA Hall of Fame inductee, Mr. Jim Smith.

Also in 2015, after retirement, at our annual awards banquet I received a Bronze Statue for Outstanding Leadership as Baseball Commissioner.

On September 25, 2015, after returning from my retirement dream vacation in Hawaii, I received a call from Dr. Brian Matney, principal at Landstown High School, informing me I had been chosen to receive the 2015 Virginia High School League Regional Award of Merit—I was asked if my wife and I were free to come to their October 2015 Region Principals' Meeting. You can imagine it took me about five seconds to accept.

One more award I was very proud to receive was the renaming of a local league's annual baseball scholarship award. It is now called the Jim Smith Baseball Scholarship award and is presented each year to a deserving graduating senior that played baseball in their league.

2001 STATE OF VIRGINIA REGIONAL
AWARD OF MERIT SELECTION

2015 GREAT NECK BOYS BASEBALL RENAMED THEIR SCHOLARSHIP
AWARD TO THE JIM SMITH ANNUAL SCHOLARSHIP AWARD

CHAPTER 9

ACCOMPLISHMENTS

O n January 1, 2015, I stepped down as baseball commissioner and turned over the day-to-day operations of the association to a new commissioner. Making sure the association was in good hands when I stepped down was my number one priority. It was one of the hardest things I have ever had to do.

I knew the association would be in good hands, as the newly elected commissioner had been in the association for over fifteen years, had a good demeanor, and was a good umpire. All of the above are in the job description. During the last two years of my term, to ensure a smooth transition, he would spend time with me at my house. We would spend countless hours going over the many facets of the association and how I had managed them. For the previous four years, he also served as the baseball delegate and my go-to man for many association decisions. Two of the jobs I tasked him with were to create a new rules and mechanics manual for umpires and to take the lead on umpire promotions and rankings. To his credit and that of many others, we turned the association into one of the largest and strongest associations in the state of Virginia.

AM I REALLY THAT OLD?

As someone who had been devoted to and immersed in the sport of baseball for over sixty years, I was not sure how waking up and not having to deal with the constant stress of day-to-day baseball issues was going to be. After being retired for three years, I know it was the right decision. Retirement allows me to share more quality time with my wife, children, and grandchildren. It also allows me the freedom to go out and evaluate umpires at my leisure. Lastly, it allows me time to go see some of the MLB and minor league baseball games I have always wanted to see. What's more, my many friends in the game welcome me, if I don't talk too long, and no one has to worry about what I will assign for them to work.

HOW I WOULD LIKE TO BE REMEMBERED

I would like to be remembered for:

- Making the association a much stronger association than what I inherited.
- Earning respect from the officials for treating everyone equally, showing no favoritism toward any one official. I hope this was evident by the way I scheduled college and scholastic games as well as recreation and summer games in the latter part of the season.
- Whenever I brought someone before the Baseball Committee for disciplinary reasons, making sure it was done in a timely manner. I never let it linger and wanted it addressed promptly.
- Providing more in-depth training to help every umpire, which would, in turn, help them become better umpires.
- Initiating a useful and strong mentorship program.
- Using our local TV stations and newspapers to help promote the association.
- Strengthening our evaluation and ranking system.

- Helping our umpires continue to get more and better games.
- Getting out and constantly seeing our umpires work. My goal was to try and see each of our umpires work at least three different times each year. I liked being visible at game sites, but sometimes I also did not want to be seen, if I felt seeing me could make umpires nervous and either not perform to the best of their abilities or kick their work up a notch just because I was there.
- Repairing and strengthening the bonds between our association and all of our customers.
- Being phone and email accessible seven days a week, twenty-four hours a day throughout the baseball season.

To steal a quote from my good friend and fellow umpire Robert Turner, "If I can help or prevent any of the guys coming up from making the same mistakes I made, I will know I have done my job." Robert was and still is one of the best instructors the association has ever had. If I have accomplished these goals or even part of them, I will know all my time and efforts were worth it. What I will miss the most is the day-to-day interactions with our customers, coaches and most of all, the umpires.

WHAT'S AHEAD?

How do I plan on filling my days in this new chapter of my life?

- Traveling and relaxing at some of the resorts I have always wanted to visit.
- Visiting my grandchildren, both in and out of state, without having to worry about getting someone to run the day-to-day operations of the association. Even when I put someone in charge in the past, I would still get phone calls and emails and was never able to truly relax.

- Staying involved with the teaching, mentoring, observing, and evaluating of umpires.
- Going to MLB spring training every year. That's a dream that can now come true.
- Visiting as many of the MLB ballparks as possible.
- Learning and using more technology. This venture would include giving up my flip-phone and moving on to a smartphone! I am sure that will come as a shock to many.
- And, oh, yes, writing this book to share a lifetime in baseball as a player, parent, umpire, and commissioner.

2012 MY WIFE, LOU, AND GRANDSON,
CAMERON, AT HARBOR PARK

2013 BRAVES VS. NATIONALS—
QUALITY TIME WITH MY SON RYAN

CHAPTER 10

NOBODY DOES IT ALONE: REFLECTIONS FROM COMRADES

This section of the book means a lot to me as it contains reflections from my career that come from the hearts of those for whom I worked, those who worked with me, and those who worked for me as baseball commissioner. Also included are reminiscences from a prominent general manager in professional baseball, professional and local scouts, other outstanding umpires, and first and foremost, from my wife and children.

LOURDES [LOU] SMITH

Over the years I have watched Jim be a dedicated, passionate, and meticulous umpire. He possesses an immense knowledge of the sport as well as a boundless, pure love for the game. During his tenure as EOA commissioner, I listened to many conversations with new umpires, veteran umpires, league directors, and coaches. No doubt these conversations could run the gamut of emotions; however, the common thread was Jim's affinity to always listen to all viewpoints.

Jim's life path has been filled with countless opportunities to help others as a teacher, an umpire, and a mentor. He has always been enthusiastic to help others. The game of baseball (and umpiring) has also afforded him a multitude of faithful friendships which he holds very dear to his heart.

There is no doubt Jim loved being an umpire, but there were times when the hardships of umpiring life were overwhelming. During those times, Jim knew he could count on his family for strength, love, and joyful times. Jim's parents raised him with strong values that would frame him to be the devoted, generous, and loving husband, father, and grandfather he is today. I am deeply proud of all of his accomplishments. I LOVE YOU, #22!

ASHLEY CHALUPKA, MY OLDEST DAUGHTER

"What's it like to be the daughter of a successful umpire?" I don't know, I guess. What's it like to be the daughter of a teacher, or the daughter of an accountant? The umpire I knew was just my dad, working hard to provide for his family. I do have early memories of Tides' games, of grape-flavored Big League Chew and salty sunflower seeds. As a kid, if I was lucky, I was allowed to tag along to little-league baseball games, where I would hiss at overzealous fathers who heckled the man in blue, questioning his eyesight. And as the oldest child, I was often thrown in makeshift batting cages in the backyard, on the receiving end of Dad's pitches. Don't tell him this, but as I much as I complained about the baseball dirt and sticky August heat, I loved being out there with my dad, proving to him that girls can swing a bat too.

As I navigated my teen years (and my dad struggled with a little girl who was growing up before his very eyes), I discovered my own passion: volleyball. I played year-round, and when I wasn't playing for my high school varsity team, I was traveling with a Junior Olympic team based out of Tidewater. This meant many hours of practice each week, with games and competitions peppered in between. To hear my dad speak of this time in our lives, he will tell you he regrets not being able to make it to more of my games due to his umpiring commitments, but I remember those years quite differently. Putting on that volleyball uniform was a source of pride for me, and I never once questioned that watching me play was a source of pride for Dad. And so he was there, not on his baseball diamond, but on my volleyball court. Because he got it. My sport was important to me, and so it was important to him. While umpiring may have kept him away from the dinner table at times, it rarely kept him away from the volleyball court. He was there, right next to my mom . . . my biggest cheerleaders.

As I got older, I began to understand that all the time he spent away from home was more than just a job to him. It was an inevitable chapter in his lifelong love affair with the game. While I never shared his passion for cleats and home runs (minus those couple of years where I pretended to be invested in the Boston Red Sox for the sake of a college boyfriend), baseball was always a steady fixture in our lives.

When I was in college, Dad transitioned into the job of assigning umpires as the local commissioner. The hangers that once held multiple baby-blue umpiring polos and freshly-pressed gray umpiring pants in the back of his 1987 Toyota came down slowly as the amount of paperwork in his office began to multiply, seemingly overnight. My decidedly 1970s Dad took to the task of learning computer programs, networking, and expecting the very best out of each umpire who passed through his association. He ran clinics, cursed at the first threat of rain in the forecast, and spent countless hours recording and re-recording his outgoing voicemail message so that his umpires would know where to find him at all hours of the day. From those who were just calling to ask how far apart to space the green-bean seeds he gave us, those outgoing messages were often met with a big groan and an eye roll.

These days, he has handed over the reins to a new commissioner. He has gone from encouraging and shaping the talent of young, excited umpires to instilling love for the game in the most difficult of customers: his three-year-old grandson. You see, in the summer of 2013, Dad bought my son his very first t-ball set. I watched as he stood outside in the dirt in that same sticky August heat, while he patiently showed a new generation to place his pudgy little toddler hands on "this end of the baseball bat" and "not that end." I know it won't be long before I watch my son take my place in the batting cages with his Grandpa. I can see my little boy now, swimming in one of the many oversized Tides' jerseys that his Grandpa has so dutifully collected for him over the past few years . . . the ones that lay folded ever so carefully in his bottom dresser drawer, waiting for the day when they hang just above his knees instead of his ankles. That day will come, and with it, Dad's love affair with baseball will come full circle, the circle of life.

RYAN SMITH, MY SON AND AN UMPIRE [DID HE HAVE ANY CHOICE?]

Baseball has always been my life, ever since I was a kid. It was and is in my blood. My Dad never forced me to play a sport, but I always knew which one was at his heart, whether he knew it or not. I can remember back when I first played coach pitch and how excited I was to play in front of him. I was only eight years old, but from that moment on, I always strived to make my Pops proud.

As I got older, the fever of always wanting to hang around my dad grew stronger, as I knew he worked hard but never understood what he did. Through so many games, I would sit and watch him officiate basketball and umpire everything from "the little guys," as he called them, to the big boys of college Division 1. To be honest, all the games run together, but there was one thing that always remains constant in my mind and heart. The talks we had traveling to games are something that as a young boy growing up meant the most to me. I did not get to see my dad much because of how much he worked, between being a teacher and a basketball and baseball official, so the times in his four-runner were what I always looked forward to.

The one saying my dad told me when I was playing ball was, "Son, I do not care if you strike out as long as you do it swinging." This always made me laugh because I was not the best hitter in the world, so this happened quite a lot.

One thing I could count on, though, was that through all the jobs my dad had, he always came to every single game he could. Coming from a man who played baseball all the way up to the college level, all of his comments toward me were meant as motivation, to see me improve to the best I could be.

Now, there was one problem. Every game, he would sit in his camping chair on the right-field foul line fence and critique everything I did. This drove me crazy because all I wanted to do after a bad plate appearance was go out to my favorite position in right field and focus on the game. My dad, however, wanted to use the time in between innings to teach me how to correct my mistakes. I wanted no part of that, and so many times I would tell him, "Okay, Dad, I got it, now please, let me play." He never took too kindly to that, because most of the time, I did not say it with the kindest intentions. Looking back at it now, I loved every word he ever said to me to make me a better ball player. Just him being there made every game I played the best game.

Weirdly though, in the games he was not able to attend, I played better. In one Pony League game I was playing second base, and there was a towering pop-up. I started to backpedal, which you are never supposed to do. Had my dad seen it, he would have corrected me. Just as I got to the outfield grass, my foot caught a rock and I fell and blacked out for a second. When I came to, there was a crowd over me, including my coaches, teammates, umpires, and of course, my mom, who ran on the field like we all see moms do when their children are hurt.

My coach asked me, "Ryan, we have to know: did you catch the ball? Because no one had seen it."

From the pounding sensation in my head I thought I had missed it entirely and only my head had "caught it." Luckily, I mustered enough awareness to open my glove and there was the ball.

Now for the reason why that story was important to me and especially my dad. The glove I happened to be wearing was one I got signed by several players from the Norfolk Tides. I had been told not to play with the glove because some of the guys whose autographs on it could become famous big-league players. I wanted to wear it, though, because it exactly because it had real ballplayers' names on it and just because I thought I would make me play better. When my dad found out about it, I never heard the end of it. It was a dumb move on my part, but hey, I caught that pop-up, and my dad was happy about that part and only that part.

The most fun I had as a kid was not going to school or watching TV or playing video games. It was traveling with my dad to his games. There were times I had to fib about my homework being done just so I could hang out with my dad! Some of my fondest memories are traveling to Richmond or Williamsburg for a college baseball series and spending the night in a hotel. I thought it was the coolest thing. Sitting in the stands of a basketball gym or a baseball field I was always asked the same question by fans who had never seen me before. "Hey, son, who are you cheering for?" The shock on their faces was priceless when I said, "I'm here with the officials, and that's my dad down there."

As a young boy, I craved the post-game talks my dad

and his partners had in the parking lot after a ball game. For all I cared, they could have gone into the next day. I just loved sitting there and hearing the old war stories and how to better themselves as officials. I gained a lot of my friends from those long talks after games and meetings. Who would have thought my dad's worst habit—talking too much—would turn into one of the things I loved the most.

Some who are reading this know what happened to me when I was fifteen. Losing my eye in such a tragic accident would shatter most kids' dreams, but my dad is one of the strongest men I know, and he proved it during one of the most significant moments of my life. The first question I asked him was, "Am I done playing ball?"

He did not miss a beat and said, "Son we will figure that out later, but right now you have to adjust to your new life."

How can a one-eyed kid play baseball? Well, my dad used every person he knew to help me even as far as trying to switch me from a right-handed batter to a lefty. I tried, but it was not in the lineup for me to be a lefty. I gave baseball one final shot. I had one year of eligibility left in our recreation league and my dad as well as my family were my support system. He changed my hitting stance, and things worked. I had a great year, and some of the guys with whom I grew up playing ball were really inspired by the fact that I was playing baseball with one eye.

Once when I walked after a good, long at-bat, my dad called out from the right field fence, "Hey, Ryan, way to have a good eye."

After I hung my cleats up I grabbed another pair of shoes, umpiring shoes. My dad had always told me "When you are ready, son, you can come into umpiring." I started when he was in his second year as the commissioner of EOA. Talk about being nervous, whew man I had played a ton of exciting games, but nothing came close to transitioning into umpiring baseball. When I started I had one goal: be the best I could be and go as far as my God-given talents would allow me. I moved fairly quickly through the ranks, going from a level-six "newbie" to a level five which allowed me to work some recreation and AAU and as a fill-in middle school games in an emergency.

One day, while I was sitting in my room, I heard my dad in a panic. He walked to my room and said to grab my gear; I was heading to a game—now—because an umpire's partner did not show! Normally this would not have been a problem except for one thing: it was a middle school game, and I had never done a game that high before as a level five. My Dad asked me if I knew where Independence Middle School was and I said no. My dad got into his truck and told me to follow him. My nerves were shot, and I was not ready, but I told myself, *You are ready, and there is no time like the present.*

When I ran onto the field, to my shock, the entire crowd applauded me because now they had two umpires. I finished the game and sat down to hear my evaluation, and I did quite well, considering I sold the heck out of a call at first that was not even close, but in my nervous state, I punched that runner out and felt great. While my dad and partner were talking to me they sarcastically said, "Great call and mechanics on your call at first for a guy who was out by three feet!" I laughed, because to me, he was out by a matter of inches.

Through hundreds of games and evaluations, I obtained my goal of becoming a level-three varsity umpire. Most of my brothers in blue had reached this status with me and before me, but to me, it was extra special. When you work your way into becoming a varsity umpire in our association, you earn a number. Several guys pick their number for a variety of reasons: it was their high school number, it was the number their son/daughter wore playing sports, etc. My reason was simple: I wanted to inherit my dad's number 22. That number meant more than just the digits on the sleeve. It represented all the car rides and all the games and memories we spent together on a baseball field. It also stood for an amazing career, his career. All the state playoffs he was selected to work and college assignments that were such important memories in his mind would become mine.

Being the commissioner's son did not come with any perks. If anything, I was held to a higher standard because of all my father had accomplished on the field and what he was doing for the association as the head honcho. My dad did the same for me as he did for every other umpire; he put us in games chosen to make us successful. I worked my tail off to earn my right to wear his number. A son earning and wearing his father's number was something that had never happened in the entire forty-four-year history of the association. The day I received my letter that I had been promoted to a level three, my dad said it was one of the happiest days of his life, and he only had one other thing to say, "That number comes with a lot of honor and integrity; now don't mess it up." Every time I was assigned a game, I wore my #22 with pride, and of course, I knew it was an honor to wear it.

I now work full time in college athletics (no, not as an umpire). My dad has taught me so much about life, how to be a good man, the benefits of working hard for what you want, and most importantly how to be a loving, supportive man. My dad juggled so much for so many people in sports. However, what he always did foremost was make sure he was a husband to my mother and father to me and my sisters. That is something I always remember and strive to be every day of my life.

DAVE ROSENFIELD, AAA ADVISOR AND FORMER TIDES GM

The opportunity to observe someone who embodies virtually all the qualities needed to handle a large and complex job does not happen often in one's lifetime. Handling as many divergent personalities as Jim does on a continuing basis is of itself a major undertaking. But the job becomes even more difficult when he has to do the assignment as well as the evaluations of all these people who want to umpire baseball games.

Having made baseball schedules for professional baseball leagues for over fifty years, I can tell you that part of the task is both times consuming and often thankless, but the follow-up Jim has to do with the teams and leagues, as well as the umpires themselves must consume almost all of his waking hours. The proof of what he has accomplished is in the desire of all of his constituents for him to continue in his important role for a long, long time.

Beyond my observance of what he does, we have become great friends, both personally and professionally. When the International League umpires were not available due to a labor dispute, Jim provided us with the best he had to fill their positions, and he has been a great help to the Tides Baseball Club, through his contacts in assisting us to schedule numerous high school games in conjunction with our home schedule.

Above and beyond all the foregoing, he is a knowledgeable baseball man, honest and forthcoming, which provides the basis for many long and interesting conversations and a sound foundation for a lasting friendship.

Editor's Note: Dave Rosenfield passed away on February 28, 2017, during the editing of this book. His legacy in Hampton Roads baseball, including his service as general manager of the Tidewater and later Norfolk Tides for forty-eight years, and his lifetime of impact on the game will likely never be matched and certainly will never be forgotten.

BRYAN CAVE, HEAD BASEBALL COACH AT THE APPRENTICE SCHOOL

As a college coach, my favorite television program during the season is The Weather Channel. My most dialed phone number during this time would be the person assigning game umpires, one Jim Smith. Not only does the weather change hourly in this area during the season, Jim and I have found there is also a great difference in the weather between the Southside (where most of his umpires work and live) and the Peninsula where we play our home games (War Memorial

Stadium in Hampton). There were many times I was on the phone with Jim and his umpires said there was no need to take off work and go to the stadium because it was pouring rain, and I was trying to convince Jim that the sun was out at the stadium and beautiful. It also worked in reverse, where Jim was telling me it was gorgeous on the Southside, and I was telling him our field was underwater and unplayable.

One key component of Jim's and my relationship was flexibility. Due to the fact that a lot of my opponents were from out of state and were usually already in the area ready to play, instead of outright canceling a game, I would normally postpone it until later in the day. There were days when I would start calling Jim in the morning to reschedule a game from a 1 PM start, and after talking a dozen times, we would finally start that game at 7 or 8 PM that night, depending on weather forecast, working to preserve a dry field, putting the tarp on and off the field, etc. This is not even mentioning when snow would come into the area and I had players shoveling snow, as I kept Jim abreast of field conditions hourly.

One of Jim's biggest challenges was my annual tournament in February where I play approximately fifteen games in three and a half days at one location. Jim's patience was tested several times, as he had to provide umpires for the entire tournament, with some games not completing until 3 AM and Jim having to supply umpires for next day's slate of games which normally started at 8 AM.

All said, it is amazing that after all these challenges over the years, and sometimes we certainly disagreed, and at times, he had to just tell me "NO," he could not support me (which was rare), we remain good friends to this day. I really admire his organizational skills and, in particular, his communication skills. As it is widely known, most baseball coaches are always right, are hard-headed, and do not like being told they cannot do something. Although Jim normally dealt with coaches in a stressful situation when emotions were usually high, he handled these situations in a very professional manner, and remains a very respected member of the local baseball community.

JIM FARR, HEAD COLLEGE BASEBALL COACH AND PROFESSIONAL SCOUT

During my years that I coached college baseball at ODU (four years) and William and Mary (thirteen years), I had many games that Jim Smith umpired. He was always very professional on the field. He was not like all umpires, in that you could discuss or argue a call on a reasonable level during the game without him getting the so-called "red ass" if you questioned one of his calls. During these years, there is one situation that stands out to me and makes me chuckle when I recall the game.

The game was the first game ever played at Plumeri Park in Williamsburg against Penn State, which happened to be where I had played college baseball as well prior to going to ODU. Thus it was a big game in a number of ways to me. The game was a tightly played contest on a cold and breezy day in late March of 1998 before a crowd of one thousand plus. The situation that arose during the game concerned the new DH rule, which the NCAA had put into effect that season. How to implement it had created a lot of uncertainty on the parts of coaches as well as umpires. The rule involved the replacement of the DH and the pitcher. If your pitcher was also the DH, this made the rule more confusing to many.

On this day my starting pitcher, Randy Leek, was also my DH; thus, we had a nine-man line-up. As Leek tired on the mound, I removed him from pitching and sent him to play LF. (Leek was also my starting LF when he was not pitching.) Robert Jones relieved Leek and now would be slated to hit in the original left-fielder's slot in the lineup who started the game, thus making it a nine-man line-up. The rule said that when a DH enters the game, you lose the DH for the remainder of the game. However, when I put Leek in LF, I moved my left-fielder to RF, thus constituting a double switch (this is a move that is very often used in the National League) and was able to hit Jones in a higher spot in the lineup and get him to the plate the next inning. Robert Jones was one of our top left-handed hitters, and with the wind blowing out to RF that day I wanted to get him to the plate as soon as possible.

This move caused a tremendous amount of confusion not only in the Penn State dugout, but also in the umpiring crew that day of Rich Humphrey and Jim Smith. There was a lengthy discussion at the time of the change between coaches and umpires . . . when all was said and done, the move was allowed, and the game continued on. Jones was the fourth hitter in the next inning and proceeded to hit a three-run home run that ended up being the game-winner.

GARY SPEDDEN, GRASSFIELD HIGH BASEBALL COACH

I am entering my twenty-eighth season as a varsity baseball coach in Virginia. I first met Jim Smith as an umpire in the regional tournament in the late 1980s to early 1990s, as I was coaching at Lafayette HS in Williamsburg. In 1993, I began coaching in Virginia Beach, and had the pleasure to work with Jim as an umpire and then as commissioner for twenty-two years (two years at Green Run and twenty at Ocean Lakes).

As an umpire, Jim always treated you with respect and was willing to listen to your concerns. He was a gentleman and a professional. I felt good when I arrived at the field and saw he was doing our games.

As a commissioner, he was again prepared and professional. He was always in attendance at our yearly preseason district meetings to help us address any issues or concerns for the upcoming season. You could call Jim and talk to him if/when there were problems or concerns about a particular game, situation, or official.

A couple of years ago, a job opportunity came open outside of coaching. It was an intriguing opportunity that would let me stay in athletics in a different aspect. I felt that a key consideration in this new position would be one's ability to handle tough situations in a respectful and thoughtful manner. Knowing our relationship over the past twenty-five or so years, I reached out to Jim for a letter of recommendation. I felt that his reputation as commissioner would carry weight and a letter from him would help my candidacy. He was willing to write one for me, and I appreciated it greatly. Although I didn't get the opportunity, his willingness to do this again shows his willingness to go above and beyond.

When Jim made the decision to step down as commissioner, we spoke again by phone. As usual, I felt like I gained from the conversation. He was more than an umpire or a commissioner. He is an ambassador for the game and its great people. I count myself fortunate to have worked with him in the game that we both love.

PETE ZELL, HEAD BASEBALL COACH AT SALEM AND OCEAN LAKES HIGH SCHOOL

Having coached for twenty-two years, in games in areas all over the country, you get to see different umpire organizations and how they handle things. The thing that really stands out to me about the association that Jim has helped to mold; I would not trade it for the world. Jim has created a group of professionals who are great to work with, easy to talk to, and most of all do a great job for the game of baseball itself.

Jim has/was/is always trying to help people do the right thing for the game, his umpires, and especially the players. Jim is a hard-working, blue-collar guy who knows where his roots came from and never seemed to forget this when he became commissioner.

When Jim took over the Umpires' Association, it was a group that was always at odds with players, parents, and coaches. Jim brought a new attitude, a fresh start to the top of this group, and in particular he did so with his great people skills. He can "work a room" with the best of them, and he can do so being real. He's confident and the same guy, day in and day out. He has a great attitude toward life and it is infectious to the people around him.

Jim has always been at coaches' meetings advocating for the game, telling us the changes that his umpires have been instructed to make and the impact these changes would have on the game. He always went out of his way to make sure the coaches knew exactly what was coming up in the near future, how the new rule changes or other items would affect the game, and how they would affect the coaches. Jim was the consummate professional, and we respected him tremendously for this. Jim's personality and professionalism permeate the Umpires' Association now, and he has created a group of professionals and an organization that works together with players, coaches, and even spectators and fans to make the game of baseball a better game.

NORBIE WILSON, FORMER HEAD BASEBALL COACH AT FIRST COLONIAL AND PROFESSIONAL SCOUT

I taught and coached at First Colonial High School in Virginia Beach, VA, for forty-three years—twenty-six of those years as head baseball coach. Our team won numerous district and regional championships, including a state championship in 1993 when we went 28-0. In 2009, I stepped down as head baseball coach at FCHS and went on to start a successful baseball program for two years at College of The Albemarle in Elizabeth City, NC, before finally retiring from coaching in 2011.

During all those years as a head high school baseball coach in Virginia Beach, it was my pleasure—and sometimes my pain—to have Jim Smith serve as umpire for many of my games. We had a good coach/umpire relationship that developed into a strong friendship based on mutual respect and a love of the game.

Jim and I used to rib each other about our college choices—I went to Atlantic Christian College in Wilson, NC, where I played basketball for two years, while Jim played baseball at East Carolina University in Greenville, NC. The two schools were only about forty miles apart, and the close proximity of the schools served as fodder for a long-running jab-fest. Jim often referred to Atlantic Christian as the "Bible School" and I would say that was better than going to "ECTC"—a reference to East Carolina University's early years as a teacher's college. Jim's comeback was that at least he played a real sport instead of just bouncing a ball.

As a coach, I was very passionate about winning. Jim would call that being hard-headed and high-strung. One of the bad things about being friends was that he knew a lot about me. His favorite expression to keep me from being tossed in a game was "Norbie! Do I need to call your wife Candy tonight and tell her you were acting like an ass?" I have to say, that helped me curb my behavior, at least some of the time.

SCOTT STUBBE, HEAD COACH FIRST COLONIAL HIGH SCHOOL, FORMER CATCHER AT BAYSIDE HIGH SCHOOL

I have known Jim Smith as an umpire and commissioner for over twenty-five years. During that time, I was a player, assistant coach, and head coach at local schools in the area. In addition, I remember his wife teaching at the elementary school I attended. I did not know him at that time, but I do remember my mother speaking highly of his wife . . . she worked with her at the time as well. I wouldn't make the connection between Jim and his wife for years to come.

When I became a varsity coach, I began to know Jim on various levels. Of course, I knew him on the field, but I also worked with him as a field director in tournaments and as the commissioner of our league when he stopped umpiring on the field. When I was coaching and Jim was an umpire on the field, he was very consistent and skilled. He knew the rules, but he also knew the nuances of the game, which made him better than most umpires. These abilities gave him confidence on the field. Sometimes he was stubborn about that confidence. When games were going my way, that confidence seemed to always work in my favor, but of course, when a game did not seem to go my way, that confidence could be frustrating. However, the confidence never wavered . . . this is what made him an excellent umpire. In addition, he would admit a mistake, but those mistakes were not made often.

When I was working with him in tournaments, I could see his ability on the field. These tournaments are sometimes coached by overzealous parents . . . as a result, they become a bit passionate. That passion often led to arguments with umpires . . . I remember Jim tossing out a coach or two during these tournaments because of their lack of professionalism. In high school games, that rarely occurred with Jim because of the mutual respect and professionalism between him and the coaches.

Finally, for the past seven or eight years, I have had the privilege of working with Jim as the commissioner. Although his job is to support his association and his umpires, he was always willing to listen to me or other coaches about concerns, compliments, or suggestions for improvement. I do believe those conversations resulted in improvements or adjustments on the field. Jim did an excellent job as an umpire and as commissioner during his tenure. He has had a positive influence on my coaching career, and the coaches in this area will miss him.

JAMES FOWLER, BASEBALL UMPIRE

I've been an official with EOA for over twenty years. Jim has been a friend, brother, and mentor throughout my career. I want to share some of our experiences and adventures along the way.

When I was a young umpire, he was my mentor. My wife would always say that she knew when Jim had evaluated me because I would get home later than normal. Jim, being the facilitator that he is, is very thorough. He could write a book on me. I've learned so much from him.

Jim always had a collection of uniforms when he was officiating. We would laugh at the number he always had in his car. Understand, Jim officiated both basketball and baseball. He would have separate uniforms in his car for high school games, college games, recreation games for grass fields, and recreation games for dirty or muddy fields. He also had separate jackets for each. Add the basketball uniforms in and it looked like a clothing store.

Rainy days are the worst. The "R" word as we call it ruins hours of intricate scheduling. I was at Jim's hose quite often on rain days. We might start talking about the schedule, and the phone would begin to ring. It always seemed like every phone in the house was ringing. This went on for hours. It was amazing to watch a perfectionist at work, answering the phone, taking down notes, and canceling games on the computer, all at one time.

Turnbacks. This was a sensitive topic of conversation with Jim and understandably so. He felt most turnbacks were due to a lack of planning. Turnbacks for deaths or illness never bothered him. Family was always first with him. Taking care of and providing for the family was something he felt very strongly about.

When he first took over he said, "I may be the boss, but the association is now going to become a close-knit family." He lived up to that expectation, not only for himself, but for all of us. He always made sure we knew about hospital trips, deaths, and births.

The eight years Jim was commissioner was a time of putting out fires, trying to please or take care of 150 different personalities, and making sure we had the best working conditions and instruction available. I salute him for a job well done. We are better for having Jim as our Commish.

RUDY RICE, BASEBALL UMPIRE

I have been officiating twenty-five-plus years, with the majority of those years in football. In 2008, I was thinking about trying my hand at umpiring baseball. I knew the name "Jim Smith" because officiating is like a family, and even though I did not officiate baseball or basketball I knew his name from talking to other officials. I made a call to Jim, told him my name, and Jim told me I had missed some of their training classes for new umpires, but if I would come to the remaining classes, the meetings and scrimmages I could start in the spring.

To my surprise, Jim Smith, the commissioner, was at every training class I attended. Again, I have been involved in many officiating associations, but never had the commissioner been at all the training meetings. I don't mean he was at these meetings because the association required it, but instead he was at these meetings because he wanted to be at these meetings. He let the instructors teach the rules and mechanics, and he would only add information if asked. I learned very quickly he was at these meetings because he truly cared about us, the new umpires, learning and carrying on the tradition of EOA..

Jim would always tell the new umpires, as well as the veteran umpires, that you never know when he might show up to watch and evaluate you at one of your games. I thought this was a statement like every commissioner in every sport makes to ensure that you would always give your best and that certainly a first-year official at a recreation league game would not be on his radar as far as who he wanted to see. Then, on a cold weekday evening in April of 2008, I was assigned a game at Fleet Park. This field is off the beaten path, and I certainly never would expect to see an evaluator, much less Jim Smith, at this field.

I am working the plate this cold evening, and my partner, another first-year umpire, is working the bases. I believe we are in the fourth inning and the game has gone very well when the batter hits a foul ball between the first baseline and dugout which is obviously going to be foul, but as I had been taught I waited, and when the first baseman comes toward the dugout and fields the foul ground ball I call "foul."

Behind the backstop I hear a voice that says, "Nice job not calling that ball foul too early." I return to my position behind the plate, and there stands Jim Smith in his winter coat, gloves, and hat. I wanted to relay this story because again this showed me how much dedication this man has for this game and how he has done everything in his power to make sure we, his umpires, were doing the things we were taught.

BOB BARRY, BASEBALL UMPIRE

Some people are said to have been given the gift of gab. Our baseball commissioner, Jim Smith, managed to get the whole store. Just ask him. Well, that might not be such a good idea, because anything that gets Jim started talking can be hazardous to your health, that is if you age at the same rate as normal humans. I swear, I started a conversation with Jim one time when I was 32, and it wasn't over until I was 34. Okay, that might be a bit of an exaggeration, but you get my point.

The Conversational Commissioner, as I call him, has never met a person or a discussion he didn't like. Jim will walk up to two umpires who are talking softly, and soon the volume is turned up and laughs are likely being exchanged all around. The triangle of talk soon becomes a circle of communication, which could be about a good or blown call, a coach with too much of his own to say, or anything else about which the Commish wishes to comment.

You see, we are a captive audience. Anyone who wants to umpire a baseball game in our area is a prisoner of Jim's preaching. You can't just walk away, 'cause you might offend him, although admittedly that's hard to do. You can shuffle your feet, maybe stifle a yawn, or cut your eyes in another direction, but none of that works. It doesn't stop Jim from pontificating on whatever point piques his interest.

I do have a secret weapon or two, though I have never used them. The easiest way to shake free is to indicate acute indigestion. My failsafe technique is to pre-program a cell call from my wife for a certain time. If I am still stuck in a conversation after the stated time, the phone will ring; I will feign an emergency, and I'm outta there, faster than the number nine batter on strike three.

Now you might assume there's an exception to the above for arguments with coaches. Not so. During Jim's long career as an umpire he never cut off an argument; he extended them. Sure, the coach was finished with his gripe long before he returned to the dugout, but you see, Jim has some secret weapons of his own. If he just talks that angry coach to death, one of two things will happen, and they're both good. The coach is much less likely to come out and argue the next time there's a close one, or after a while, Jim will have talked him into meeting for a beverage later that evening. Works like magic.

I have to admit I am a lawyer, and as such, I have been accused, wrongfully of course, of acting like I get paid by the word. Well, anyone who ever thought that of lawyers has never met Jim Smith. This guy has an incredible talent for letting you know something that can be said in one minute in, oh, about twenty. Of course it's not that he needed twenty minutes to get his point across; he just likes to hear himself say it twenty times. Perhaps I exaggerate, but I can confidently state that I grasp most of what Jim has to say on the tenth or eleventh repetition. To borrow a phrase once pronounced by Winston Churchill, an orator almost the equal of Jim, "Never has so much been said by so few that meant so little."

I close with my own very personal Jim Smith memoir. He and I started officiating at about the same time in baseball and basketball. It was a very long time ago, not much past the two-thirds post of the last century, make that millennium. After parts of four decades of juggling a law practice, family and officiating, I had reluctantly decided to give it up. Well, more precisely, my lovely wife decided that for me. Goodbye, ball field; whoa to my well-chewed whistle. Home was I at a decent hour without stinky laundry, black and blue bruises, sore feet, or pulled muscles. Sixteen seasons went by without a rhubarb or calling a technical. Not all that bad, come to think of it, but then I chanced to see my old friend Jim.

We met at an awards banquet, and I suddenly was defenseless and all his once again. It was like no time had passed. He had taken over as commissioner of our baseball program, and no spousal, pre-planned rescue call could save me. An hour of cajoling later (or was it two?), I was coerced into making a search for my mislaid mask, shaking off my sooty shin guards, and relearning the mechanics and customs of the Eastern Officials Association, some thirty-nine years after I had begun umpiring for that organization in the then-mandatory black sport coat and stiff white button-up shirt with a skinny black tie. That was ten years ago, and now, as I get ready for my next baseball season, exactly fifty years after I started, I realize that Jim Smith has been the constant, the guide, and in a very real sense, the reason I am still at it. He just kept talking that evening ten winters ago, and he wouldn't stop, wouldn't take no for an answer. So thanks, Jim; I am much better off for having refereed with you, having umpired with you, having laughed with you, even having argued with you, but most of all for having just listened to you.

THE LATE BOB CAMPBELL, LIFELONG UMPIRE, ASSIGNER, EVALUATOR, INSTRUCTOR

It as an honor to be asked to submit some of my memories. I started umpiring with Jim way back in 1979. Most of the games I worked with him are hard to remember since nothing occurred out of the ordinary. We worked our game{s} and afterward had a few libations and talked and talked, enjoying our time together. This was the way of EVOA. Work your game and socialize. We were one big family.

In 2006, Jim became the EVOA baseball commissioner. He held that position for eight years, longer than any other baseball commissioner EVOA has ever had. During his term, he more than doubled the membership of baseball officials, more than doubled the number of games available, and more than doubled the money earned by the officials. His dedication to the officials was outstanding. He ensured that all of them had the opportunity to be evaluated, which is a requirement to be advanced in our association.

I was fortunate enough to be assigned by him to be the head of the evaluation committee. During my tenure at this position, Jim constantly provided input, making my job a lot easier. His recordkeeping and attention to detail made our association what it is today. We spent many a night on the phone talking for hours about baseball, and those memories I will treasure forever.

RICHARD RUCKA, UMPIRE

Jim is very organized and a type-A person. He hates laziness and for people to dress sloppily or be late. He sets up monthly meetings and is up front about fining umpires who show up late to those meetings.

If you ever talk to him about baseball, you soon find out that baseball and umpiring are his true passions. Jim also loves to talk, except during the time when games are getting canceled due to rain.

Jim also loves to watch/evaluate umpires. He understands how to develop them, as evidenced by the way he schedules them. He frequently schedules new umpires to work with veterans. One of the favorite places he likes to schedule them is at the Great Neck Boys Baseball complex. This way, he can watch three games and six umpires at one time. Quite often, he will schedule two sets of umpires there so he can see twelve umpires in one day. They also feed him there, which he doesn't refuse.

The one thing about Jim is you never know where he will show up. So we always need to be ready and at our best. He always tells us he doesn't know where he will go to observe. It just depends on whether the light is green or red at the end of the street. Thinking he won't drive a hundred miles to go see a game has gotten some umpires in trouble. If you think you have the worst game in town that day and so he won't show up, think again.

Jim Smith loves to eat wings. When he decided to step down as commissioner, the EOA umpires decided to gather together for two nights as he was finishing up his term and let him know how much he was appreciated. There were a lot of surprise guests to help celebrate his retirement as EOA commissioner. There were about forty umpires/coaches who attended the get together each night.

MANNIE SURRETT, UMPIRE

Working with Jim Smith over the past five years has been an excellent learning experience. As the game assigner, Jim would always be willing to work with your schedule in order to maximize the association's ability to meet the customer demands.

He understood the value of family and respected each umpire when family situations arose and you were unable to meet your obligation. I remember I was assigned a Pony doubleheader in Western Branch one Saturda,y and my wife received an unexpected call to report to a military function. I immediately called Jim about two hours before game time and explained the situation and asked to be removed from the game. Although it was at the last minute, Jim removed me from the game, did not count it against me, and found another umpire to fulfill the obligation. Honesty is what Jim demands and nothing less.

One of the fine attributes Jim displayed as the baseball commissioner is his ability to reach out to each of the association customers on a regular basis. I have not seen another commissioner of any sport that is more engaged and travels to every site for which the association is responsible. Jim makes site visits and provides instructional critique to umpires during live play. It does not matter if you are a first year or twenty-year veteran, Jim would always utilize his forty-plus years of experience to educate you on the game, whether it was your timing, missed rotation, strike zone, or your position in the field of play.

Jim was a fair-handed commissioner. He often threatened to fine umpires for turning back games but always found it in his heart not to take action. His decision often came from his forty-plus years of baseball experience because he understood real-life situations do happen.

I remember my third year as an umpire I wanted to be awarded my number as a level-three umpire, but unfortunately the Evaluation Committee did not promote me that year. Jim said, "Mannie, you are one of our best and brightest new umpires, but do not take it to heart. Just continue to work hard, and I will see that you get promoted."

I did the things he instructed me to do, and indeed I was promoted. His leadership and ability to help you understand will be missed. Under his leadership the association has grown by leaps and bounds. The training program he put together with his fellow board members is the best in the area. The association has gained a reputation for being the best around, and other schools and youth leagues have requested our services under his leadership. Still, he maintained the business posture of knowing how much he could bite off and still provide outstanding services. He never allowed the lure of better financial contracts to influence his decision on providing good service. Jim was a realist and knew what he could provide to his customers even though that sometimes went against some person's wishes, and that is true leadership.

ROQUE AGUON, UMPIRE

I was seventeen years old, just barely the minimum age to umpire with EVOA. I had played baseball since I was five and was interested in umpiring, but I knew nothing about how to become an umpire. My baseball coach gave me Jim's name and number as an umpire contact.

I talked with my mom about umpiring and she called Jim

Smith to get some more information. By the time she got off the phone with Jim, she was so excited about me umpiring, and this was due to Jim's enthusiasm and love for it. Jim was excited to hear that I was a young man and was interested in umpiring. He explained the process of training required, as well as the dedication it was going to take.

I met Jim at the first umpire meeting of the season, and at that point, I was sold. It was obvious that Jim not only loved umpiring but took it very seriously. I knew right away that I had to work hard to learn all the rules and mechanics, as Jim sets a very high bar. Jim was very strict and supportive at the same time. It seemed like he put a little extra effort into me because he knew that I was going to be challenged on the field due to my age. Don't get me wrong; he never let me get away with not knowing a rule or proper mechanic, but he gave me extra encouragement and advice to help me succeed as an umpire.

I am in my fourth year of umpiring now, and I honestly feel I am a better umpire because of Jim. I don't think he saw my young age is a disadvantage, which I really appreciate. I put all my effort into learning the game and in turn, Jim encouraged me and pushed me so that I would be successful. He complimented me when I did well and he definitely let me know when I didn't. But either way, it always made me want to try harder and do better.

One of the things I really enjoyed about our classroom instruction was that Jim was always trying to trick me as well as the others in the class. He would give us a rule, lead us down a path that may be the right or wrong one, and then challenge us to defend it. I was one of the few umpires whom he could never trick, but that was because I was always reading the rulebook and doing my homework. I always remember him saying, "Do you want to bet me on it?" I would always say no, but boy, did he make you wonder.

RICH HUMPHREY, FORMER PROFESSIONAL UMPIRE

I joined EVOA in 1987, and that is when I first met Jim Smith. As a quick background, I began my officiating career at the age of thirteen and was fortunate enough to become a professional umpire for eleven years, two years part-time in the American League.

Even though I had umpired professionally, I still considered myself just another umpire. Jim Smith was one of the first umpires I met in EVOA, and at times I felt Jim was impressed by my background and wanted to associate himself with me even more than every other umpire. Honestly, not what I really wanted at the time.

As I got to know Jim better, I saw an umpire who was extremely dedicated, passionate, and committed to his profession and one who wanted to get better at his craft. He was in the top five or ten rated umpires in the association at the time, and only wanted to get better by attending every clinic and always asking questions. Not only was he a baseball umpire, but also a basketball official. I think this helped him in many ways in learning how to manage games.

One of the things I always noticed with many umpires was that they would know the rules, but not know how to apply common sense when applying the rule. I taught umpires not to use the rulebook as a Bible, just a guide. I was the first to admit I did not fully know all the rules. Case in point, working over two thousand professional games with their DH was not the same as knowing the collegiate and high school DH rule.

You can imagine how confused I was when the situation came up at William and Mary during a game I was working with Jim. Jimmy Farr, coach of William and Mary, was the master of switching the DH around. They were playing Penn State, and Coach Farr came out to make his DH change, which made no sense to me. Because I was still interpreting the rule from a professional stance, I called Jim down to assist me. Thankfully, Jim was diligent enough with the rules. He also had his cheat card which covered all the possible scenarios with the DH. He was able to get me out of the situation. He, along with Coach Farr, even went further and explained the rule to the Penn State coach, which took a lot of doing.

When I joined the association, Jim had a nickname of "Smooch." This term is a somewhat polite name for an umpire who would always go out of their way to be nice to the coaches, ballplayers, etc. Among umpires it is not considered to be a compliment. However, I did not see a lot of evidence of Jim being a smooch. What I observed was an umpire who had figured out that umpiring was more than balls and strikes, outs and safes. It was about getting along with people and getting them to respect and like you, thereby making your job easier on the ball field. Jim's approach was much different from some of the prior leadership, who felt you should not even talk to players or coaches. Because Jim was good at this, he was able to avoid an argument.

I was head of the Baseball Committee, which was in charge of evaluations, clinics, etc. Jim was a very valuable asset and member of the group, and his opinions were always without bias. He positioned himself in line for the commissioner job when it became available and led the association through some very difficult times to where it is extremely successful today, in large part because of his time and efforts.

Eleven years ago, I founded a memorial golf tournament in memory of one of the boys I coached in 2002. Jim has played a huge part in the success of the event. His monetary contributions are only a small part of what he does for the event. For the time he served as commissioner, he arranged clinics to help support the event. Even though Jim is not a golfer and never had to be there, he was always there, helping me out on the sixteenth hole.

JEFFERY NEARY, UMPIRE

I first talked to Jim Smith on a random day in November of 2012. I was interested in getting into umpiring, and after looking at the EOA website, I wanted to ask him how I would go about getting started. I was too late to start that fall, and after I explained to him my love for the game and how I just wanted to be on the field again, I noticed he had a similar passion. He loves the game's every aspect, and it was apparent he cares a great deal for the umpires in the organization. The phone conversation lasted about twenty minutes, and it was the first time I ever talked to him! He is a straightforward, honest, and non-dismissive kind of person. It was clear that I called the right organization.

When January of next year rolled around and the training clinics started, he was at every single one.

After about three months the classes were over, and I started getting games assigned to me. It's obvious to me he really wants me to improve my game (as an official), and my willingness to learn really benefited our relationship. He often does travel to different sites to watch the product we're putting on the field. I was in my first season when he saw me umpire for the first time. That game changed everything. After the game he came up to me and my partner and suggested that a good official must both play the part and look the part. He explained that when we get lazy on the field it makes a bad perception in the eyes of the coaches and fans. Also, when he sees laziness it affects his assigning. A bell rang in my head, and it was apparent that hustling and being completely involved makes you not only look better, but actually call a better game.

In the second mandatory session of training clinics (we're now in the fall), I kept learning, and he kept giving me opportunities to get not only more games but higher-level games under my belt. He goes out nearly every weekday and certainly every weekend to watch everyone work. He does this not because he has to, but because he wants to see where everyone stands as far as officiating skill. He could watch me work for a mere four innings and provide excellent insight to help me improve not only my positioning but subtle mechanics that only a veteran would know.

My fiancée, at the time, came to a lot of my games, as did

Jim, and he would literally sit next to her and help her help me, he would make her get a notepad out and take notes! It's funny and serious at the same time, and it does help. Again, this is not something he has to do. It is great to know that while I'm out there, there are people on the sidelines not rooting for a team but observing me and genuinely taking an interest to help me be the best I can.

In the second fall of umpiring I realized how much of a brotherhood our organization is, and it defines who Jim really is. My own brother was in a near-fatal car accident, and there was a week and a half where the doctors couldn't even tell if he would survive. Without prying, he asked about the situation and let me know that if I needed time off from a game, he would find someone to cover (not easy to do on short notice). This shows how much he is willing to help out our officials. I ended up keeping the games, and it was a good way for me to keep my mind off the current situation with my brother. He came to the game to support me and told me if there was anything I needed, he would help out. The overwhelming support I received from everyone in EVOA opened me up to this fraternity that he molded.

STEVE KANTER, UMPIRE

A little over seven years ago, I was coaching my oldest son's Mustang baseball team during the spring together with Mike Dejaeger. During that time, I always struck up conversations with several of the umpires working our games. Immediately, the gears in my brain started to spin, and I began to think how interesting it would be if I could be an umpire. In the middle of this game, Mike pointed me in the direction if a gentleman who Mike said was "in charge" of all the baseball officials. I introduced myself to the man named Jim and told him I was interested in umpiring.

Within the next couple months, Jim Smith had emailed me the information about the upcoming umpire class, and I jumped in with both feet! During the umpire classes that winter, I then started to become friends with Jim and enjoyed his jovial manner. It was comical to watch Jim with his Bluetooth microphone/earpiece always, and I mean always, tucked into his ear. I always thought to myself, "What clown thinks he is more important than everybody else and would wear that in their ear constantly?" I later came to find out just how many calls he really got each day.

My first season, for whatever reason, Jim assigned me games as a new umpire that were normally given to more experienced second- and third-year officials. When Jim would watch me in these games, he would always give me criticism and never say anything positive about how well I was doing. He constantly wanted me to strive for excellence and always be in the absolutely correct position every time during every play or potential play. Jim knew I wasn't a "yes man." My personality, for lack of a better description, clashed with many of the guys in the group. Jim saw the potential in me but had to routinely remind me about staying under the radar. However, this tension sometimes got under Jim's skin too, and I knew I had better listen to someone who had been where I wanted to go.

Yes, I did some things that irritated Jim and some of the other leaders of the association. What I thought were minor incidents eventually would bring me before the Baseball Committee for discipline. I was suspended. The other members of the Committee wanted to remove me from the association. However, Jim saw the good in me and asked the other Committee members to allow him to give me a stern lecture and one last chance. Jim stuck his neck out for me and for any other umpire when they deserved his support. It seemed like Jim was constantly on my case, yet he would never raise his voice. Every time there was a conflict, there would be a peaceful resolution.

Jim has a great heart for people and, of course, for umpires. He works very hard to help his umpires excel.

KRIS DENSON, BASKETBALL OFFICIAL

Jim assigns and teaches in a style that is in the best interest of the official. He is far from a self-booster, nor did he take advantage of his position as an assigner.

As a rookie and a woman in a male-dominated field, I found he would stick up for me with veteran officials, i.e., not let one put me down or let them get away with saying he's over his head putting me in advanced games. He would push to make sure promising rookie officials got a fair chance to make top fees, work fun tournaments, convenient games, or challenging games.

Jimmy was a protector of what sometimes could be a "dog-eat-dog" world of officiating. For some veterans, instead of a quick mirror check, it was, "Boo-hoo for me because this rookie and that rookie are getting more court time than ME or better games than ME." There was no one else I knew better than Jimmy who would respectfully put one in his or her place for that type of mentality, especially newer, successful, upcoming officials.

Jimmy recognized me as a "new and upcoming official with raw talent." With hours on the phone, locker room talk, or multiple Hooters visits with Ryan after AAU games, he sat me down and taught me the lessons of Referee 101 with layers upon layers of the X's and O's.

As for my assignor, Jim intentionally put me in uncomfortable, higher-level games with experienced veteran partners who would genuinely take care of me. Because of these opportunities Jimmy afforded me, I got to see quicker plays to the basket, true athletic talent, and how to handle tough coaches and difficult plays from early on.

One of the most memorable nights was a Wednesday night in January, when I was assigned to my first men's game. I kept trying to find out who my partner was so I could call him. This was one of Jimmy's pet peeves, communication. He kept telling me he was still working on it. Finally, the day of the game, I called Jimmy again and he said don't worry about it as he had just talked to him.

Twenty minutes before game time, Jimmy came walking in wearing a warm-up suit. I had no clue that ten minutes later he would peel off his warm-up suit and there he would be in full uniform. This scared the life out of me.

He told me they were going to try me, being how I was one of the very few women he had put in a men's game. He told me not to take any mess from them and if I needed to, throw a technical. At the end of the first half, I asked him how I was doing. He said, "Great, but you are taking too much lip from them."

Twenty seconds into the second half, I threw a technical foul on one of the guards for complaining about being fouled. Jimmy just smiled. At that point, I knew I had arrived and would be good with every adult game that followed.

Little did I know that just a handful of years later, because of Jimmy's seed watering, I was going to work two Women's Division 2 Final Fours and one national championship, or have an opportunity in the NBA Development League, NBA Summer League, and WNBA Pre-Draft Camp.

Jimmy's initial gardening has planted multiple seeds for me as I continue to work on the next level of becoming a solid and reliable NCAA Division 1 women's basketball official.

More than anything, eleven years later, after working a short three years for Jimmy, my most meaningful takeaway has been the everlasting friendship. As I often remind myself of my beginning in stripes, Jimmy's mentorship is the trunk of every branch. I am forever grateful that such a good person took me under his wing and am confident hundreds of officials and umpires would say "ditto."

Though your own stripes are hung in a place of honor, an everlasting friendship was created. Thank you, Jimmy.

MIKE BREWER, UMPIRE

My first encounter with Jim was rather interesting. It was my first year umpiring with EVOA, I was a young, up-and-coming umpire and was working a Mustang game at

Kempsville Pony Baseball, which coincidentally is where Jim's son Ryan played. As luck would have it, this was Ryan's game. I was working with an evaluator. After the game, we were reviewing the things I needed to work on, which were quite a few, especially if you ask all the fans who were giving me grief during the game. As we were reviewing the game at our cars, a man, who I just assumed was a parent, came over to us and began to give me a few things to work on. After he walked away I asked my partner, "Who was that guy and who does he think is?"

He told me, "That was Jim Smith and he umpires with us. He's one of our senior level umpires who evaluates and works college baseball" (a level most amateur umpires aspire to work).

Over the next few years, I would get the opportunity to work with Jim as my evaluator. One of the most memorable games we worked together was a middle school game at Beach Middle School (my first middle school game), which was a pretty good game. Back then my wife, who was my girlfriend at the time, would go to a lot of my games. After the game we went back to our cars, and before he gave me my evaluation, my girlfriend asked if she could sit in and listen. He told her if she wanted to hear her boyfriend get bashed to sit right down. It wasn't so bad. I was definitely nervous that game. I was getting to work with a college-level umpire. I did have quite a few things to work on. I believe that is where our family bond began.

Over the next few years Jim and I got to work together quite a bit. He became a mentor to me. That's probably why I'm not the best with the rules, but mechanically sound as anyone. Jim was never a rules guru; rather, he was an umpire that umpired using common sense. He always told me, hustle and be in position, and most coaches will leave you alone. Seriously, though, it meant so much to me that someone would put that much effort into teaching me how to umpire.

After Jim stopped umpiring, he became the commissioner of EVOA baseball. We became even closer during this time.

As the years went by, Jim's son Ryan became an umpire. This was another pivotal point in our relationship. I was scheduled to work a middle school game and my partner never showed up. I called Jim to let him know, and he was a little upset with me because there had been no prior communication between me and my partner. Instead of going ballistic, very calmly, he started trying to figure out who he could send. We were fully booked, and he said he only had three guys open, one in Norfolk, one in Chesapeake, and his son Ryan. When he said Ryan was sitting at home, I said, "Send him."

"He is not ready."

"Send me Ryan, and I'll work him through the game."

He was hesitant, but he sent me Ryan. The significance here is that I worked my first middle school game with Jim, and his son Ryan worked his first middle school game with me. I think that meant a lot to all of us.

Jim has a great sense of family. Once I had children, it became a little harder to manage my officiating schedule. Jim always made it easy for me. If my boys had a game of their own that came up after my schedule was already made, Jim would find a later game for me to work. He would have me and my family over for cookouts, and my boys loved going. Jim and his wife became another set of grandparents for my boys. To sum it up best, Jim has been a mentor to me, a commissioner to us all, and most of all, my friend.

ZACH HANEY, UMPIRE

My first encounter with Jim occurred on the baseball field during my 2003 high school season. My school's team started out as a nobody during my freshman year, and as we continued to win games and appear in state tournaments, the quality of umpiring continued to improve. As a young kid, I had no idea about "quality" umpiring, but I could tell that the older veterans of yesteryear and new umpires were no longer participating in our games. Instead, in came these seasoned officials, and games became more serious and competitive.

My father, an up-and-coming umpire in EOA, took note of these umpire advancements much sooner than me, and it was after this game that he expressed his awareness of better games, better umpires.

"You know that was Jim Smith," he said after that game. "He is one of the top umpires in this area, and it was a big deal for him to come umpire your game."

I thought nothing of it until an umpire meeting a few years later. I would return from college to work during spring break. Jim, the new assignor of the group, led the meeting, and while I knew him through emails and handshakes as the Commish, I never made a connection to him as one as my own umpires during school.

During my first official meeting as a full-time umpire, Jim mimicked his out call and it all came back to me. This signature move nearly incorporates all forms of martial arts into one swift denial of reaching a base. It is a quick jab punching the top of a midget's head, followed by a graceful side hook, only to add the back leg into a stylistic flair to complete the move. In ump school it is called a mechanic, but there is nothing mechanical to the Jim Smith punchout. The move is the art behind the science of calling the play.

No one knows his strike-three mechanic, because everyone jokes him about never working the plate. That is definitely a false statement, as that is where I saw him work the most. I remember once when he threw out an All-American player at Clemson after calling three strikes. The batter's attitude had, let us say, enlarged the strike zone. The story made its ways through the ACC world, just as it has through my conversations with Jim and sometimes whenever someone new is around. Ejecting anyone isn't the most peaceful experience, but it also portrays another side of umpiring that only a few can understand: the on-field relationship with players and umpires.

Jim helped me move quickly from Pony-level baseball to becoming an NCAA certified umpire, while serving as

decision-making process for every umpire.

Since my first year under Jim Smith was a good year, I decided I would come back. This time, Jim approached me about being more involved with evaluations and training. I came to realize Jim was the best fit for the job as commissioner, and I agreed to start teaching and evaluating. Right then, I knew Jim took care of his people and that trait is a trait that makes up good leaders. EOA was coming to a prosperous time with Jim at the helm, and I was happy to be part of it.

Now as the years went on, every year, I looked forward to officiating because the atmosphere was always positive, due to the way Jim was running things. Young and up-and-coming umpires had opportunities, and games were split fairly. The association was getting young guys involved and giving them a chance.

As an association, we work a lot because our customer list has grown, and that too is because of what Jim did. He went to all the fields we worked and watched the umpires to ensure that we were giving the customer a good product. I overheard many league officials say they were glad that when they called the commissioner, they actually got someone on the other end and not a voicemail. Jim's name got around fast and that really helped our association grow.

I would like to share one short, funny story. Another umpire and I were working a game, and next to our field were two AAU teams getting ready to play a game. The only problem was they didn't have any umpires to work their game. One of the coaches came over and asked us if he would work their game because their umpires didn't show up. We told the coach we couldn't for liability reasons. He understood and asked if we worked for Jim Smith. We responded "yes," and he said he needed to get with Jim because the association they were using was not professional, seldom on time, and not willing to work with them on game changes. EOA's good reputation was being spread around as a professional group to the leagues, and this in a big part was because of Jim

Smith and the umpires of EOA.

I would like to share one last story where the professionalism of our association and the selling skills of Jim Smith came into play. It was at the Bronco U11 World Series. Our first year, Jim was asked to send four umpires to work one of the two fields. The other field was to be manned by another four-man crew from a North Carolina association. Jim and our crew had decided that even though the field was small, we as a crew were going to work the games as we would any other four-man crew game: rotating, going out on trouble balls, doing it the professional way. Present at this tournament was the president of Pony Baseball. He noticed our professionalism and the way Jim debriefed the umpires after each and every game. This so impressed the Pony officials that they decided to drop the North Carolina group and accept another crew from EOA.

Jim took care of all the umpires on and off the field. He always said that family came first, and when you had a family issue, he had no problem working with you and getting you time to be with your family. Jim's eight years was a prosperous time for EOA baseball, and he got us to be the best umpires around. We are in demand, and that has a lot to do with what Jim Smith has done.

JOE FULLER, UMPIRE

I was the baseball coach for my two sons for twelve years. After a contentious high school playoff game in 2001, the then-commissioner overheard me complain about the ejections my son's team had suffered after a scuffle at home plate. He suggested that if I thought I could do better, maybe I should come out and become an umpire. I agreed that might be a good idea. So he wrote down his phone number on a slip of paper and handed it to me. I put that slip of paper in my wallet with no immediate intentions to follow through.

After ten years of watching my kids play high school sports, I no longer had that outlet. My wife Karen suggested that I follow through on the threat to become an umpire. After eight years, I still had that folded slip of paper, so I called. Understandably, the number was no longer in service. After some checking around, I got the number of Jim Smith, the current commissioner for the Eastern Officials Association. I called and left a message.

The next day, I was in Charlottesville for a UVA football game. Jim Smith called me on my cell phone. I explained my situation and Jim explained in great detail why EOA was the best umpiring association and how they needed guys who loved baseball to join. It was too late to get going for that fall, but the winter classes were right around the corner, and by springtime, I'd be ready to hit the field.

Having been in a number of large organizations, I immediately recognized how well EOA was run. As a leader, Jim was confident and firm, yet approachable. As I imagined what it would be like to manage 150 headstrong guys from all walks of life, it became clear Jim was the perfect guy for this job. He had umpired for twenty-plus years, so he had street cred. He was a big guy with a big voice, so he commanded the room and the role. But he also had a sense of humor, enjoying a good story with the best of them. And he had stories. His facility with the spoken language was renowned. I don't know how he remembers all the details of all the situations he was in, but he does. He was modest about his umpiring accomplishments, but it was clear he was well respected for his umpiring ability and experience as well as his management style.

I've worked my way up to being a varsity-level umpire. That rise may have taken longer than I wanted it to, but that was fair. Jim Smith and his veteran colleagues in the association had laid out what it took to move up from day one. Expectations were high. You had to look sharp. You had to show up early. You had to embrace positive and negative feedback, and you had to talk honestly about your and your partners' performance. Jim took hours to meticulously pair less experienced umpires with veterans and evaluators to give us the best chance to advance, improving ourselves and the association as a whole. I tried to help Jim by making myself available and saying yes if he called needing someone in a tight spot. He'd show his appreciation by recommending me for a tournament game or a game or some other plum assignment that stretched my experience. If you did all the right things and attacked the opportunity with optimism and energy, you might get better games or get more consideration for promotion. If you showed up sloppy, never volunteered to do anything extra, or complained that the evaluators (who were working for free) were arbitrary, you might get the less desirable assignments. At the end of the day, it was fair.

Jim also brought organized charity to our association, and thousands of dollars were donated to charities and association families from the regular meeting fundraisers. Jim would let us all know when someone needed thoughts and prayers, and I know many families were comforted by his and the association's genuine concern.

My development as an umpire was accelerated by Jim's advice and counsel. He built an incredible organization that has tremendous momentum. For the eight years of Jim's tenure, he was one heck of an effective commissioner. The result of his energy and care can be seen every day from March through October on fields across Hampton Roads. I wish Jim the best in the future, as he spends more time with his precious grandchildren. And maybe now he can take up gardening and discover that the "R" word is not so bad after all.

DUCKY DAVIS, SCOUT FOR THE LOS ANGELES DODGERS AND UMPIRE

I have known Jim for over forty-five years. To save he loves the game of baseball is an understatement. He was and still is a true ambassador of the game. There isn't anything constructive that he would not do for those involved in it.

Over the years we have officiated many games together.

Jim was a very good balls-and-strikes umpire, and his judgment on calls behind the plate and on the bases was outstanding. His handling of coaches and keeping them in the game when they went ballistic was impeccable. I remember one game at the College of William and Mary where we could easily have thrown out the visiting coach and several players. Jim found a way to keep them in the game, yet still let them know we were in charge of it.

Every day he was either out umpiring or observing umpires. When out observing, he would give the umpires valuable tips so that they would not make the same mistakes he and others made during their careers.

When Jim took over the duties of commissioner, he did an excellent job. He was a big help to the various major league scouts coming to games in our area when games were canceled or game times were changed. This saved many of the scouts time. His phone line was always open to us.

During his time as commissioner, he brought the EVOA back to the high standards it had once maintained in regards to the training and quality of umpires as well as improved customer service. I am proud to say he is a friend.

CHRIS BURTON, COLLEGE AND SCHOLASTIC UMPIRE

Mr. Commish, as you will always be to me, I want to start off by saying thank you for all that you have done for me as an umpire and for the association over your eight years as our Commish.

I started my umpire journey the same year you took over as commissioner. Until recently, you've been the only commissioner I have known. I still remember those first classes at Point O' V elementary and more so those chilly evenings outside at the old Kempsville Pony Baseball field. Some of those nights you and a few of the instructors busted my chops about my mechanics, all fond memories. Most memorable was the interest you took in my skills early on; that made me work that much harder on my craft as an umpire. I could not have asked for a better organization to join with a great leader at the top. I know I would not be the umpire I am today without you and the structure of EOA.

I had never had a mentor, like I hear most of the vets talk about, that one person who took them under his wing. I knew early on I could always call Larry Gordon, and we could talk situations and mechanics for hours. Vets like Bob Campbell and Bill McInnis helped too, and finally, I received a chance to work with the likes of Robert Turner and Jeff Doy. That was a great opportunity to learn and having those gentlemen take an interest in me, wanting me to get better and succeed, truly meant a lot.

I thank you for the times you put me with the late, smooth Mike Brown "24." He taught me a lot about how to handle myself on a field, interact with coaches and how to look and be smooth on the field. I truly learned a lot from those umpires and they have all made quite an impact on my umpire journey. I know I left off a few others, but this is about you, Commish!

If I had to say I had one mentor, it most likely would be you, Commish, the one who took, at the time, a young umpire who was hungry to learn, and you showed him you had a lot of confidence in him. If I never told you, I really did and still do appreciate that gesture, the opportunity. You followed up on that trust in me by giving me a varsity game late in my second year with the association. I still remember the phone call . . . you asking me as soon as I picked up the phone "Chris, are you ready for the big time?" I worked that game with Larry Gordon at Kellam, I remember thinking the kids were so much bigger and faster! Then you gave me other top-notch Beach District games. I remember the conversations we had after big games. I cannot tell you how much this has all meant to me . . . Gosh, I'm gonna miss you, Mr. Commish.

TERRY SIZEMORE, UMPIRE

I've always felt Jim was extremely passionate about his love for the EOA organization and its members. He went over and beyond the duties of his position as commissioner. You could contact him at any time during the day or night. He always provided wisdom and thoughtful insight with a splash of humor mixed in on any issue you may have had. He always looked out for the umpiring group, whether it was an issue that occurred on the field or different ways to provide better training or providing evaluations or suggestions that he observed at a game you had just finished. His evaluations were honest and meaningful, and he strived to provide the Hampton Roads area and the state of Virginia with the best-prepared and best-trained umpiring staff that could be offered. Jim's goal was to make every umpire in his organization the best that he could be, and he wouldn't accept anything less.

Some quick observations about Jim. There was never a short conversation. His conversations would develop from a specific question. Then from there it could go anywhere, from questions about how members of your family were doing, to recent games he had watched, to game situations he had run across during his travels, to players who had made an impression on him, to coaches he admired and some he may even have questioned.

If you were umpiring a game in the heat of the summer or late evening and Jim was there, in the parking lot, after the game, he would always have a cold drink ready and some good advice to offer to his crews. That was just the way Jim operated.

I hope Jim realizes just how much he was and is admired and respected by the umpires, coaches, administrators, league officials, and players. I truly wish he would have stayed on a little longer, but I understand the stress and the time required to do the job right. Jim did the job RIGHT!! I wish him the best, and I'm privileged to be able to call him my friend.

CHAPTER 11

EXTRA INNING

nd so in the bottom of the tenth (or is it eleventh?), I have stepped off the diamond, out of the court, and even away from my computer used to assign so many thousands of games. Wouldn't you know it, the thing just got worn out and gave up as I was finishing this book. Well, I guess I am a bit worn out, but I'm definitely not giving up.

Truth be told, I just bought a new computer that has a lot of life in it, and with blessings from the Man Upstairs, I hope so do I. There are still plenty of games to watch, umpires to observe and train, and baseball folks who might enjoy some oldie-but-goodie stories.

Along with Lou, I hope to be a good grandparent, travel a fair amount, and set up my folding chair near quite a few ballfields. So if you live in or visit Hampton Roads and see a distinguished, white-haired fellow with an EOA hat or shirt and a notepad sitting behind a fence or backstop, there's a good chance that would be me. Please come over and say hello.

ACKNOWLEDGMENTS

I have to begin by thanking my late mother and father, who supported and encouraged me during my playing days and who made sure I got my high school and college degrees just in case a career in professional baseball did not work out. They allowed me to pursue my dreams, and for that I am most appreciative. Life came full circle at my first big conference series game as a Division 1 college baseball umpire—I will never forget looking up and seeing my parents in attendance. That moment was so profound that it brought tears to my eyes.

Thank you to all the instructors and clinicians with whom I have had the privilege of working during my longtime basketball and baseball career. They helped so many, including me, become the best umpires we could be.

A sincere thank-you to my brothers on the baseball diamond—the umpires—whom I worked with for nearly forty wonderful years, both as a fellow umpire and commissioner. You gentlemen are part of the strongest and most talented officials' association I have ever known, and it has been an honor. I also owe much gratitude to the coaches and other friends who shared memorable moments to be included in my book.

There are not enough words to express my appreciation for my dear friend, Bob Barry. Bob began this journey with me. He unselfishly invested countless hours to help me tell my story. I am grateful for his dedication, his diligence, and his never-ending support. Thank you also, Bob, for your encouragement, your motivation and positive spirit!

I am truly grateful to Joe Fuller for contributing his artistic and talented visions. I am in awe of his creative abilities in editing and formatting photographs for the book. It was a delight to work with Joe! Thank you, Joe, for your generous and kind support!

I am grateful to all the school officials and players who gave our association a place to hold instructional clinics and trainings. I especially thank my longtime friend, Ed Timlin, former principal of Point O' View Elementary School, who allowed us to use his school up until his retirement; as well as Pauline France, who so generously continued this gesture of goodwill when she began her tenure as principal of this wonderful school.

To the entire Norfolk Tides organization—thank you. To Ken Young, owner and president, Joe Gregory, current general manager, and the late and certainly great Dave Rosenfield, longtime general manager, executive vice president and senior advisor to the president—a million thank-yous for giving me a place, if only for a few hours, to take my mind off of the stress of serving as baseball commissioner.

Thank you to Randy Mobley, president of the International League, for providing me a pass to any minor league game I ever wanted to attend. Your generosity has meant so much.

I appreciate Roy Bateman with Olde Masters for taking decades-old photographs and bringing them back to life. How amazing it has been to relive moments through your work.

I definitely need to thank Andy Altman and his staff at Atlantic Physical Therapy and Mike Pishioneri and his staff at Bon Secours for keeping my body parts functioning. They took care of two shoulder surgeries, two back surgeries, and multiple episodes of plantar fasciitis.

I can't thank my sisters, Mary Alice Rhodes and Karen Brock, enough for so generously coordinating efforts to photograph the very first ballpark in which I ever umpired. Thank you for your love and support.

I also must acknowledge my children Ashley, Lauren, and Ryan. No father could ask for three better children. They have each played a role in my baseball life, and they accepted and understood how I had to be away at times, working hard to make a better life for our entire family. Their memories of the baseball diamond will always be intertwined with mine.

As a young girl, Ashley would tag along to baseball games I was officiating, yelling at anyone who dared to speak negatively about the ump. She often suggested I collect and record my memories and encouraged me once I started. Most recently, she has contributed her time helping me edit sections of this book where I struggled to find the right words. Thank you, Ashley.

Lauren has always been a calm voice of reason, helping her technologically-challenged father understand new assigning programs and computer glitches. As a teenager, she helped assign games and often answered the phones for me on busy days, probably speaking to many of you at one point or another. Thank you, Lauren.

JIM'S DAUGHTER, LAUREN WELCH

Ryan, my youngest, learned the ropes of officiating as a young boy and followed in his dad's footsteps to officiate games himself as a young man. I have always appreciated his knowledge of and enthusiasm for baseball. Thank you, Ryan.

Most importantly, I could have never experienced the longevity and measure of success I had in my years of baseball without my wife, Lou. In my many decades of officiating and being commissioner, she was a huge support to me. She never complained about the hours or my time spent away from home. She encouraged me to pursue my dreams, all while raising our children. After many years and upon my consideration of retirement, Lou simply advised me to "do what makes me happy." She knew I would somehow always be involved in the world of baseball, and she was there to support whatever decision came next. I appreciate her for the wonderful wife and mother she has always been.

Whether it was baseball or basketball, Lou was always behind me. She always asked me about games when I came in the door. It was always the same question, "How did the game go?" I would always tell her the truth. Seldom would I keep it to myself and not say anything. She was always very supportive of me as she knew I was doing something I loved and at the same time providing an additional income for the family. Thank you, Lou.

To everyone in my baseball family: a heartfelt thank-you for your love, friendship, generosity, and support as for the last time I now call, "Time!"

—Jim Smith

-- can't come Now — — I'm on the computer and the mouse died and there's an excessive ringing in my ....
Ring ring ring
UMPS RULE
U GOTTA PROBLEM with that?
7.30.11

CPSIA information can be obtained
at www.ICGtesting.com
Printed in the USA
FSHW01n2107250618
49655FS

9 781633 936782